*The Symbolism and
Sources of* Outlander

ALSO BY VALERIE ESTELLE FRANKEL

Women in Game of Thrones*:*
Power, Conformity and Resistance (2014)

Buffy and the Heroine's Journey:
Vampire Slayer as Feminine Chosen One (2012)

From Girl to Goddess: The Heroine's
*Journey through Myth and Legen*d (2010)

EDITED BY VALERIE ESTELLE FRANKEL

The Comics of Joss Whedon: Critical Essays (2015)

Teaching with Harry Potter: Essays on Classroom
Wizardry from Elementary School to College (2013)

FROM MCFARLAND

The Symbolism and Sources of Outlander

The Scottish Fairies,
Folklore, Ballads, Magic and
Meanings That Inspired the Series

Valerie Estelle Frankel

McFarland & Company, Inc., Publishers
Jefferson, North Carolina

LIBRARY OF CONGRESS CATALOGUING-IN-PUBLICATION DATA

Frankel, Valerie Estelle, 1980–
    The symbolism and sources of Outlander : the Scottish fairies,
    folklore, ballads, magic and meanings that inspired the series / Valerie
    Estelle Frankel.
        p.   cm.
    Includes bibliographical references and index.

    ISBN 978-0-7864-9952-6 (softcover : acid free paper) ∞
    ISBN 978-1-4766-2116-6 (ebook)

    1. Gabaldon, Diana. Outlander novels.   2. Symbolism in
literature.   3. Magic in literature.   4. Folklore—Scotland.
5. Folklore in literature.   6. Scotland—In literature.   I. Title.

PS3557.A22O9834 2015
813'.54—dc23   2015011465

BRITISH LIBRARY CATALOGUING DATA ARE AVAILABLE

© 2015 Valerie Estelle Frankel. All rights reserved

*No part of this book may be reproduced or transmitted in any form
or by any means, electronic or mechanical, including photocopying
or recording, or by any information storage and retrieval system,
without permission in writing from the publisher.*

Cover images © 2015 Thinkstock

Printed in the United States of America

McFarland & Company, Inc., Publishers
  Box 611, Jefferson, North Carolina 28640
    www.mcfarlandpub.com

Table of Contents

Introduction   1

Symbols
  Book Titles and Covers   5
  Clothes   18
  Jewelry   30
  Animals   37
  Plants   42
  Television Symbols   44
  Character Symbols   47

Literature and Music
  Literature   57
  Writing on Writing   65
  Literary Anachronisms   66
  Music   74

Myth
  Myth and the Standing Stones   81
  Sun Feasts and Fire Feasts   95

Scottish Folklore
  Introduction   105
  Fairies and Their Kin   107
  Gods, Saints, and Devils   125
  Local Legends   135
  Magical Animals   139
  People and Their Talents   143
  Rituals and Ritual Tools   164

Other Cultures' Folklore
  Caribbean-African/Vodou   173
  China   176
  Europe   180
  Native American   190
  Norse Myth   195

Conclusion   196
Appendix 1: Titles in the Outlander Series   197
Appendix 2: The Starz Series Cast and Creators   199
Bibliography   201
Index   205

Introduction

Outlander has finally reached television. Begun as a series of massive, eight-hundred-plus page novels (standing at eight books) complete with a spinoff series, short stories, guides and more, it has been entertaining many readers for decades. As well as offering romance and adventure, the series incorporates the myths of the ancient Celts into a world on the edge of rationalism. Claire Randall, a World War II nurse, brings her modern sensibility to the past, but even she is overwhelmed by a world of ghosts, monsters, and above all, the enchanted standing stones. Centuries before her own birth, her true love Jamie Fraser has seen the Wild Hunt and believes in the Fair Folk, even with his worldly upbringing. The ancient Sun Feasts and Fire Feasts open the standing stones, but unwary travelers may die inside them, rather than find enlightenment. Literature, myth, and symbolism permeate the series, connecting it with the history and culture of the period.

Workers sing folksongs, soldiers sing songs of the battlefield, travelers sing dirty ballads in the taverns. Funerals offer the Coronach—loud praise songs of the deceased—with the *ban-treim,* or professional mourner, wailing along. The television show of course is dominated by the Skye Boat song, memorializing Bonnie Prince Charlie's frantic flight after losing his rebellion. Scottish instruments from the bodhrán and penny whistle to the Uilleann pipes and a variety of bagpipes dominate the score. Specific 1940s songs also accompany some scenes, emphasizing Claire's perspective as she hears them even in the past. The first episode features "I'm Gonna Get Lit Up" and "Shuffle Rhythm" on Frank's car radio, with "Run Rabbit Run" as Claire flees British soldiers centuries before it was written.

Literature abounds, beginning with the Bible and the classics of Latin and Greek Jamie studied at university. Along with Shakespeare and well-known classics, he quotes from the poem "The Hounds of Fingal" about the culture hero Fionn Mac Cumhaill who sleeps under an Irish hill until he'll be needed once more. Claire, by contrast, quotes English romantic poets she learned as a child. She sprinkles her references with the anachronisms of Robbie Burns and Sir Walter Scott, which nonetheless fit smoothly into the culture around her. There's additional symbolism: the blue vase, strawberries and thistles, marvelous gowns of silver, white, or gold Claire is forced to wear. More prominent is jewelry: the pearl necklace or dragonfly in amber, wedding rings and betrothal bracelets, and the many perfect gems Geillis collects for her magic. Many precious stones bestowed for protection also bear traces of family love—garnets from Roger's mother or the ruby of Jamie's father's ring.

Mythology and folklore touch every aspect of the adventure. In the modern age, standing stones transport Claire through time after she spies on an ancient Beltane dance. From there, small traces of magic continue to fill the world. Provocatively, Geillis asks a skeptical Claire, "Have you never found yourself in a situation that has no earthly explanation?" (Episode 103). The Loch Ness Monster appears to Claire after the men tell stories of a Scottish waterhorse around the fire, then Claire encounters a tiny changeling. In a more frightening moment, Claire is condemned as a witch and nearly killed by the mob, while Geillis more proudly claims this heritage for herself. Dougal takes her to a saint's spring, while another one bubbles under the Abbey of Ste. Anne de Beaupre, both Celtic sacred places incorporated into Catholic life. Through this all, the prophecy of the Brahan Seer concerning the family of Fraser lingers, awaiting fulfillment.

In North America, wendigos and ghosts haunt the heroes, while Claire learns herbs and charms from the wisewoman Nayawenne. The West Indies offers a terrifying scene of zombies and Vodou ritual given power with blood and sacrifice. Lord John is haunted by a *loa* there, even as he tries to govern a myriad of mixing cultures. Meanwhile, the Chinese Yi Tien Cho instructs Claire in acupuncture and astrology, increasing her knowledge of other cultures' mysticism.

Europe offers many old tales as the series continues: succubae, carved figurines and reliquaries, and the ever-present hauntings. Claire is called a White Lady in France, tied into legends of ghost women rising from their lakes to heal or kill. Master Raymond in Paris knows much of alchemy and astrology, the medicine (both New Age and ancient) of herbalism and auras. Scottish culture itself incorporates many European traditions: the Norse god Odin features in legends, as do Roman gods and *genius loci*. Witchcraft, spells, and the casting of runes are all Norse, while Claire often sees Jamie as a berserk Viking warrior from a century gone by. Though the show omits some of the magical references (like the Loch Ness Monster) it too performs a balancing act between the world of the present and that of the supernatural past.

While avoiding the dread "spoilers" to focus on symbols and myths in the Highlands (and beyond), it's hard to ignore that at this time the book series is more than eight times longer than the show. Thus, while significant events are left vague, a small introduction to all the characters seems necessary. Season one/book one offers Claire, Jamie, and Frank in their love triangle, along with Jamie's scheming uncles Colum and Dougal MacKenzie, Jamie's faithful Fraser cousin Murtagh, and Jamie's nemesis, Black Jack Randall. There are also Jamie's dead parents Ellen and Brian Fraser and his living sister Jenny with her husband Ian Murray and their children. The conniving witch Geillis Duncan is significant, as is the Reverend Wakefield, a historian and Frank's close friend back in the 1940s.

Main characters in the later books include the next generation: time-travelers Brianna and Roger and Jamie's adopted children Young Ian, Fergus, and Marsali. Colum, Dougal, and Ellen's sister Jocasta Cameron appear as well. Lord John Grey, an English soldier introduced in the second book and Jamie's friend, has significant plot threads, as well as a spinoff series of his own.

Books one and two (and presumably the corresponding seasons) follow the Jacobite Rebellion of 1745 in the Scottish Highlands with additional aid sought in Paris. The later books show Claire and Jamie off to the New World to carve out a home together ... just in time for the Revolutionary War. Through it all, they encounter significant ceremonies, creatures, and symbolism from ancient myth as they struggle through love, trauma, and adventure.

Symbols

Book Titles and Covers

Cross Stitch

While the show and the American book are called *Outlander,* the British edition is not. Diana Gabaldon named her first book *Cross Stitch*, which, as she calls it, is "a play on 'a stitch in time,'" also referencing Claire's occupation as a healer and seamstress of wounds (*Outlandish Companion* 323). If Claire had time traveled both ways in book one, as first planned, the story would have made a cross shape. This is a powerful image, not only of a common stitch but of perfect balance, going and reversing.

An X is a crossroads, a moment when one must decide which way to turn. Claire encounters these several times, usually regarding whether she will travel through time or risk her life to save Jamie's. Jung comments, "Where the roads cross and enter into one another, thereby symbolizing the union of opposites, there is the 'mother,' the object and epitome of all union" (qtd. in Cirlot 71). Thus Claire is seeking the feminine principle within herself—the goal she most desires, that will bring her the greatest spiritual fulfillment. Each return to the crossroads represents a small descent into the unconscious. It also suggests a pilgrimage to the axis of the world, a place, like the standing stones, of ancient earth magic. On her reemergence, she understands herself and her purpose better.

The X's four legs represent the four elements of matter. When represented by the symbol X, the crossroad portrays creation or decision in the material realm—the place of Claire's physical existence. This is where she chooses her home and life partner, choices she finds herself making again and again, in a constant pattern of stitches.

The cross-stich symbol also links with women's art and creation, a subtle celebration of female readers and the feminine magic found in sewing and embroidery. Thread is used to link things—hands, mind, and art in a chain of creation. Many myths feature the world being sewn or woven together, and indeed, human bones are attached with stringy sinews and joints were once conceived of as the knots of the body. Sewing and healing are linked metaphors, while stitchery is also an act of creation as humble thread is turned into marvelous works of beauty. Claire, too, transforms plants and later mold into near-magical cures, emphasizing the power of women's skills to reimagine the world.

Outlander/Sassenach

"'Sassenach.' He had called me that from the first; the Gaelic word for outlander, a stranger. An Englishman. First in jest, then in affection" (*Dragonfly in Amber,* ch. 5). Jamie indeed seems to regard Claire as *his* Sassenach, his English wife. Pet names like this one are both affectionate and proprietary—Jamie is the only one to call Claire this, and he uses it almost constantly (though there are various Gaelic endearments as well). As such, the word emphasizes their special bond as well as its constancy through the series.

Sassenach was proposed for a book title, but as it was difficult to spell and pronounce, Gabaldon and her publisher settled on *Outlander,* the translation. (Nonetheless, episode one of the show is "Sassenach" in a possible homage.) Gabaldon adds that the American publisher worried that calling the book *Cross Stitch* would suggest embroidery and asked, "Can you think of something else, maybe a little more ... adventurous?" (*Outlandish Companion* 323). However, changing it to *Outlander* meant having it perpetually confused with the Sean Connery movies *Outland* (1981) and *Highlander* (1986). The double titling also leads to some misunderstanding. *The Outlandish Companion* is called *Through the Stones* in England as the original American title wouldn't make sense.

While the British edition cover art appears to be landscapes, the cover of the American *Outlander* is a striking cobalt blue with a crown and thistle, suggesting the start of the Jacobite Rising and its war for British kingship. The thistle has long been a symbol for Scotland, a symbol of national pride in the violent era of the novels. A crown also represents success, as in, a crowning achievement. While book one's cover suggests the crown of Britain is the goal, in fact, the Jacobite cause is doomed. Historically and in practice (as Claire already knows and Jamie discovers) the Highlanders have no chance. Thus a suggestion appears of a greater goal beyond Prince Charlie's famously failed campaign.

As Jamie and Claire try to survive the Rising and its aftereffects, and then join the American Revolution, the story becomes one of resisting kings rather than supporting them, even while managing conflicting agendas, spying, and double-dealing. A crown represents the existing hierarchy, and Jamie and Claire flee from this to find refuge in the wilderness and create a new land of independence and safety. Another possible foreshadowing here is the Brahan Seer's prophecy that a descendent of the Frasers of Lovat will rule Scotland. Those terrorized by the ruling class may one day supplant them.

Dragonfly in Amber

Hugh Munro gives Claire a piece of amber with a dragonfly inside it in chapter nineteen of the first book and episode eight of the show. Gabaldon notes that the dragonfly in amber symbolizes Jamie and Claire's marriage "not only via the token Hugh Munro gives Claire—but as a metaphor; a means of preserving something of great beauty that exists out of its proper time" (*Outlandish Companion* 368). Amber symbolized frozen tears of the gods in Norse and Greek myth, indicating the sorrow of this precious time that will soon end (Bruce-Mitford 38). Indeed, the moments described with amber symbolism are precious but also heartbreaking in their transience. Jamie gives Claire a second piece of amber to celebrate a year of marriage near Hogmanay, "a good time for beginnings" (*Dragonfly in Amber*, ch. 33). This is their last time of safety together before the Uprising.

Trying to banish memories, Claire burns up a stick of wood with a "tiny golden bead" of sap. As she thinks, "Crystallized and frozen with age, it would make a drop of amber, hard and permanent as gemstone. Now, it glowed for a moment with the sudden heat, popped and exploded in a tiny shower of sparks, gone in an instant" (*Dragonfly in Amber*, ch. 38). This wood, like this moment, must not be preserved. By this time, the war has begun and Claire longs to forget the violence around her.

Gabaldon adds that "amber is a rather mystical substance that's been used for magic and protection for thousands of years" (*Outlandish Companion* 368). In fact, "amber was also worn to protect from deafness, digestive troubles, catarrh, jaundice, loss of teeth from looseness, and as a child's amulet against convulsions when teething" (Thomas and Pavitt 197). A source of healing and guardianship, it was often made into children's amulets. As such, Claire's gifts from Jamie and Hugh are talismans, symbols of their protection, which appears throughout the first two books.

In contrast with the amber, dragonflies are a symbol of evanescence, fragile beauty that will shortly be lost. As such, they parallel the clan way of life and Jamie and Claire's love, all under terrible threat. The dragonfly also symbolizes free will, as the glistening creatures fly wherever they wish. Incredibly swift, they can move in all six directions, radiating a sense of power and poise. This is the kind of mobility that comes from experience, allowing transformation through self-understanding. Even knowing their doom, Claire and Jamie defy history and predestination, as the power to choose is one of the most vital in the series.

In creating the show, Ron Moore describes including Munro's gift of the dragonfly in amber as a "nod to fans" who recognize the title of the second book (Podcast, 108). While naming her novel, Gabaldon first considered *Firebringer* and *Pretender*. Nonetheless, while she was working, someone asked her what had happened to Hugh Munro's gift. As she adds, the dragonfly in amber is "a visually arresting image, rather poetic in sound" that connects with the book, "insofar as notions of fate and inevitability, helplessness in the face of circumstance, references to antiquity, etc., are concerned" (*Outlandish Companion* 324).

The static nature of the dragonfly in amber appears several times. When Jamie doesn't come home, Claire worries, thinking "for the hours of the night, I was helpless; powerless to move as a dragonfly in amber" (*Dragonfly in Amber,* ch. 19). Gabaldon uses this metaphor again, describing how even a tiny child has a "small streak of steel" representing the individual personality. "In the next years, the hardening spreads from the center, as one finds and fixes the facets of the soul, until 'I am' is set, delicate and detailed as an insect in amber" (*Dragonfly in Amber,* ch. 4).

For modern readers, the image evokes ancient times, with the insect a moment of history frozen in the sticky sap, forever trapped and preserved. Indeed, preserved art constitutes a major trope. In a lecture within Claire's dreams, Frank emphasizes the remoteness of portraits, with their subjects fixed in time. "The artists we know," Frank says. "But the people they painted? We see them, and yet we know nothing of them. The strange hairstyles, the odd clothes—they don't seem people that you'd know, do they?" He shows off a miniature of Jamie, with his hair "braided and ribboned into an unaccustomed formal order," then a miniature of Claire. "Undated. Unknown. But once ... once, she was real" (*Dragonfly in Amber*, ch. 10).

Upon meeting Brianna, Roger sees her as a painting. "Brianna had that brilliant coloring, and that air of absolute physical presence that made Bronzino's sitters seem to follow you with their eyes, to be about to speak from their frames" (ch. 1). All of these moments emphasize art's static nature—time and history move forward, but objects do not. As Gabaldon adds:

> You'll see dragonfly-in-amber imagery all over the [second] book (not just insects <g>, but images of things static/stuck/preserved/clinging), and water/voyage/identity/discovery all over the third. They pretty much all have that kind of thematic resonance, but it isn't really meant to be noticed explicitly, so people only see it when they read analytically (or multiple times <g>) ["Outlander Reread Thoughts"].

The amber imagery continues even after the book has ended. In *Voyager,* Claire valiantly digs through history to find Jamie once more, transforming the cold published sentences back into her living husband. Describing him, Claire remarks:

> He had been fixed in my memory for so long, glowing but static, like an insect frozen in amber. And then Roger's brief historical sighting, like peeks through a keyhole; separate pictures like punctuations, alterations; adjustments of memory, each showing the dragonfly's wings raised or lowered at a different angle, like the single frames of a motion picture. Now time had begun to run again for us, and the dragonfly was in flight before me, flickering from place to place, so I saw little more yet than the glitter of its wings [*Voyager*, ch. 26].

Whether through his faint gift of second sight or some other quirk of personality, Jamie receives magical moments that stamp themselves "on heart and brain, instantly recallable in every detail, for all of his life," like photographs but of smell and warmth and emotion all tied together. "He had such glimpses of Claire, of his sister, of Ian ... small moments clipped out of time and perfectly preserved by some odd alchemy of memory, fixed in his mind like an insect in amber. And now he had another" (*The Drums of Autumn*, ch. 27). Likewise, in the stillness of the forest, Claire feels "part of the slow and perfect order of the universe" standing in a river, surrounded by minnows and the ubiquitous dragonflies (*The Drums of Autumn*, ch. 25). These memories turn into art of a sort—perfect, unalterable pictures of the mind. They are preserved, even as time races forward.

Much later, William Ransom discovers that he has lived in a frozen state, unaware of his heritage. When he learns the truth, he smashes a crystal chandelier. As Claire describes it, "Tiny rainbows danced on walls and ceiling like multicolored dragonflies sprung out of the shattered crystal that littered the floor" (*An Echo in the Bone,* ch. 102). Like the secret, the dragonfly is loosed. During wartime, Claire has a nightmare of her time in World War II, struggling to bring morphine to the suffering men and clumsily smashing shards of glass and dripping blood on the floor "both as bright as dragonfly wings" (*Written in My Own Heart's Blood,* ch. 52). Here, lives are revealed as fragile and impermanent, easily lost.

The chalice on the book's cover has a whiff of Gethsemane, as Jamie wishes the cup would pass to another. He loathes sacrificing his men and his own life in the hopeless cause, but his honor demands it. Duty-bound, he becomes Charles's best friend even while disapproving of his lifestyle and playing a dangerously double-sided game. With a faint Celtic pattern, the cup also suggests royalty and kingship, linking to the Cup of the Druid King intended for another Jacobite rebellion in *The Scottish Prisoner.*

Voyager

Gabaldon also describes how she came to name book three:

> To me, *Voyager* conjured up not only the superficial meanings of journey and adventure—and the very concrete reference to an ocean voyage—but something a bit more. Growing up in the sixties as I did, I was exposed to the U.S. program of space exploration in a big way, and found the whole notion unspeakably romantic. Of all the different missions, Voyager was one that particularly caught my imagination. This was commitment to the dark unknown, in the search for unimagined knowledge. Courage and daring, in the service of hope. Very suitable, I thought, for a book dealing with dangerous journeys in search of self and soul [*Outlandish Companion* 326].

The moon landing in 1969 was witnessed by 600 million people and became "the ultimate symbol of man's indomitable spirit and urge for conquest," notes Miranda Bruce-Mitford in *The Illustrated Book of Signs and Symbols* (11). Following this came the Voyager missions, to fly to the outmost planets and beyond, photographing places no human had ever seen.

Before sailing to the New World in an extensive journey across the ocean, Claire journeys through time to rejoin Jamie. Both are risky acts of faith and love in order to reunite. "From the spiritual point of view, the journey is never merely a passage through space, but rather an expression of the urgent desire for discovery and change," J.E. Cirlot explains in *A Dictionary of Symbols* (164). Journeying is linked with new experience, with a dissatisfaction and eagerness that leads to adventure.

There are many references to travel, though the moon landing doesn't appear in the series until the following book. Jamie tutors Young Ian in *The Odyssey*. On the ocean, Claire quotes Longfellow's "The Building of the Ship": "She moves! She stirs! She seems to feel/The thrill of life along her keel!" (*Voyager*, ch. 41). Likewise, Jamie reads from *Robinson Crusoe* on the journey, emphasizing their great adventure, and quietly foreshadowing the shipwreck to come.

The brooch on the cover is abstract Celtic or even Viking, emphasizing the ancient myth into which they sail. The two ends, comprised of circles (feminine) and squares (masculine), suggest a man and woman yearning towards each other, linked through the center with the fastening pin. Gabaldon describes a horseshoe shape to the arc of *Voyager*, as the plot follows Jamie, then Claire, with Roger attempting to link their stories through his historical research (*Outlander Podcast*). The brooch shares something of this shape, with the pin, like Roger, bridging the sides.

The Drums of Autumn

> And then, along came the fourth book. The Colonies—New World, whiffs of revolution, lost daughters, gallant quests through time, Native Americans up the gazoo.... *Next to the Last of the Mohicans? One If by Land, Sick If by Sea? There's a Wet Dog in My Wigwam?*—*Outlandish Companion* 326

Gabaldon explains after this spirited brainstorm that she chose the title *The Drums of Autumn* to sound something like *Dragonfly in Amber* and also evoke the mood of the fourth book. Chapter one begins, grimly, with an execution. A drummer precedes the condemned to the gallows, emphasizing the upcoming danger for Jamie and Claire in the New World. Drumbeats appear in primitive ceremonies worldwide, marking beginnings and endings. Shamans use them to evoke spirits, and indeed, ghosts and Native American ceremonies play a notable role in the story. The Iroquois execution near the end of the book caps the story off as it began.

Drums also hint at the upcoming Revolutionary War, which hovers in the rapidly-approaching future. At the time, drums were a staple of battle, used to terrify the enemy with their inexorable pounding (as Roger does with a *bodhran*, or Scottish war drum, in *Snow and Ashes*). They also kept time for marching soldiers, emphasizing the countdown toward the war, much like that toward Culloden.

In a completely different trope, the most ancient drums were a feminine symbol. The first sound an unborn infant hears is the mother's heartbeat, and drums reflect this most primal pounding. The book features a significant pregnancy (along with several others) as the new generation is born. "Drumming was once an integral part of childbirth rituals, intended to entice and direct the baby's path from the womb" (Illes 302). Thus the drums signal more approaching than war.

Autumn is also significant. By this point, the characters could be said to be in the autumn of life, with Claire and Jamie in their late forties to early fifties and the next generation grown into adults. Nonetheless, aging together becomes a gift for them, especially Jamie, who has had so many close calls. "To see the years touch ye gives me joy, Sassenach," he explains, "for it means that ye live" (*The Fiery Cross,* ch. 85). They both begin to plan a future of stability together, with less voyaging, as Jamie exclaims, "I am more than five-and-forty! A man should be settled at that age, no? He should have a house, and some land to grow his food, and a bit of money put away to see him through his auld age, at the least" (*The Drums of Autumn,* ch. 13).

In the northern hemisphere, the Autumn Equinox is the moment of transition from the Moon's chasing the Sun to the Moon's outdistancing it and ruling the heavens for half the year. As the female power symbolically overtakes the male power, Brianna and Claire find themselves making many choices for their men and households as well as for themselves. According to myth, the Autumn Equinox is the time of year when Persephone, youthful goddess of flowers, bids farewell to her mother Demeter in the magical world of the gods to make a dark trek to the underworld, seeking her lover in the primitive world of darkness. As such, Brianna's journey in the book, leaving civilization and finding love in the primal wilderness, corresponds clearly.

The tree on the cover functions as a family tree—this book highlights family and the need for connection. The first children of the next generation are born in the new world, even as Brianna meets her many cousins and finds herself part of a larger community.

The cover symbol also suggests the wilderness—the main characters have left the cities of the earlier books and are venturing deep into the forest. Forests symbolize a return to the female principle or the Great Mother. Hidden from the patriarchal symbol of the sun, life can thrive in secret mystery, much like Jamie and Claire in the backwoods.

The World Tree, appearing in many traditions, indicates the axis mundi, the center of the cosmos. This connects the earthly realm of matter below with the heavenly realm of spirit above, and is a classic place of initiation. Many gods were sacrificed on this tree in order to find enlightenment: Odin hung from an ash tree for three days, Osiris's corpse was swallowed by a tree, and the Buddha meditated under one, until all were transformed spiritually.

In *The Drums of Autumn,* not only do the heroes venture out into the wilderness to find their best destiny, but Claire and Roger have significant encounters there. Hiding in a cave in the uncharted forest, Claire meets a ghost who both saves her and shows her the consequences of subverting history. In an equally climactic moment, Jamie abandons Roger in the forest to choose between life in the past and the future. Roger, injured and suffering, makes his decision and returns transformed and finally filled with certainty. There are also the quieter moments, as Jamie and Claire lie together in a tiny snow shelter or Brianna and Jamie camp deep in the forest. Ian ventures farther and farther on his own journeys until he surrenders to the call of the wilderness. In a smaller way, Claire does the same. As she tells it, standing by a stream, "I moved with the rhythms of water and of wind, without haste or conscious thought, part of the slow and perfect order of the universe" (*The Drums of Autumn,* ch. 25).

The Fiery Cross

The symbol of the fiery cross was part of Highland life, as well as a significant scene in the book of that name. E. J. Guthrie explains in the book *Old Scottish Customs:*

When a chieftain wished to summon his clan on any sudden or important emergency, he killed a goat, and, making a cross of light wood, burned its extremities in the fire, and then extinguished the flames in the animal's blood. This was called the Fiery Cross, also Crectu Toigh, or the Cross of Shame, because disobedience to what the symbol implied inferred infamy. This cross was transferred from hand to hand, and sped through the chief's territories with incredible velocity. At sight of the Fiery Cross, every man from 16 to 60 was obliged to repair at once to-the appointed place of meeting. He who neglected the summons exposed himself to the penalties of fire and sword, which were emblematically denoted by the bloody and burned marks, upon the fiery herald of woe [ch. 18].

As Gabaldon adds, "Now, given that at this point in the story, the American Revolution is looming on the horizon, and the Scottish Highlanders had quite a bit to do with it (though mostly fighting on the wrong side, as usual), this seemed a very good title to me" (*Outlandish Companion* 327). She describes lots to do "with clan and community" in the book, building from the one powerful image of the title. The book also offers a "sight of the very last Highland charge ever" as Jamie lights the Highland call to battle in a new land (*Outlander Podcast*).

A book earlier, Claire notes that the MacKenzie clan badge, a burning mountain, is the image of a Gathering, "the fires of families burning in the dark, a signal to all that the clan was present—and together. And for the first time, I understood the motto that went with the image: *Luceo non uro; I shine, not burn*" (*The Drums of Autumn*, ch. 71).

Fire becomes associated with strength and clan pride as Jamie recruits his soldiers on the edge of war. The book begins with a significant clan gathering, and continues through Jamie's actual fiery cross, summoning his people to battle. The prologue, speaking of family, war, honor, fire, and blood, in fact sounds more like Jamie than Claire: "I have lived through war, and lost much. I know what's worth the fight, and what is not. Honor and courage are matters of the bone, and what a man will kill for, he will sometimes die for, too."

Gabaldon also reminds readers that Jocasta MacKenzie Cameron, one of the book's main characters, is caught up in many secrets and plots: "Warlike foreshadowing aside, the word 'cross' implies 'double-cross,' which is always a good bet when you're dealing with people named MacKenzie, and then there's all the crisscrossing of storylines, too" (*Outlandish Companion* 327).

This book has a cloak brooch on the cover, indicative of family and clan loyalty. It is Jamie's running stag brooch, reminding readers of his personal pride and the ominous vision of his ghost to come. He received the brooch in France before Culloden, and now he embarks on a different rebellion, linking the two stories.

A Breath of Snow and Ashes

> He reached forward then took me in his arms, held me close
> for a moment, the breath of snow and ashes cold around us.
> Then he kissed me, released me, and I took a deep breath of
> cold air, harsh with the scent of burning.—*A Breath of Snow
> and Ashes*, ch. 102

Following *The Drums of Autumn*, the title suggests the characters are reaching the winter of life—Jamie and Claire are grandparents to a vast clan of adopted and blood relatives. There is also a sense of doom as the Revolutionary War begins in earnest—last book came the call to arms and now the journey to war. The passage of time as well as ashes is referenced in the prologue:

> Time is a lot of the things people say that God is. There's the always preexisting, and having no end. There's the notion of being all powerful–because nothing can stand against time, can it? Not mountains, not armies. And time is, of course, all-healing. Give anything enough time, and everything is taken care of: all pain encompassed, all hardship erased, all loss subsumed. Ashes to ashes, dust to dust. Remember, man, that thou art dust, and unto dust thou shalt return. And if Time is anything akin to God, I suppose that Memory must be the Devil.

This story has a particularly touching parting, emphasizing the loss and pain described above. The novel to Gabaldon is shaped like a great tidal wave, but in two parts, only calming its wave at the end (*Outlander Podcast*). As she adds on the Compuserve posting board:

> *A BREATH OF SNOW AND ASHES* isn't a tempest, though—it's a double tidal wave. <g> If you look at the Japanese wood-block print I mentioned in describing it (Google "The Great Wave Off Kanagawa"), you see the enormous cresting wave, spilling bits of water from the crest (these would be the various plot elements), towering over several small boats full of people—and in the background, Mount Fuji stands unmoved. That—Mt. Fuji—would be Jamie and Claire's relationship, if you want to get symbolic, while the "crest" of the first wave is reached with Claire's rescue and Grannie Wilson's resurrection (which is the symbolic spiritual resolution of that particular episode). The second wave then begins to build from a much lower point of tension, rising to (we hope) an even higher peak as it threatens all the characters in their frail little boats. And at the end, Mount Fuji is still standing <g> ["The Shape of the Books"].

While this isn't an identical image to a great storm of snow, it has a similar feeling of overwhelming natural power. Through it all, of course, the mountain of Claire and Jamie, which rose through the earlier books, remains steadfast. Their relationship is no longer one of outlanders and strangers or evanescent dragonflies soon to perish, but a long-standing marriage, inviolable in the face of trauma or revelation.

The snowflake on the cover fits the title, though its many-sided complexity also emphasizes the growing number of viewpoint characters. Its six arms emphasize how the plotlines have grown past the double-headed brooch patterns of earlier books to many intersecting branches. "Snow represents coldness and hardness in human nature, but the fragile beauty of a snowflake symbolizes truth and wisdom. The snowflake is also a symbol of individuality, since no two are alike" (Bruce-Mitford 37). War brings coldness and deprivation, but it is made up of vulnerable individuals who, through their clever choices and strong personalities, shape what is to come.

An Echo in the Bone

The seventh novel, *An Echo in the Bone*, follows several groupings of characters on parallel plots that indeed seem to echo: Jamie and Claire; Brianna and Roger; Lord John and William; and Young Ian. Death is a heavy current, as the book begins and ends with significant passings. At one funeral, Claire thinks, "I wondered what sort of man—or woman, perhaps?—had lain here, leaving no more than an echo of their bones, so much more fragile than the enduring rocks that sheltered them" (ch. 75). In the future, the children play among the gravestones and know that Jamie and Claire are watching over them, even long-dead in the past.

"An Echo in the Bone" also means something known deep in the self—body knowledge rather than that of the mind. This seems to refer to the secrets of William's heritage, as well as the truths the loving couples must face as they decide where they belong. William explores the past in the chapter called "Bred in the Bone," emphasizing this link.

On the cover is an old-fashioned caltrop, used to injure horses in battles of the era. Its four points also suggest the four scattered storylines. Gabaldon calls the caltrop "close to the structure of the book" with four plot threads, which "ends in a triple cliffhanger," as she only closes one of the four (*Outlander Podcast*).

Written in My Own Heart's Blood

"I have loved others, and I do love many, Sassenach—but you alone hold all my heart, whole in your hands." Jamie's words in the book's final scene emphasize his love for Claire, heart deep, just after he spills blood in her defense. The eighth (but not final) book continues all the divided characters' personal journeys. On a more individual level, biology asserts itself as William and Jem's heritages grow more pronounced in their actions. The title suggests suffering and personal sacrifice as many characters risk everything in order to save a loved one or win back that person's trust. Separations from the previous book begin to recombine, with more torment and trauma as well as happy endings. The Revolutionary War stretches onward, through 1778 at this point.

There is also the knowledge of the body and bone once again. Claire remembers Jamie viscerally, thinking of his breathing in the night and "the sudden, magical well of his blood in dawning light when I'd cut his hand and marked him forever as my own. Those things had kept him by me" (ch. 47). She employs this knowledge as her medical expertise grows. As she explains:

> A trained surgeon is also a potential killer, and an important bit of the training lies in accepting the fact. Your intent is entirely benign—or at least you hope so—but you are laying violent hands on someone, and you must be ruthless in order to do it effectively. And sometimes the person under your hands will die, and knowing that ... you do it anyway [ch. 117].

The red seal on the cover emphasizes particular letters through the series, especially the many Claire and Jamie send Roger and Brianna. The cover resembles a folded letter with blood-red seal. Looking closer, there's a calligraphy mark inside the wax. Gabaldon had wanted an octopus, but settled for an "octothorpe, otherwise known as the lowly hashmark" with two infinity signs and a Mobius shape, emphasizing the time travel. To Gabaldon, the book is octopus-shaped: There are eight viewpoint characters and eight interconnected plotlines in the eighth book radiating out as if from an octopus's body (*Outlander Podcast*).

The Lord John Novels

Covers on most of the Lord John novels feature their hero looking through a sort of square peephole that obscures part of his face. The face is the symbol of identity, because it distinguishes us from others. Hence a partial face suggests anonymity or spying, both major tropes of the series. Lord John investigates mysteries and occasionally acts as a British spy, but through it all runs his secret life as a homosexual among the elite of London. Partial faces or bodies (generally women's) have been popular on recent book covers, subtly suggesting this is a women's series, even though it features a man. The fractured image also hints at Lord John's torn desires as he is valued physically as a companion but fails to find a deep, lasting love that his partner can return. Alternate covers have symbols like those on the Jamie and Claire novels—a pentagram for the *Hand of Devils*, compass, signet ring, and drug bottles for the others. All suggest plot elements as well as the items of everyday life.

The titles are intriguing because several hint at the occult as well as adventure mysteries: *Lord John and the Succubus, Lord John and the Haunted Soldier, Lord John and the Hand of Devils,* and *Lord John and the Plague of Zombies* evoke ghosts and monsters as well as the detective like Sherlock Holmes or Miss

Marple determined to root them out. *Lord John and the Hellfire Club* references a real society in London's history, though also with the suggestion of the paranormal and evil. However, the titles are the most supernatural things about these stories (originally published in fantasy or paranormal anthologies), as Lord John discovers superstition and hoaxes lie at each mystery's heart.

Lord John and the Private Matter and *The Custom of the Army* have titles emphasizing the stuffy propriety of manners and London society, even within the military. Lord John spends much of his time on morning calls or sitting in the Society for the Appreciation of the English Beefsteak, even as he struggles to solve mysteries and murders. *Lord John and the Brotherhood of the Blade*'s titles is similar but more ironic, as it features his sexual relationship with his stepbrother, a fellow "brother of the blade" in the army with him and their mutual responsibility to each other.

The Scottish Prisoner's title varies from the others—likely because it's half Jamie's story. The cover, unlike the rest, is along the lines of the Jamie and Claire books with a single object decorating it—in this case, a ring of keys. These emphasize his status as prisoner of course, but also the tantalizing possibility of freedom. In fact, he is paroled to embark on a grand adventure ... with the mission of arresting a traitor. Keys also symbolize freedom and secrets, tantalizing bribes that surround Jamie during his adventure. They can indicate access to spiritual wisdom or even the Gates of Heaven. In fact, Jamie does gain a higher level of understanding, but at a terrible cost to another.

A Trail of Fire

A Trail of Fire collects four Gabaldon novellas:

- "A Leaf on the Wind of All Hallows"
- "The Custom of the Army"
- "Lord John and the Plague of Zombies"
- "The Space Between"

This book is available for readers in the UK, Australia, and New Zealand (U.S. rights are still tied up with their original anthologies; a bibliography is available at the end of this volume). As Gabaldon explained on her site's blog (May 1, 2012):

> Why A TRAIL OF FIRE? Well ... as the cover copy says ... "Trails of tracer bullets in the dark, and the fiery trail of a wounded Spitfire falling out of the sky. The trail blazed by night by the handful of heroic Highlanders who fought their way straight up a vertical cliff to stand on the Plains of Abraham in a fiery dawn. The burning of plantations in a Jamaican night, in a trail leading down from the mountains, straight toward Kingstown. And the trail of a torch burn-

ing green as it moves through the eerie surrounds of a Paris cemetery, down into the mysteries of the earth."

A leaf on the wind means a person being carried about beyond his own control—certainly the case for Roger's father Jeremiah in his plane and then time-traveling. Further, he is carried on the wind of All Hallows—the force of Samhain that opens the passages into the past and the holiday that brings ghosts back to see their loved ones. His one moment of existence back in the present is like a ghostly visitation, as is his momentary meeting with his adult son.

"The Space Between" features an in-between story with barely-mentioned characters from the Jamie and Claire books. It also stars characters in states of transition as St. Germain and Raymond, poisoned between life and death, take on time travel and Joan decides on her future. Michael Murray too is caught in a transition stage, living in moments: Ian tells him, "Ye find a way to live for that one more minute. And then another. And another.... But after a time, ye find ye're in a different place than ye were. A different person than ye were. And then ye look about and see what's there with ye. Ye'll maybe find a use for yourself. *That* helps" (171).

On the cover is a circle of seven glowing jewels—jewel magic is important in the stories, as it is in the larger series. One could even argue seven travelers appear (Geillis, St. Germain, Raymond, two Rogers, and two Jeremiahs). Thus this book joins the others with meaningful titles and additional symbolism for readers, as they deepen their journey into Gabaldon's world.

CLOTHES

1940s Fashion

Clothing in both book and show clearly reflects the period. Frank wears mostly all brown or gray, very faded into the background, very correct. By contrast, Jamie lives rough and works in the stables sometimes, but his blues and greens on the show give him much more color. Claire's blue suit and blue paisley scarf make her seem quite vivid in contrast with Frank's beige, suggesting he's already a vanishing memory.

Frank's fedora sets him in the time period, as do his suits. Clothes rationing, prevalent through 1949, meant Utility suits with low-wool fabric in plain navy, brown, or grey, with narrow, single-breasted jackets and trousers without pleats or turn-ups. Waistcoats were gone, while children's clothes were generally pieced together or cut down from worn garments. The women's utility suit had a knee-length skirt and simple square cut, with three buttons only and very few pockets.

Terry Dresbach, the show's costume designer, adds, "The later scenes with

Frank, these are the stolen moments in the midst of war, and the peachy blush color of the peignoir coveys the romance they are trying to hold onto in spite of the war that surrounds them." The peignoir, a departure from Claire's simpler clothes, suggests a single extravagant indulgence in the midst of constant rationing.

Claire's Shift Dress

In the time travel scene, Claire's gray plaid shawl makes her seem a part of the past already before she travels there. She soon loses both shawl and the belt on her simple white dress, and then tears off the button at the neck, transforming the garment into a classic shift. Her buckled brown loafers can arguably fit in with both times as Jack Randall notes the "very fine shoes" she wears. By the time Claire reaches Castle Leoch (where Mrs. Fitz disapproves of her outfit), she's in a loose, stained, torn, knee-length garment that certainly resembles a battered shift—the innermost layer of eighteenth century underwear.

On her blog, Terry Dresbach describes creating this shift and calls it "One of the most difficult designs I have ever had to do" (Sept 2014). As she adds:

> It had to serve two very difficult and specific masters. Be a convincing 40s dress, and then change to an 18th century shift, two completely different structures. Plus to make it even more fun, the season for the show changed to autumn instead of spring, as it was in the book. At least if it had been spring, I could have had Claire in a cotton voile or even a lightweight linen dress. But in the fall, in cold rainy Scotland, my options got even narrower.

In the book, in May, she wears a cotton dress, described as being sprigged with peonies in *Outlander* but not in *Cross Stitch* (ch. 3). These flowers are absent from the show. As Dresbach explains:

> There came a moment when we all had to decide if we were going with the descriptions in the book or going to do the look that we wanted. This dress is not what is written in the books exactly. When we make choices that are not exactly as they are in the book, they are never done casually or dismissively. They're always done with tremendous consideration because we're fans too [Bell].

In the comic Claire wears a knee-length blue 1940s housedress—less like a shift in obvious appearance. Gabaldon explains in her Afterward that "using a solid color instead of a print makes the composition of the panels more striking." It's not a large change. However, the top of the comic's dress rips severely, leaving Claire spilling out of it for all her scenes as she rides with Dougal's men and tends Jamie. It's no wonder they think her a wet nurse (complete with illustration). The comic repeats this image: Claire's gown for the Gathering is low cut, and as she gets drunk at the bar before her wedding, she's (oddly) spilling out of a slightly-ripped dress once more.

Back on the show, after Claire reaches the castle, Mrs. Fitz removes the shift and her modern underwear. Onscreen, she dresses Claire in all the layers of the time, showing audiences (along with a brief nude scene) the classic shift, wool petticoats, bum roll, bodice, and everything else a respectable woman would wear. Moore notes that it took twenty minutes to dress Claire for each take, but considers the scene important in showing "Part of her transformation from a twentieth-century woman to an eighteenth-century woman" ("Inside the World," 102).

The book mentions two brown overskirts and a pale yellow bodice for this scene, with a pair of yellow slippers that are leather oblongs with no differentiation between left foot and right foot (*Outlander*, ch. 6). On the show, Claire often wears brown gowns, but collars of fur or knitting accessorize them, and there's often a gold stomacher, interesting embroidery, or exotic textures around neck and sleeves. The gowns thus seem very touchable, combined with alluring low cleavage for evening occasions.

Dressing Up

When Claire weds Jamie in the books, she wears a "low-necked gown of heavy cream-colored satin, with a separate bodice that buttoned with dozens of tiny cloth-covered buttons, each embroidered with a gold fleur-de-lis. The neckline and the belled sleeves were heavily ruched with lace" (*Outlander,* ch. 14).

Claire puts on the gown mildly unwillingly. As she notes, "I looked at the port-wine stain on my grey serge skirt and vanity won out. If I were in fact to be married, I didn't want to do it looking like the village drudge." She stands there "like a dressmaker's dummy," barely participating in the proceedings. As such, she comes across like *The Hunger Games'* Katniss, gowned and perfumed against her will, for an event she has agreed to under duress. As various critics have noted in different works of literature, greedily wanting the beautiful gown (and in this case the handsome Scott that comes with it) would be immoral of the heroine. If however, she's forced to accept all this, she's allowed to remain the "good girl" entrapped by circumstances.

She's finally ready "complete to white asters and yellow roses pinned in my hair and a heart pounding madly away beneath the lacy bodice," as she says. She feels "quite regal, and not a little lovely" but the point is that she's been forced to primp and wear expensive satin. The story builds on this, as Dougal demands that Jamie and Claire consummate their marriage properly—if they do not, Jack Randall could still claim Claire. "Six weeks ago, I had been innocently collecting wildflowers on a Scottish hill to take home to my husband. I was now shut in the room of a rural inn, awaiting a completely different husband, whom I scarcely knew, with firm orders to consummate a forced marriage, at risk of my life and liberty," she notes (*Outlander,* ch. 15). Thus the following romance, sex, and disloyalty to Frank are also forced on Claire and she must submit to save her life ... no matter how much she might also relish it. As she notes, "I supposed it would be harder if I found him unattractive; in fact, the opposite was true."

"Not only was I a bigamist and an adulteress, but I'd enjoyed it," she adds on the show. More beautiful gowns follow at Lallybroch and in France, mixing the romance of period drama with more of the good girl persona—once again, Claire must wear the luxuriant gowns to establish her status and impress others—she is never seen purchasing them through greed or vanity.

Jamie by contrast is proud to dress up and show Claire a different side of himself. When he marries Claire he arrives in a "fine lawn shirt with tucked front, belled sleeves, and lace-trimmed wrist frills" (*Outlander,* ch. 14). He decides the squire's son he borrowed it from is "a bit of a dandy." He wears the best of everything he has or can borrow, including his father's ruby wedding ring.

Earlier, Claire is given a striped green overskirt with a bodice of silk to wear to Colum's Hall (*Outlander,* ch. 6). In the comic it's bright yellow. More to the point, she's forcibly dressed in it by Mrs. Fitz, even as she's desperately plotting her escape from the Hall. On the show, Mrs. Fitz drags her off as she stammers excuses and stuffs her into a fine dress for the Gathering, delaying Claire's escape.

After Claire arrives at Lallybroch, Jenny and Mrs. Crook make her a dress for important occasions such as Quarter Day. It's "primrose yellow silk" that fits her like a glove, "with deep folds rolling back over the shoulders and falling behind in panels that flowed into the luxuriant drape of the full skirt" (*Outlander,* ch. 31). The upper bodice is reinforced with deconstructed stays, as Claire refuses to wear a real corset, but that's the only impact her wishes have.

When Claire and Jamie are invited to a ball at the Palace of Versailles by King Louis, Jamie asks Claire to have a dress made that will allow her to stand out in the crowd. The gown is red silk, of the most fashionable color of the season, called Christ's blood. (While this may be historically accurate, she and Jamie both will be sacrificed in different ways soon enough). The dress has a huge overskirt with filmy gussets of silk plisse. The bodice, a single layer of silk, darts quite low (*Dragonfly in Amber,* ch. 9). Jamie is horrified that the white charmeuse lining under transparent lace looks like Claire's skin and from his height, he can see all the way to her navel. At Jamie's request, she brings a larger fan to cover her bosom and occasionally beat off pushy gentlemen.

Considering a seduction to save Jamie, Claire dresses in "white for purity, red for ... whatever this was" (*Dragonfly in Amber* 380). In fact, once again, she's dressed by others, with Mother Hildegarde and her nuns first telling Claire what she must do then decorating and perfuming her and stuffing her in a carriage.

On several other occasions, Jamie asks Claire to dress up and appear "fine" or "respectable." Their trip to Edinburgh is no exception, as she has a new gown that's "a heavy coffee-colored silk with a close-fitted bodice and three lace-edged petticoats to show at the ankle," all because they have business and "Jamie had said firmly that we could not appear as ragamuffins and had sent for a dressmaker and a tailor as soon as we reached our lodgings" (*An Echo in the Bone,* ch. 74). When Claire points out she could work in "a grey flannel petticoat" in *Written in My Own Heart's Blood,* Jamie retorts, "I like to look at ye now and then in a fine gown, lass, wi' your hair put up and your sweet breasts showin.'" He adds that he's judged by how well he provides for her and what he buys for her to wear (ch. 142).

Though she cares little for fashion, the dictates of others see her reveling in her period drama. When traveling in time once more, she finally chooses something for herself. This is a dress of "a deep, tawny gold, with shimmers of brown and amber and sherry in the heavy silk." There's some awareness of others' judgment, as she rejects the white dress, which will dirty too easily, and the red dress which might suggest she's a prostitute (*Voyager,* ch. 21). Nonetheless, she notably shops on her own, and ignores the seller's suggestions. The dress matches Claire's sherry-colored eyes, emphasizing it comes from her own willpower and choice as she returns to Jamie.

Wedding Gown

Claire actually has two—the tailored 1940s pale suit and the indescribably elaborate gown. Costume designer Terry Dresbach comments: "If you look closely, you'll notice that both wedding outfits are silvery gray" (Friedlander). As she adds on her blog, Claire's 1940s suit was pointedly simple (July 2014):

> Claire and Frank are getting married just as the war is breaking out, and while there is still optimism in the air, it is a more somber time. Ron [Moore, the show's creator and Dresbach's husband] wanted the clothes to be very faded as in an old photo, so we used tones of grey and brown. But Claire is in love, and it shows up in her jaunty little hat, tipped over one eye. We wanted her suit to carry through some of the deco lines of the 30s, but showing the direction of women's fashions to come during the war years. It is a very tailored, masculine style, nothing frilly or frivolous.
>
> This suits Claire's character very well, and tells us a lot about who she is. She is a strong and savvy young woman, filled with optimism.

While not detailed in the American book, Claire's 1940s wedding clothes appear in the British *Cross Stitch*:

> Last time—next time?—I had been married in a white linen suit with alligator pumps. Frank had worn grey Harris tweed. I caught myself thinking wildly of Uncle Lamb, who had witnessed the wedding. "Pity to waste the surroundings with this modern stuff," he had said, casually patting Frank's tweed sleeve.

"It's a genuine eighteenth-century Scottish chapel, you know. You ought to have got yourselves up appropriately, kilts and dirks and long gowns and such." Looking up at the formidable sight of my intended bridegroom, I had a sudden unhinged vision of Uncle Lamb nodding approvingly.

"Much better," he said, in my imagination. "Just the thing" [273–274].

As with the show, the book stresses the jarring contrast between the time periods as Claire's two weddings reflect their surrounding cultures. Her first time, she chooses a startlingly modern, practical suit, rather than a traditional gauzy gown. The second time, she allows others to garb her as a classic lady, with a binding corset and such large skirts bursting with gold or silver she can't fit through the door. Dresbach adds:

We wanted [the suit] to be the polar opposite of the 18th century gown as there's nothing frilly about 1940s Claire. There's actually nothing frilly about 1740s Claire either. Both pieces have in common a structure and clean architecture to them. Neither are soft or loose. We were taking a period that was very ornate and elaborately embellished and still retaining the character of Claire. We wanted people to feel like despite not having much choice in the matter, our character would still be happy wearing the dress [Bell].

The ornate wedding gown is silver and white with a pattern of acorns and falling leaves (though the latter somewhat resemble rising birds). Acorns and oak leaves are a symbol of strength and fidelity in a marriage, the costume designer says in the accompanying podcast.

"It was as if I stepped outside on a cloudy day and suddenly the sun came out," Jamie says sweetly. The gown gleams with endless layers of glittering mica as well as silver embroidery. As Dresbach describes the wedding gown in further detail, she notes:

I had really had gotten directions from Ron that this needed to be a fairy tale; a beautiful moment that cements and entire book series and an entire television series. It's a series about a marriage and the foundation is this moment, but it's two people who didn't know each other and who didn't plan to be married and are being forced into this. And yet, we had to make it so impossibly romantic that we could believe that our heroine and our hero could just fall in love so completely at that moment.

So, I wanted a dress that would be incredible in candlelight. And in the 18th century metallic fabrics were made with actual metal woven into the fabrics. When you put them in a room filled with candles, they just glow. They're quite remarkable. There are museum exhibits that actually show the dresses in candlelight so you can see the effect.... But that dress took us—we calculated it out at about, I think if one person had done it, it would have been about 3,000 hours' worth of work. We did a technique of embroidery that was done hundreds of years and is no longer used. The embroidery is done with metal [Friedlander].

Geillis's Clothes

Geillis's gray dress has a touch of Gandalf, while the bodice she wears seems made of feathers or fur—likewise with a touch of the forest-wise wizard about it. Her Gathering outerwear resembles a filmy Greek tunic. As Dresbach notes in her blog (August 2014):

> Geillis is wearing an Arisaid, a Scottish woman's plaid. It is purely an ornamental garment, obviously, as it is made of sheer fabric, and clasped at the shoulder with a Lovers Eye brooch.
>
> I used a man's leather belt, with a jeweled buckle, at her waist, as both a nod to Highland men, and as a way to provide contrast to her delicate, translucent costume. Feminine, but dangerous.

The painted eye of the brooch belongs to Charles Stuart. Presumably Geillis thus shows her loyalty subtly—most people would have no idea whose eye is painted on her shoulder, but she is fully aware and can wear it in public. While the lover's eye jewelry was popular at the time, it too has an occult association for modern viewers. The disembodied eye seems a guardian for Geillis, suggesting occult powers of perception.

Mobcap

To Claire the mobcap represents wifely conformity and subservience as well as ridiculous levels of modesty. Thus Claire refuses to wear it on every occasion. These were traditional in the Highlands for modest married women, but Claire has no interest in being one of them. Her bouncy, wild, untamable hair springs around her at every opportunity, subtly declaring her independence. When she receives "an enormous mobcap, liberally embellished with lace and trimmed with lavender ribbons," Claire privately thinks "a few choice things" about the woman who's sent it as a gift (*The Fiery Cross*, ch. 10). Even when her hair is cut off, after constant offers of these caps, she walks about proudly with almost no hair to cover her skull.

Nonetheless, in *An Echo in the Bone,* Claire realizes that being taken for a harmless, respectable grannie is a powerful tool that will allow her to spread Revolutionary War propaganda from a humble marketing basket. Thus she discovers the cap's value. The cap also has an emotional connotation. When she thinks she has lost Jamie, she mechanically allows her hair to be tucked under a cap. Her spirit has been visually quenched at last, and rebellion no longer matters to her. When she discovers he's alive, however, she throws her cap off, noting, "I had a feeling that my status as a respectable woman wasn't going to be important for much longer" (ch. 101). As always, she's correct.

Kilts

When asked about the appeal of a man in a kilt, Gabaldon notes that while "really tired" she said, "Well, I suppose it's the idea that you could be up against a wall with him in a minute" ("The Doctor's Balls," Kindle Locations 376–379). The interview was immediately reprinted everywhere. As she adds:

> A man who you know is running around with his dangly bits so immediately accessible is plainly a bold spirit, up for anything at the drop of a hat (or some more appropriate garment) and entirely willing to risk himself, body and soul. The English Government understood this very well; hence the DisKilting Act, passed after Culloden, which—as part of a program of cultural punishment and ethnic cleansing—forbade Highland men to wear the kilt or possess tartan ["The Doctor's Balls" 382–385].

In a later book, Claire tells Jamie, "Actually, it's your kilt that makes me want to fling you to the floor and commit ravishment.... But you don't look at all bad in your breeks" (*The Drums of Autumn*, ch. 13). Kilts are a romantic image, seen on many novel covers as a departure from dull, mannerly trousers.

Claire reveals that she's noticed on the rent-collecting trip that usually there's nothing under the kilt. In episode six, the British officers joke about what's under Dougal's kilt until Brigadier General Lord Oliver Thomas finally announces in snotty fashion, "The question of the kilt will remain an enigma." In a later book, Roger (who has heard many kilt jokes) has the line, "As my auld grand-da used to say, when ye put on yer kilt, laddie, ye ken for sure yer a man!" (*The Drums of Autumn*, ch. 4)

The evolution of the kilt may have begun with the Irish, who adopted a version of the Roman tunica, a striped shirt which descended to the knee. A medieval quilted coat with pleats was later worn in place of armor. There are numerous historical records of the kilt, both in pictures and text, revealing how far back the Scots wore such a garment:

> Some years ago a sculptured stone was dug up from the ruins of the Roman Wall (which was constructed in the year 140), representing three figures dressed exactly in the ancient garb of the Highlanders.
> Herodian, who wrote about the year 204, in speaking of the dress of the Caledonians says, they were only partly clothed, which would agree with the opinion of many subsequent writers on the Highland dress.
> The Sculptured Stones of Scotland also give clear and decided evidence of the great antiquity of the dress, and their period may be said to extend from the sixth to the ninth century. There is one at Dupplin in Perthshire, Forres in Morayshire, Nigg in Rossshire, each representing figures in the Highland dress.
> There is also a sculptured slab in the Antiquarian Museum, Edinburgh, which was found at Dull in Perthshire, some years ago, and represents several figures in the Highland dress. In Kilmuir, Skye, there is also a rock bearing a natural repre-

sentation of the dress. It is called "Creag an fheilidh," or the rock of the kilt, from its marked resemblance to a man dressed in the kilt. This name must be coeval with the arrival of the Gael in Skye, for being a natural representation, it could not get the name through any event or accident.

In the Norwegian Sagas, in reference to the expedition of King Magnus to the Western Isles, in the year 1093, it is said that he, adopted the costumes in use in the Western lands on his return, and likewise many of his followers; and for this he was called Magnus Barefoot.

The seal of King Alexander I., whose reign began in 1107, represents that monarch in the Feileadh-beag, and also with the round Highland target. King David I., who began to reign in 1124, and Malcolm IV., in 1153, used a seal identical with that used by Alexander I., and their adopting it proves conclusively that they wore the dress represented ["The Highland Garb"].

Thus in one form or another, the Scottish kilt goes back millennia. In a song composed to commemorate the battle of Harlaw in 1411, M'Mhuirich, bard to the Lord of the Isles, describes the rest of the Highland dress item by item: "A jacket, vest, and feile-beag or kilt; a belted plaid or breacan-feile, a full-trimmed bounet, set of belts, a pair of tartan hose made of cloth, a pair of knitted hose, a pair of garters, a silver-mounted sporran, a targe [Scottish shield], with spear, a claidheamh-mor [great sword], brace of pistols, dirk, with knife and fork, a sgian-dubh [sock knife], a powder horn, and shoulder brooch" ("The Highland Garb").

It was not until the 16th century that a simple length of cloth, belted round the waist, came into use. The "feileadh breacan" or "feileadh mor" (the great kilt) was several yards long and the Highlander had to lay it on the ground, gathering the cloth into pleats from the waist with a length over his shoulder. Jamie, stuck borrowing an old fashioned great kilt, explains the operation of it at one point:

> "It's a bit undignified to get into, but it's verra easy to take off"
> "How do you get into it?" I asked curiously.
> "Well, ye lay it out on the ground, like this"—he knelt, spreading the cloth so that it lined the leaf-strewn hollow—"and then ye pleat it every few inches, lie down on it, and roll."
> I burst out laughing, and sank to my knees, helping to smooth the thick tartan wool [*Dragonfly in Amber,* ch. 36].

As one historian describes it,

> The breacan-feile was twelve yards of tartan, i.e., six yards of double tartan, and was plaited and fastened round the body by a belt, the lower part forming the kilt, and the other half being fixed on the shoulder by a brooch, hung down behind, and thus formed the plaid, in the same shape as the belted plaids now used by the military, which is an imitation of it. There was great neatness displayed, in arranging the plaits so as to show the set of the tartan. This was a par-

ticularly convenient style of dress, as the plaid hung loosely behind, and did not encumber the arms, and in wet weather could be drawn over the shoulders, and formed a sufficient covering for a Highlander, while, in the event of a camping out at night, it could be thrown loose, and covered the whole body ["The Highland Garb"].

In both books and show, Jamie most often wears separate pieces of little kilt and plaid, using the plaid as sleeping bag or ground cover, or quite often to cover Claire's ripped garments. The plaid was six yards by two, a voluminous garment that could be wrapped in several different ways, depending on the weather. He has a jacket and waistcoat for more formal occasions, but when he's working in the stables, he generally wears only the kilt and a long shirt. On later adventures, Claire notes that while men from other cultures might do heavy or hot work in just their trousers, Jamie, like other Scots, loses the kilt and plaid and works in his long shirt, with the tails of it tied between his legs. At night he customarily sleeps in the same shirt or in nothing.

The present-day kilt—the "feileadh beg" or "little kilt" evolved in the mid-eighteenth century, losing the upper length of cloth. There is a controversial claim that an Englishman named Rawlinson introduced it as a way of reducing accidents at his iron-smelting works. Of course, a simple skirt, even with pleats, is not a complete innovation.

By now, and for centuries before, the kilt and plaid have been part of the national consciousness. Worn by rich and poor, they symbolized nationwide pride and the Scottish heritage. As the folklorist J.F. Campbell proudly describes it in *Popular Tales of the West Highlands*:

> Speaking from the experience of one who wore no other dress in his youth, and has worn it at odd times all his life, it is the best possible dress for shooting, fishing, wading, walking, or running one of the worst possible for riding, or boating; it is inconvenient at first for cover-shooting in whins or brambles, or for watching at a pass when the midges are out on a warm evening. It is a capital dress for a healthy man, and tends to preserve health by keeping the body warm and dry. Many a man has caught cold when he changed his dress, and exchanged the thick folds of a kilt for a pair of trousers. It is commonly worn by boys in the Highlands till they grow up to be striplings. It is hardly ever now worn by labourers, boatmen, or farmers. It is the dress of individuals of all classes—gamekeepers, deerstalkers, peers, pipers. It is worn by Highland regiments, and occasionally by all classes of the community as a gala dress, when they attend Highland demonstrations, or go to court; but it can no longer be called the common dress of the country, though there is not a Highlander in it, or out of it, whose heart does not "warm to the tartan" [Vol. IV, 347–348].

Burt, who wrote in the year 1729, mentions several Highland chiefs as wearing the kilt, as well as Prince Charlie and some of his close court. "There is a picture in Taymouth Castle of the Regent Murray in full Highland costume (breacan feile.) There are also pictures at Holyrood Palace, and Armadale and Dunrobin Castles, of gentlemen dressed in the kilt" ("The Highland Garb"). John, Duke of Argyle, and Greenwich, the author of the well-known song, "Argyle is my Name," says in the third verse:—

> I'll quickly lay down my sword and my gun,
> And I'll put my plaid and my bonnet on,
> "Wi' my plaiding, stockings, and leather heeled shoon,
> They'll mak' me appear a fine sprightly loon;
> And when I am dressed thus frae tap to tae,
> Hame to my Maggie, I think for to gae,
> "Wi' my Claymore hinging doon to my heel,
> To whang at the bannocks o' barley meal.

Tartans

On the show, Jamie typically wears the blue and brown MacKenzie tartan, presumably because he's hiding among them. His wedding tartan in Fraser plaid is mostly blue-green with a little red. The costume designer describes making the Fraser tartan similar to the MacKenzie one to show the relation between the families—the Fraser tartan has only a thin red stripe in an homage to the traditional red tartan (Podcast 107). The MacKenzie tartan in "earth colors" was also created by the design team—neither is the authentic clan pattern.

Many clans had a hunting tartan to blend in with the forest, in contrast to the brighter one for formal occasions. Nowadays, patterns are sorted into this category and also "Modern" and "Ancient," with modern dyes contrasting with authentic vegetable dyes from the 18th century. As J. F. Campbell describes the dyeing process:

> Old wives still colour worsteds of their own spinning with plants that grow on their own Scotch hills.
> With the root of the bent they make a sort of red.
> With "máder" they dye blue and purple. With some other root, whose name I have forgotten, I have seen thread coloured yellow by boiling it in a pan, and thus the Highlanders still produce the three primitive colours from native dyes. Wool and goat's hair give black and white.
> Green they produce with heather, and a very rich brown of various shades from yellow to black with a species of lichen which grows on trees and rocks, and is called "crotal" [Vol. IV, 335].

Each clan thus has several official patterns, registered in books and databases of the official patterns for each clan—or often separate patterns for separate clan branches. These patterns are widely known, and are especially displayed in Scottish games and gatherings today.

The MacKenzie tartan in *Cross Stitch* (ch. 6) is described as a "plaid of dark green and blue with a faint red and white over-check" and in *Outlander* as a "plaid of dark green and black with a faint red and white over-check" (ch. 6). In fact, in the Scottish Tartans World Register, it is green and blue plaid with a black background and a faint red and white over-check.

In the books, the Fraser dress tartan is a brilliant crimson, blue and black in *Cross Stitch* (ch. 14), but just crimson and black in *Outlander* (ch. 14). Jamie's has a faint white stripe to distinguish Lallybroch from other areas (*Dragonfly in Amber*, ch. 7). The Fraser hunting tartan in the book is green and a bark colored brown with a faint blue stripe (*Outlander,* ch. 6). The actual Fraser of Lovat Clan Tartan (WR391) is mostly red, with green and blue behind, or for the hunting tartan, green and blue with a thin red stripe.

Jamie arrives for his wedding looking far different from the rough working stable boy he's been before this. As Claire sucks in her breath, she notes, "A Highlander in full regalia is an impressive sight—any Highlander, no matter how old, ill-favored, or crabbed in appearance. A tall, straight-bodied, and by no means ill-favored young Highlander at close range is breath-taking."

> His tartan was a brilliant crimson and black that blazed among the more sedate MacKenzies in their green and white. The flaming wool, fastened by a circular silver brooch, fell from his right shoulder in a graceful drape, caught by a silver-studded sword belt before continuing its sweep past neat calves clothed in woolen hose and stopping just short of the silver-buckled black leather boots. Sword, dirk, and badger-skin sporran completed the ensemble [ch. 14].

While the book leaves it unclear how Jamie suddenly acquires a fine tartan marked with his own clan's pattern for his wedding, the comic book adaptation clears it up, as Murtagh has brought it for Jamie to wear back to Lallybroch "so ye'd not look a beggar." Of course, by the time he and Claire finally reach home in the books, they're both in rags. On the show, Murtagh borrows the plaid and kilt from a Fraser widow. Murtagh complains that Jamie in his traditional tartan is making himself a redcoat target, while Dougal says the same in the book. After sex, Claire on the show wraps herself in Jamie's plaid, suggesting her closeness to him.

Gabaldon mentions in her notes for the artists of the comic book that one plaid for each clan is actually not historically accurate. As she adds, "You would see groups of related men wearing similar colors and patterns, just because they were all getting their cloth from the same local weaver." In 1581, George Buchanan described a multicolored, striped garment. However, there is no evidence at this point of a pattern for each clan. The pieces of tartan found from this time do not match the modern patterns and show little trace of clan uniformity.

After the Rising, clans were forbidden from wearing tartan, owning weapons or playing bagpipes from 1746 to 1786. However, later on, Victoria and Albert romanticized the Highland tartans as did Sir Walter Scott, and the tartans became fashionable once again. "Whereupon the Lowland woolen merchants ... recognized a Good Thing and swung into gear, producing 'traditional' clan tartans," Gabaldon adds. In 1886, James Grant established this further with his book *The Tartans of the Clans of Scotland*. Likewise, *Old and Rare Scottish Tartans* by D. W. Stewart (1893) aided with the designations. Thus the culture of tartans in the Highlands was in fact invented over a century later by the merchants of the Lowlands. Admittedly, these were often reconstructed from portraits, demanded from clan chiefs and recovered from weaver's notes, but the accuracy is less-than-perfect. As Gabaldon adds, this invented tradition is far more well known that the truth so she "had to sort of walk the line between what I knew to be historically accurate, and this very popular misconception."

Regarding tartans, Terry Dresbach comments:

> There's a huge debate—I talk to fans all the time who are still having a debate with me about the weaving of the 18th century. There's a school of thought that the really bright-colored tartans that we see today were invented by the Victorians and there were those who say no, they were always there. That's often the case where you have a lot of conflicting opinions on what was worn historically, so we made it a creative choice based on talking with Ron about the look of the show [Friedlander].

James Grant responds in "The Tartans of the Clans of Scotland": "The particular *setts* or patterns, appropriate to each clan, must have been long fixed ... by which a man's name and clan were at once recognized." J.F. Campbell makes much of the gorgeous plaids, but does not mention any particular clan patterns, suggesting this is a modern conceit not authentic enough for his book of 1890. Though as he adds, "There are plenty of bits of old tartan preserved in Scotland. There are pictures at Dunrobin, at Taymouth, at Armidale, at Holyrood and elsewhere, all of which prove that tartan was anciently worn, and that particular patterns were worn in certain districts" (Vol. IV, 335). The debate rages on.

JEWELRY

Jewel Symbolism

Jewel symbolism abounds in the first book, long before Master Raymond's obsession with crystals or Geillis's revelation that jewels can protect travelers. When Jamie gives Claire her wedding ring, a bottle on a shelf gleams like lapis. After Jamie rescues Claire from Cranesmuir, the grass is described as emeralds, the heather, amethysts and the rowan tree berries, rubies.

Finally, when Claire comes back down from the stones, she sees Jamie asleep, with tears that have made silver tracks on his golden skin. As Claire prepares to "ransom a man's soul" at book's end, she notes, "There was a feeling, not sudden, but complete, as though I had been given a small object to hold unseen in my hands. Precious as opal, smooth as jade, weighty as a river stone, more fragile than a bird's egg." Like the dragonfly in amber (another jewel in book one), these treasures suggest a precious moment frozen in time and also the beauty and richness of the romantic past.

The stones also represent a tie with lost family. There is a great deal of heirloom jewelry, as Jenny digs through her mother's jumbled box of baubles, or Jamie weds in his father's rubies. Jocasta Cameron wears "a handsome cairngorm brooch," the national stone of Scotland and a tawny gold in color, to remember the place of her childhood (*The Fiery Cross*, ch. 11). Linking with the family he's lost in *The Scottish Prisoner,* Jamie keeps a rough amethyst to remind him of Claire (ch. 38) and other pretty-looking stones for other family members.

The choice of an amethyst is significant in itself. "Pliny says the Magi believed that if the symbols of the Sun and Moon were engraved upon the Amethyst it made a powerful charm against witchcraft, and procured for its wearer's success" (Thomas and Pavitt 274). In medieval times, the amethyst soothed those who were stressed and alerted wearers to traces of poison. Its medicinal ability evokes an image of Claire the physician. "In religious art it was regarded as emblematic of resignation under earthly sufferings, patience in sorrow, and trust unto death," suggesting their relationship (Thomas and Pavitt 274).

In the books, Jamie gives Claire a dagger with a moonstone in the hilt, on which he swears never to beat her again. "Camillus Leonardus says it is powerful in reconciling lovers, and helpful to consumptives when the Moon is increasing in light, but when the Moon is waning, its stone will only enable its wearer to foretell future happenings" (Thomas and Pavitt 182–183). A gift of love, healing, and foretelling together is appropriate for Claire, more than the humbler bone-handled knife Jamie makes for her in North Carolina.

A ghost of a Native American traveler from the future saves Claire and gives her an opal, carved with a spiral pattern. Jamie is instantly skeptical, commenting with Highland superstition that opals are "unlucky stones" (*The Drums of Autumn,* ch. 23). Young Ian corrects Jamie that his mother says "an opal takes on something of the owner"—a good owner brings good luck and a bad owner evil. In fact, the concept of the opal as unlucky may be an anachronism, as one source suggests the superstition came after Jamie's time. An opal can mean varying luck, in fact, good or bad:

> The idea of its being an unlucky stone had its origin in the misfortunes that befell Anne of Geierstein in Sir Walter Scott's novel, her principal jewel consisting of a large Opal; they are not, in reality, more unlucky than other stones,

though being a Libra gem and essentially a pledge of friendship, they are not fortunate for any one having Venus afflicted in their horoscope. In the East it is regarded as a sacred stone which contains the Spirit of Truth, and in Ancient Greece the Opal was supposed to possess the power of giving foresight and the light of prophecy to its owner.

...

All Opals are very sensitive to atmospheric conditions, varying in brilliancy according to the temperature, their colouring being at its best when worn and kept warm and dry. This sensitiveness was believed by the ancients to make them susceptible to influences of an occult nature, so that when the colour of an Opal was bright and lively it indicated success and good fortune to enterprises or travel, and when dull and lifeless it warned of failure and disappointments [Thomas and Pavitt 219–220].

From Geillis after their adventure in the third book, Jamie keeps an emerald, opal, turquoise, golden stone, and the black diamond. While the last of these, like its fellows, is intended for time travel, it has further significance as Jamie notes the adamant gives its owner "The knowledge of joy in all things" (*Voyager,* ch. 63). While he sells the other jewels, Jamie keeps this one for Claire so she can return to the future if necessary, suggesting his love and joy in her. In the seventh book, Lord John gives Claire diamond earrings. These are the hardest stone, as well as one of the most beautiful and expensive, and thus, a salute to her strength.

For many years, Lord John keeps the sapphire he confiscates from Jamie. When pressed, he doesn't return it, but instead gives Jamie the sapphire ring his first love Hector left him—he considers his talisman from Jamie (though given unwillingly and representative of a strictly platonic relationship) more significant that one given by the beloved. Lord John sets it in a semicircle of gold or silver (different in two books) to make a sapphire paperweight that always journeys with him. He also gives away Hector's ring as an engagement ring in *The Drums of Autumn.* Sapphires symbolize a higher spirituality with "truth, chastity, and contemplation," since they're the color of the heavens (Bruce-Mitford 40). John uses his path with sapphires to show his growth toward a more elevated love. The "Star Sapphire was much valued by the Ancients as a love charm; they considered it peculiarly powerful for the procuring of favours, for bringing good fortune and averting witchcraft" (Thomas and Pavitt 156). Both his sapphires bring him love and luck in the accompanying relationships.

"In most symbolic traditions, jewels signify spiritual truths" (Cirlot 163). As jewels protect people while traveling in Gabaldon's mythology, this works as a metaphor of spiritual defense. Pope Innocent sent King John of England four jeweled rings as a gift—the roundness of the rings signified eternity to lead the king "by the form of them to pray for a passage from earthly to heavenly, from temporal to eternal things." There was additional significance: "The number four, which is a square number, denotes the firmness of mind which is neither depressed in adversity nor elated in prosperity, which will then be fulfilled when it is based on the four principal virtues—namely justice, fortitude, prudence, and virtue" (Jones 94). As such, the gleam of jewels suggest heavenly guidance as well as beauty and perfection.

Brooches

Circle brooches were worn historically by the Highlanders to secure their plaids, so it's no surprise that many appear. Colum and Dougal secure their plaids with large jeweled brooches on formal occasions. Jenny's grandmother had a silver crescent moon brooch with a single diamond shining above the tip (*Outlander,* ch. 31). The silver and the moon of course are feminine symbols, appropriate for a matriarch. While Jamie wears a rather simple abstract silver brooch of his mother's on the show, in the book he wears a brooch of two deer chasing each other. It is described as "a beautiful thing ... made in the shape of two running stags, bodies bent so that they joined in a circle, heads and tails touching" (*Dragonfly in Amber*, ch. 22). This appears on the cover of book five, while book three shows a U-shaped brooch with a pair of abstract ends, possibly symbolizing Jamie and Claire questing for each other and joining once more.

Jamie buys Claire a fish pin carved from black coral in the West Indies, celebrating their lengthy voyages. Fish also represent joy and sexuality in the ancient world. In the next book, Jamie considers getting Claire a brooch for their anniversary but prefers a doctor's kit when he finds one in a pawnshop. Claire reflects that he's not one for impractical gifts.

Pearl Necklace

"The pearl signifies humility, purity, innocence, and a retiring spirit," Jones notes in *History and Mystery of Precious Stones* as he describes the "modest splendor and purity of the jewel" (94, 113). In fact, these last do not well describe Claire, or indeed Ellen MacKenzie, who eloped with her husband against her clan's wishes and only returned when heavily pregnant. Both women are pale, especially Claire, and both have a faithful marriage blessed with the pearls and other gifts, but neither are especially humble or innocent.

On their wedding day in the books, Jamie gives Claire his mother Ellen's necklace as they go into church. It is a necklace of baroque pearls interspersed with tiny gold roundels with smaller pearls dangling from these (*Outlander*, ch. 14).

> "They're only Scotch pearls," he said, apologetically, "but they look bonny on you." His fingers lingered a moment on my neck.

"Those were your mother's pearls!" said Dougal, glowering at the necklace.
"Aye," said Jamie calmly, "and now they're my wife's. Shall we go?"

On the show, they have a more classic look, a larger simple long string. Jamie gives them to Claire on their wedding night when she's looking distraught. He tells her he values them and her, and they engage in sex with her wearing only them, dangling between her breasts. "Since the neck has an astrological association with sex, the necklace also betokens an erotic link" (Cirlot 227). Pearls are also a symbol of beauty that "have long been the jewel of love" (Bruce-Mitford 87). They were said to be a combination of masculine and feminine, male fire and female water. Paradise has been equated with pearls and also sexual completion: "Aphrodite's 'pearly gate,' the symbolic yoni leading to her sexual paradise, also became a Christian tradition" (Walker 517). In the episode, Claire describes forgetting her previous life, losing the incidents like "pearls on a string ... rolling into dark corners." While this links with the pearls, in fact they are an heirloom, kept intact for Claire's years in Scotland and beyond. Thus they provide a link with memory rather than its dissolution.

Of course, "pearls have for ages been significant for tears" (Jones 119). Margaret Tudor, wife of James IV of Scotland, dreamed she saw her husband mangled at the bottom of a chasm and also dreamed that her chains and coronets of diamonds suddenly turned to pearls "which are the emblems of widowhood" (119). The queen of France had a similar dream a few nights before the assassination of her husband Henry IV.

> The idea that Pearls are symbolic of tears arose from this fact, and illustrates the old adage that the most noble achievements have their origin in painful and enduring effort. Nowadays in the Pearl Fisheries, particularly in the Bay of Ago, (Japan) foreign matter is intentionally introduced into the shell, but the results do not equal the Pearls found as the outcome of natural influences, a considerable time being required to bring them to perfection.... This gem is, however, considered unfortunate for those in love, and if worn by the married signified "torrents of tears," and for this reason is seldom used in engagement rings, even at the present day [Thomas and Pavitt 184–185].

Mrs. Graham the fortuneteller and housekeeper wears three strands of artificial pearls when Claire meets her for the first time (*Outlander,* ch. 2), suggesting the sorrows the fortune telling predicts as Claire is catapulted to another world. As such, Jamie anoints their wedding with sadness, and indeed, suffering, death, loss, and partings follow them through their adventures.

Other intriguing significances follow. "There is a magic charm in the pearl that seems to have fascinated the world in various ages and countries" (Jones 113). A gift of magic for Claire the time traveler is more appropriate, and indeed, the gold in the necklace protects her on her travels according to Gabaldon's lore.

Also, powdered pearls had many medical uses: for stomachs and the voice. "They also comforted the heart and rendered their possessor chaste" (Jones 123). These physical cures and charms for the heart thus suit Claire the physician.

Lovely and valuable, the pearls appear on several formal occasions. Claire also pawns them for the money. The pearls most often function as a sign of recognition for those who know Jamie and acknowledgement that Claire (and anyone else who has them) is Jamie's family and heir. Claire tries to use them as a bribe in the first book, only to have them recognized. Her host, Sir Marcus MacRannoch, explains that he gave them to Jamie's mother for a wedding gift, after he'd hoped she'd be his bride. He returns the pearls to Claire with a wish that she'll wear them in good health, to which Claire responds tartly, "I'll stand a much better chance of doing so ... if you'll help me to get my husband back" (*Outlander,* ch. 36). In memory of Ellen, he does, and sends her a matching bracelet later, acknowledging her courage. It is described as a single row of large baroque pearls set between twisted gold chains (*Outlander,* ch. 41).

A bead necklace symbolizes unifying diversity—in this scene, Claire recruits many forces—and even a herd of cattle—to save Jamie. Regarded as a string, the necklace becomes a cosmic and social symbol of ties and bonds. All this is what Claire calls on the scene above.

Rings and Bracelets

"Like every closed circle, the ring is a symbol of continuity and wholeness. This is why (like the bracelet) it has been used both as a symbol of marriage and of the eternally-repeated time cycle" (Cirlot 273). Of course, there are Claire's wedding rings: a gold one for Frank and a silver for Jamie.

Gold symbolizes the sun, patriarchy and masculine principle. Thus is apt for Frank, in his world of military hierarchy in which Claire learned to operate. Only her trip through the standing stones saves her from a future as housewife to an Oxford Don, another masculine order. Gold is popular for wedding rings because of its sunny, undimmed color, suggesting untarnished joy. Malleable as it is, gold is a symbol for adaptability as well as untarnished constancy and the indestructible—gold buried for millennia will emerge from the earth in the same state it was buried. Frank is frozen waiting for Claire in the future, a lightpost to guide her home if she chooses to return. A constant in her life, he also represents continual temptation and the possibility of a modern life to resume. He proves surprisingly adaptable; though in books and show he refuses to believe in the power of the stones, he's found cautiously exploring, driving there in episode eight and researching the possibilities in the books.

Silver is the less expensive, simpler metal. It represents the feminine principle—a surprising symbol for manly Jamie, but indeed he has a softer side.

Claire has more sexual experience, as well as more scientific knowledge; Jamie is better in literature, languages and more liberal arts. He swears less than the other men—thanks to the strong-minded nuns who trained him. As Caitriona Balfe describes Jamie:

> His emotional intelligence is what, for me, stands out. In this very rough and barbaric world, here's a young guy who's, emotionally, so much more modern. And he's willing to learn and he's looking for that guidance. And I think that's the beautiful thing that they find in each other. I truly believe that she was very much in love with Frank, but I think that this is something that she has never experienced before... [Prudom, "Strong Female"].

As he asks Claire to share her emotions and encourages her to use her many strengths, he helps her complete her journey to womanly power. Silver is associated with intuition, self-reflection and inner wisdom, qualities he evokes within her. It is also a metal of protection, emotion, purity, and love. In the book, Claire's ring is "a wide silver band, decorated in the Highland interlace style, a small and delicate Jacobean thistle bloom carved in the center of each link" (ch. 23). It echoes the small, delicate love, blooming in the Highlands like the tough, hardy flower of Scottish survival and fortitude. The sinuous continuing pattern suggests an everlasting nature, something like the single circle of gold, but in this case delicately embellished. On the show, the wedding ring is forged from the iron key to Lallybroch, Jamie's home, of which Claire is now mistress.

For Claire, both wedding rings suggest obligation to these contrasting husbands. She wears them balanced between her two hands, acknowledging her tie to one husband while she lives with the other. As she describes a scene with Jamie after he gives her the ring:

> He held me, arms outstretched, wrists pinioned. One hand brushed the wall, and I felt the tiny scrape of one wedding ring chiming against the stone. One ring for each hand, one silver, one gold. And the thin metal suddenly heavy as the bonds of matrimony, as though the rings were tiny shackles, fastening me spread-eagled to the bed, stretched forever between two poles, held in bondage like Prometheus on his lonely rock, divided love the vulture that tore at my heart [ch. 23].

Bracelets too symbolize marriage and continuity. Ellen Fraser owned a pair of "magnificent, barbaric bracelets" made from circular boar tusks, capped with silver and etched with flowers. They were given to her by an admirer, finally revealed as Murtagh. Claire wears them on Quarter Day at Lallybroch (*Outlander,* ch. 31). As such, she continues Ellen's legacy, even as Murtagh fights to defend Ellen's son.

Later, Roger gives Brianna a silver bracelet that says all the different ways he loves her. It "looks like prescience" as they decide that they only want to be together when they know it's forever (*The Drums of Autumn,* ch. 18). Nonetheless, Brianna considers the bracelet an engagement gift of a sort, as the one token he gives her before their ringless handfasting. She carries it with her, inheriting the protection of the silver and symbolically the protection of his love.

Brian Fraser's wedding ring is a cabuchon ruby, used as Claire's wedding ring in the book ceremony (*Outlander,* ch. 15). Jamie wears a ruby stickpin as well. Rubies are the color of love and passion as well as vitality. They can symbolize blood as well as courage and martyrdom, all of which Jamie will offer. In chapter 6 of *Drums,* Jamie gets Claire a ruby necklace, with similar associations.

A final set of rings are the three Jocasta Cameron hides away in the fifth book: one a plain band set with a beryl, another with an enormous emerald, and the last with three entrancing diamonds (*The Fiery Cross,* ch. 41). All three are ostentatious, reflecting her three marriages that seem to have more of wealth about them than love. In a way, these rings, so carefully hoarded but not worn, parody Jocasta's marriages. It's revealed later that after getting her three daughters killed, her husband gave her the three rings in remembrance. Thus they're an inversion of the love and trust of marriage, in contrast with Claire's simpler bands. It's no wonder Jocasta doesn't wear them.

ANIMALS

Birds

Colum's many caged songbirds offer a moment of strangeness for Claire, though of course they're a reasonable hobby for someone living indoors. However, as Colum tells Claire she must stay at the castle, she feels as trapped as the birds themselves. In the comic adaptation, which uses more points of view than Claire's, Murtagh quarrels with the MacKenzie brothers about Jamie's best interests and captures a bird in his hand. He squeezes in a subtle threat and then leaves the bird unharmed on Colum's head.

"Every winged being is a symbol of spiritualization," as the mind reaches like the bird for the heights (Cirlot 26). Thus caged birds suggest the caged mind, one unable to find divine spirituality. Colum is concerned with the mundane—ensuring an heir for his clan and keeping Claire under his control, remaining neutral and safe as Jacobite sentiments rise. He is not portrayed as one of the great risk-takers or heroes in the story.

Later, in the wilderness, birds' restlessness echoes the immanent war. As Jamie describes it:

> It was as though they felt the imminence of flight, and the pull of it—and that disturbed their rest. The stranger it was, because most of the birds that he had

were young ones, who had never yet made the journey; they hadna seen the place where they were bound, and yet they felt it there—calling to them, perhaps, rousing them from sleep.

He calls it "Zugunruhe ... the wakefulness of the wee birds, getting ready to leave on their long flight." As he explains, the roots of the words add up to "a restlessness—the uneasiness before a long journey" (*The Fiery Cross,* ch. 107).

Later, Claire and Jamie go visit a local tribe, only to be surrounded by a great wave of birds, so dark they resemble a storm. The tribe panic and several children begin to cry (ch. 82). Claire considers it a dark omen when she realizes they're passenger pigeons, condemned to become extinct. She and Jamie may soon follow. Birds, as well as a source of spirituality and free choice, represent delicacy and the natural environment. Thus they are the first to sense change and even die as the fortunes of the world spin on.

Cat and Fly

The night before her wedding of the books, Claire gets terribly drunk at the bar and watches "a green-bellied fly struggling on the edges of a sticky puddle on the table." In the background, she hears Jamie arguing with Dougal for his wedding conditions. She adds: "With a certain amount of fellow-feeling, I nudged it out of danger with the edge of my glass." However, the fly finds itself back into the sticky whiskey and "was floundering in the middle, hopelessly mired" (ch. 13). As it twitches and struggles, her "fellow-feeling" increases. The fly is obviously herself, deprived of freedom and "hopelessly mired" in a political tangle—she can wed the near-stranger Jamie (though she's married to Frank in the future) or face Jack Randall's interrogation and torture. All her efforts to escape have gotten her more entangled until she isn't completely sure she wants to get free.

In the wedding episode, the fly is gone (obviously, it is disgusting and difficult to film). Instead, a cat wanders downstairs eating scraps in several scenes. The meaning of the grey cat is not fully explored, but in its color it seems to mirror Claire in her silvery gown. Cats are a feminine symbol, suggesting the pride and power of the lion, though much smaller and sleeker. They were associated with powerful, independent goddesses Diana, Freya, Kybele, and Bast. "The cat, that animal that famously does *not* come when called, has long been an emblem of independence—and of free, independent, autonomous women" (Illes 44). Obedience is foreign to their nature ... something that might also be said of Claire.

Symbolically, cats are sexually insatiable (the *fe* is the Latin *felis* means to bear young and also appears in words like fecund and fetus) (Illes 45). Cats are sensual creatures, accustomed to fine food and soft sleeping places, offering mystery and beauty when they choose to appear. As the cat roams freely during the wedding night instead of being caught in a sticky puddle while Claire despairs, it represents Claire's cautious then eager consummation upstairs. Both are independent, proud, and willful, but willing to be domesticated.

In Celtic legend, the cat represents the guardian of the Otherworld, suggesting an initiation into the mysteries (of marriage in this case) and a deeper level of wisdom upon returning. It allows the human heroine of the story to touch her inner wildness and primitive longings. The animal, according to Jung, stands for "the world of subhuman instincts and for the unconscious areas of the psyche" (Cirlot 13). Notably, the cat runs off when Dougal makes a pass at Claire. Below conscious thought (though admittedly, not very far down), Claire is repelled by Dougal and feels trapped by the forced marriage. Yet, like the cat, she comes to accept family life as a way to rule over the household and complete her spiritual journey.

Horses

Jamie is employed as a horse trainer at Castle Leoch (because he's hiding from the English soldiers). As such, Claire gets to know him as a humble stableworker, one who soothes and comforts horses all day before he becomes her lover and husband. Claire notes several times that Jamie's training with horses has taught him a great deal of gentleness, which he most often uses when trying to relax her. She describes him as "horse-gentling" with his touch on their wedding night. In the second episode, Jamie is training a white horse—when Claire makes a noise, the horse is spooked and hurts his injured shoulder. However, Jamie dismisses the incident and notes, "She's just a girl with spirit is all. That's always a good thing." He certainly seems to be talking of Claire as well.

Later, Old Alec offers Claire the use of the horse Brimstone. He tells her she's not really devilish, only called this, "like calling a tall man 'wee.' She's no fast, but she's sweet and can go for days. Only thing is if yer not minding her every moment, she'll turn for home first chance she gets" (Episode 104). This description also seems to echo Claire—called Sassenach, witch, and devil-woman, but really a force for good. And she certainly turns for home whenever she's not watched.

Jung suggested the horse symbolized "the magic side of Man, 'the mother within us,' that is, intuitive understanding" (qtd. in Cirlot 152). Jamie uses his body knowledge from training horses to connect with troubled children and animals as well. Years later, he walks a pregnant Brianna around her room "like a horse with colic" (*The Drums of Autumn*, ch. 64). He's also seen working with horses at the estate of Helwater. The most important thing that happens to Jamie there is the birth of young William and Jamie's time spent with him. Once again, nurturing and caring are central, with the horses providing the link: Horse training provides an excuse for Jamie to spend any time with the young earl. His Christmas gift to baby Jem and his parting gift to William are both hand-carved horses.

> Elements of the cult of the mother-goddess (essentially a neolithic fertility cult) remained in medieval Ireland in the ritual matings of patrilineal Celtic dynasts with white mares symbolizing the land of Ireland: Mother Earth. This symbolic act was the remaking of the original mating of the Celtic male sun-god with the mother-goddess of pre–Celtic Ireland [Cairney 27].

After hearing this lore by the fireside, Jamie awakes in chapter one of *The Fiery Cross* dreaming that he's about to make himself king of Ireland by copulating with a white horse. However, in his dream, he discovers the horse is black. This book will have several surprises and reversals that are more ominous than lucky. Further, he has the dream as Claire dreams Frank is visiting for Brianna's wedding. While Claire is visited by her old husband, Jamie has trouble controlling the white horse—it changes color then vanishes, emphasizing this lack of control, not only over Claire, but over the politics and family plots that are about to appear. In fact, later at the plantation, Claire notes, "There were horses in my dream; glowing black Friesians with flowing manes that rippled in the wind as the stallions ran beside me. I saw my own legs stretch and leap; I was a white mare" (ch. 48). In dreams, a black horse often signifies mystery, wildness, and the unknown, as Claire and Jamie gamble with the events of the American Revolution. Once more, she is the wild horse and Jamie, the man struggling to tame her.

Rabbits and Fish

Around their weddings, Claire and Brianna are presented with gifts of rabbits and fish. Both are obviously a small food source, taken from a well-wisher's personal supply to add to the young couple's. The modern women tactfully accept the dead animals—marriage will not be all sweetness and perfection, but will have its unsavory moments as well.

Along with food in the ancient world, these animals represented fertility, prosperity, and new life. As such, they're wishes for fruitful and satisfying unions. "Fish have always been viewed as an 'aphrodisiac' food because of their ancient associations with the Aphrodite type of goddess" (Walker 374). Rabbits, with their month-long gestation period and many babies, are a sign of fertility and womanhood. "Sacred rabbits, female and male, had dominion over women's reproductive abilities. Vestiges of that pagan belief survive in the bunny that delivers eggs, emblematic of birth, at Easter" (Illes 85). Jamie's wedding poem to Claire as they honeymoon echoes this sentiment, listing badgers, otters, and fish, all prolific lively creatures of the natural world:

"Thou daughter of the King of bright-lit mansions
On the night that our wedding is on us,
If living man I be in Duntulm,
I will go bounding to thee with gifts.
Thou wilt get a hundred badgers, dwellers in banks,
A hundred brown otters, natives of streams,
A hundred silver trout, rising from their pools..."
[*Carmina Gadelica* Vol. II, 281]

Wolves

In book one, Claire confronts a lone wolf. She finds herself connecting with it, looking into its "wicked yellow" eyes and judging the moment it will jump. Wild animals often represent the hunting instinct, the inner wildness within a person. This Claire finds struggling with the beast:

> I drove a knee viciously into its chest, eliciting a strangled yelp. Only then did I realize that the odd, growling whimpers were coming from me and not the wolf.
>
> Strangely enough, I was not at all frightened now, though I had been terrified watching the wolf stalk me. There was room in my mind for only one thought: I would kill this animal, or it would kill me. Therefore, I was going to kill it.
>
> There comes a turning point in intense physical struggle where one abandons oneself to a profligate usage of strength and bodily resource, ignoring the costs until the struggle is over. Women find this point in childbirth; men in battle [*Outlander*, ch. 35].

Physically in a life-or-death battle for the first time in her life, she harnesses this wolfish power and fights savagely for her life. She wins the battle, and when the wolf's pack shows up, her terror has transformed into "black rage." Wielding this fury, she might take on the entire pack, and indeed, she uses this strength to save Jamie several times. Her encounter has transformed her and awakened the raging power within. Later, an admirer sends her the wolf's pelt to salute this wildness within Claire.

In the New World, Young Ian wins Rollo, a dog who's part wolf. Adopting a wolf emphasizes the power and primitiveness of the wilderness around them as Jamie, Claire, and Ian struggle to survive. With the animal always at his side, Ian soon becomes known as Wolf Brother. He joins a tribe for a time, symbolizing a descent into wildness, a pathway to becoming a man—and indeed, he returns far different. Rollo is his constant companion on his many journeys into the forest.

Rollo himself symbolizes wildness, mirroring the predatory spirit in others. As Claire watches, she sees that "Jamie and Rollo regarded the possum with identical looks of calculation, assessing its plumpness and possible speed." When the possum leaves, "The two hunters let out identical sighs, and relaxed again"

(*The Drums of Autumn,* ch. 9). Deep in the forest, Claire has her own encounter as she dreams of herself as a wolf, "the scent of blood hot in my own nose, running with the pack" (*The Drums of Autumn,* ch. 23). She too is becoming part of the wilderness, encountering ghosts and beginning to train in New World mysticism. She wakes up nose to nose with Rollo, who has not only found her here in the forest but is blessing her as one of his own.

PLANTS

Forget-Me-Not

Claire returns to the standing stones to pick this flower and carries it with her when she time travels. Moore describes the scene when Claire silently finds the flowers as important to him as an "interesting texture" along with a motive for Claire to return (Episode Podcasts 101).

Forget-me-not plants symbolize true love because of their strong color. They're used to decorate gifts of remembrance, of course. They also symbolize faithful love and memories. Claire feels these emotions for both her husbands, torn as she is between the pair of them. Blue also signifies striving for spiritual heights, seen as it is in the heavens. By returning for the flower, Claire is seeking knowledge of herbs but also enlightenment as to her place in the world, which she indeed discovers.

Heather and White Roses

In *Dragonfly in Amber,* Brianna and Roger visit Culloden, the site of the Jacobite Highlanders' last stand, and see the heather left at the clan stones. He tells her it's more common to be placed on the mounds when it's blooming in summer: "then you'll see heaps like that in front of every clan stone. Purple, and here and there a branch of the white heather—the white is for luck and for kinship; it was Charlie's emblem, that and the white rose" (ch. 4).

Heather has always been representative of Scotland, much like the thistle. Meanwhile, the white rose appears as a coded symbol in Jacobite documents through the series, especially in *The Scottish Prisoner.* It was once the emblem of the House of York, and when they allied with Lancaster and ended the War of the Roses, they combined their white and red roses into the Tudor rose. Some generations later, James Francis Edward Stuart, the "Old Pretender" and father to Bonnie Prince Charlie, was born on 10th June 1688, the Summer Solstice, when the white rose is traditionally said to flower. The day is called White Rose Day, so James's supporters chose the York rose for their symbol. According to legend, Prince Charlie stayed overnight at Fassfern House en route from Glenfinnan on August 23, 1745. As he departed, Charlie plucked a white rose from a nearby bush and attached it to his blue bonnet, making the famous White Cockade, another Jacobite emblem.

Roses and heather are both sweet-smelling symbols of beauty and femininity. Claire wears white asters and yellow roses in her hair for her wedding of the books, and Jamie's mother's roses twine around the entrance of Lallybroch like a blessing. In traditional circles it's good luck to wear a sprig of white heather for a wedding. According to legend, the famous bard Ossian had a son named Oscar. He left his sweetheart, Malvina, behind, and when he died, he sent her a spray of purple heather as a last gift. In her grief, Malvina ran over the hillside, weeping. Where her tears fell, the purple heather turned pure white. When she saw this, she said, "May this white heather forever bring good fortune to all those who find it."

Strawberries

"D'ye believe in signs at all, Sassenach?"
"What sorts of signs?" I asked guardedly [*Drums of Autumn*, ch. 60].

Jamie explains that the strawberry is the emblem of Clan Fraser, shown in its heraldry. As he adds, "It's what the name meant, to start with, when a Monsieur Fréseliére came across from France wi' King William that was—and took hold of land in the Scottish mountains for his trouble" (*The Drums of Autumn,* ch. 14).

The Fraser coat of arms is azure: three silver strawberries quartered with three antique crowns gules (heraldic red). It seems the Frasers go back to William the Conqueror in 1066 and France before that:

> The Frasers (Friseal) descend from a Norman family named de Frisselle (Norman-French "the Friesian") or de Freseliere that settled in Tweeddale and Lothian, where the name is still extant. Some of them, including the main line of the family, adopted the alternate name of Fraissier, which means strawberry bearer, as a pun on their name because they adopted fraisses, or strawberry flowers, as armorial bearings in the twelfth century. The first of the family recorded in Scotland was Sir Simon Fraser, who in 1160 held part of the lands of Keith in East Lothian [Cairney 136–137].

Jamie adds that the red-white-green of the fruit has meaning, with white flowers for honor, red fruit for courage, and green leaves for constancy, with the fruit in the shape of a heart. Claire thinks this describes him perfectly. The strawberry traditionally symbolizes perfection and righteousness, so the fruits often decorate altars and the tops of pillars in churches and cathedrals. In the last chapter of *Written in My Own Heart's Blood*, Claire calls the strawberries encircling the house "tiny, sour-sweet red hearts" and she and Jamie sit among them and lovingly reminisce about where their lives have brought them (ch. 145).

Thistle

The thistle of Scotland is said to be the oldest national flower on record. From 795, Vikings launched frequent raids on Scottish lands. In 1263, King Haakon of Norway invaded with a sizeable fleet. Landing at Largs in Ayrshire, the Norse tried to surprise the sleeping clansmen, so they removed their shoes to creep close to their camp. However, as they skulked, they crossed ground covered in thistles. One of Haakon's men stepped on one and shrieked out in pain, alerting the Clansmen. The Vikings were soon turned back. Scotland took the thistle as its symbol in gratitude.

The legendary King Achius is said to have founded the Order of the Thistle in the ninth century, then James VII refounded it based on this legend in 1687. Their motto is "Nemo me impune lacessit," which translates as "No one assails me with impunity." Hence Claire's wedding ring from Jamie carries this tough Scottish survivor of a flower, rather than something soft and delicate. The gentle sentiments are inscribed on the inside, carefully hidden. It also marks her as a Scot from that day forward, devoted to protecting the men of Lallybroch and the other Highlanders, rather than the English cause.

TELEVISION SYMBOLS

Key as Wedding Ring

Claire's wedding ring on the show is not silver, carved with thistles, but a simplistic, blocky iron ring. The original concept was a nail, rejected by costume designer Terry Dresbach for its ugliness. Nonetheless, the producer wanted a ring with sentiment to it, rather than one Jamie simply bought (as in the book, though he has that one engraved). Thus, Jamie wants to use the door key to Lallybroch, his lost home. Ron Moore explains that each of their friends needs an assignment to make the wedding come together (Dougal took the priest and Ned Gowan the dress), so he wanted Angus and Rupert to go fetch it. It becomes a "key to my heart" reference as well (Podcast 107).

Keys are a feminine symbol, as the lady of the house was generally the keeper of the keys and dispenser of goods. At Jared's townhouse in France, Claire notes, "Aside from the occasional call to open the linen cupboard, the wine cellar, the root cellar, or the pantry with a key from my bunch, my time was then my own" (*Dragonfly in Amber*, ch. 8). Jamie is thus acknowledging her as the Lady of Lallybroch and giving her the key's symbolic power and status. Spiritually, a key can indicate freedom, success, and secrets. Claire's marriage to Jamie brings her all of these, as does her time spying as lady of the townhouse in France.

This is a mashup of symbols, as iron is firmly masculine. With its use in weapons as well as plows and farm tools, it signifies mankind's conquering energy and power over the natural world. It evokes aggression, progress, dependence and protection. As the most human metal, it also protects against fairyfolk and supernatural attack. While the book's silver wedding ring indicates Jamie conveying Claire to a higher spiritual understanding of herself, transmitted through silver's love and clarity, iron indicates he will protect her with all a man's strength.

Shinty Game

Moore added the shinty game (known as *camanachd* in Gaelic) to episode four ("The Gathering") in an attempt to show the culture. After researching what games they might actually have played, he had real shinty players as extras in the episode ("Inside the World," 104). Jamie apparently plays in the books, though this only appears as a brief nod: "What on earth makes ye mention Letitia?" he asks. "I lived at the Castle for a year, and had speech of her maybe once that I remember, when she called me to her chamber and gave me the raw side of her tongue for leading a game of shinty through her rose garden" (*Outlander*, ch. 24).

Dougal and Jamie show the complexities of their relationship as they play—violence and competition as the student, a soldier, begins to surpass his teacher, the war chief. At the same time, strong affection binds them, and the pair are only playing a game ... for now at least. Graham McTavish (Dougal MacKenzie) discusses working with the cast, just after his friend Geordie's death: "coming on the back of ... such an emotional scene, it's an outlet for Dougal, for him to basically take it out on Jamie" (Bertone).

Waulking Wool

In the book, Claire occasionally visits a cottage for a cup of milk while on the rent collecting trip, and she does what doctoring she can for the families (*Outlander*, ch. 11). The show adapts this, following Claire into the women's community of the Highlands for the first time. In the original script, a group of women were supposed to invite Claire for tea and cards—Gabaldon pointed out that in the remote Highlands neither of these existed and suggested waulking wool, which was then added to the scene (Loughlin). Waulking or shrinking by hand the tweed to make it proof against the northern weather was a communal task, kneading the heavy cloth with strong hands or sometimes by the bare feet after it was soaked in hot, stale urine.

The television crew even found waulking songs from the Highland Folkways Museum (Loughlin). The women sing "Mo nigh'n donn ho gù" (an homage to Claire's nickname of brown-haired lass). They also sing "Gille Bòidheach."

In his essay, "The Traditions of the Northern Celts," Peter N. Williams calls waulking songs "perhaps the most important group of songs in the entire tradition":

> These songs, the *drain luadhaidh* have remained, even after the heavy work of "waulking" was replaced by electric looms. In them are preserved some of the most ancient historical and mythological material providing a wealth of information on the traditional life of the Highlands that would otherwise have been lost forever. They include ballads, fairy tales, clan lore, songs of love and battle and purely local stories about the idiosyncrasies of purely local characters.... The rhythmic movements of the task were accompanied by the voice of the leader who sang the narrative, with the team, seated around the large worktable, taking up the refrain. The whole process was unique in Western Europe, an extraordinary experience that helped preserve so many rare aspects of the folk tradition.

Waulking appears in several historical texts. As Keltie records: "They use the same tone, or a piper, when they thicken the newly-woven plaiding, instead of a fulling-mill. This is done by six or eight women sitting upon the ground, near some river or rivulet, in two opposite ranks. With the wet cloth between them; their coats are tucked up, and with their naked feet they strike one against another's, keeping exact time." In the books, the waulking scene appears in book two. Claire accepts the process philosophically, and thinks, "Smell aside, the waulking shed was a warm, cozy place, where the women of Lallybroch visited and joked between bolts of cloth, and sang together in the working, hands moving rhythmically across a table" (ch. 34).

On the show, Claire is drawn from the camp because she hears an unusual song, much like the way she was drawn to the standing stones. Raised by only an uncle, and then serving among soldiers, Claire presumably has not spent much time with women. She mentions in the books that Jamie's sister Jenny is the closest (and basically only) female friend she's ever had. Thus she finds herself drawn to this other culture so different from the male world surrounding her. This is Claire's first introduction to the women's world—Mrs. Fitz cares for the men of the quite masculine Castle Leoch, and Geillis is strange and witch-like. By contrast, the village women are leading an ordinary life with women's songs and culture. They welcome Claire among them. She in turn joins in the fun, to the point where she's squatting over a bucket to, er, add to their working materials, when Dougal's man interrupts them, rudely intruding into the women's hut without knocking, just as Claire has her skirts up. This represents a male intrusion into the female domain, an area only shown in a few of the often-masculine epic series.

In a humorous interlude in the third book, Claire and Jamie stay overnight at a brothel, and in the morning the prostitutes assume she's one of them. Over a friendly breakfast, they offer her sex tips, remark on her body and give her many pieces of advice, to the horror of the madam. This is one of Claire's rare moments in a female space, as she's soon adventuring with Jamie once more.

CHARACTER SYMBOLS

Blue Vase

The show starts almost at once with the image of the blue vase in Claire's voiceover.

> Strange, the things you remember. Single images and feelings that stay with you down through the years. Like the moment I realized I'd never owned a vase. That I'd never lived any place long enough to justify having such a simple thing. And how at that moment, I wanted nothing so much in all the world as to have a vase of my very own. Somehow in my mind, V.E. day, the end of the bloodiest and most terrible war in human history, grows fainter with each passing day. But I can still recall every detail of the day when I saw the life I wanted sitting in a window.

Gazing in the shop window, she longs for the vase she sees there since she's never had a real house or chance to practice domesticity. "I sometimes wonder what would have happened if I'd bought that vase and made a home for it," she adds. By this she seems to mean, what if she had resolved to settle down permanently instead of continue wandering. A vase was the token of Mother Rhea in Greek myth, suggesting the beneficent mother doling out enormous gifts to the people. Thus it symbolizes heavenly generosity but also the maternal world. Blue is a color of striving and celestial enlightenment, as it's the color of the sky. "It is also the infinite and the void from which all life develops" (Bruce-Mitford 107). As such, it suggests striving for spirituality and self-improvement rather than settling.

While Claire's time travel is an accident, she makes several decisions, including seeking the flower in the first place—which she might not have made if she'd chosen to settle. There's a disturbing hint here that if Claire had been satisfied with domesticity—buying vases and homemaking instead of herbalism and combing the countryside for plants, she wouldn't have left. The book mentions that Frank "suggested" Claire take up botany "to occupy [her] mind" once she was finished with nursing (ch. 1). After the war, she is restless and seeking occupation. Gathering forget-me-nots is the best she can do, before she must settle down to the life of an Oxford don. Instead, of course, she travels to a place where her medical skills are needed and finds her destiny.

Colors

Black Jack Randall is so named for his character: Jamie reminds Claire, "that's with reference to the color of his soul, not his hair" (ch. 16). "In the

West, black is the color of death, mourning, and the underworld. It also has associations with evil magic" (Bruce-Mitford 106). Black Jack's name is, as Claire notes, "A common name for rogues and scoundrels in the eighteenth century. A staple of romantic fiction, the name conjured up charming highwaymen, dashing blades in plumed hats" (ch. 35).

But he's no longer a romantic character from the past but a living sadist determined to torture her and Jamie. As she adds, "One never stops to think what underlies romance. Tragedy and terror, transmuted by time." Now the time is gone.

Red Jamie as he's later known provides a striking contrast. "Red is the color of life—of blood, fire, passion, and war" (Bruce-Mitford 106). To Claire, he is the most vibrant person in an all-too real past, contrasting with the fading present (especially on the show, where the film is deliberately tinted). Jamie's hair emphasizes his extreme vitality, along with his passion. Too, violence and war follow him through the books. Red is the traditional color of martyrdom, as he sacrifices himself or demands to be whipped in another's place in nearly every book. In nature, red signals "Back away! Danger!" and Joan calls it a devil's mark in "The Space Between." Indeed, Jamie can be quite dangerous. His red hair and height also mark him as singular—eyes are drawn to him in every room.

Claire's pale skin is emphasized repeatedly—the French call her a "White Lady," and the Native Americans, "White Raven." White is a symbol of purity, saintliness, and virtuous magic, of course, emphasizing her role as a force for good. "It is the color most associated with sacredness: sacrificial animals are often white" (Bruce-Mitford 106). White is the color of the untried maiden, as Claire quests like many other mythic heroines and experiences the powers of red and black after meeting her true love and his deadly foe. As *From Girl to Goddess*, a book exploring the stages of the heroine's journey, says of the mythic heroine: "She is a maiden (white) longing to become a grown woman (red). To accomplish this, she faces death and gains powers of the spirit (black)" (Frankel 57). As Claire experiences love and devastation at the hands of these two men, she follows a similar spiritual path towards deeper understanding.

Nonetheless, Jamie often calls her "my brown one," "mo duinne," or later, "mo nighean duinne," "my brown-haired lass." When Claire, disconcerted by his intensity on their wedding night, calls brown a "dull color," he responds that it's "Not dull at all." but "like the water in a burn, where it ruffles over the stones. Dark in the wavy spots, with bits of silver on the surface where the sun catches it" (*Outlander,* ch. 16). Brown symbolizes the earth, tying Claire with the magic of plants and healing. Jamie loves the natural world, so it's unsurprising he connects Claire with it. The color also can signify humility or a renunciation of the world, as seen in friars' robes. Claire has left the world of modernity and hot baths to live in primitive times when bright colors cannot be made. She is indeed Jamie's brown one, though around Frank, she wears brighter clothing.

The Home

Ron Moore notes:

I think it's a show that I've never seen before. It's a different kind of story. There's not a home base—it's not like there's the police station or the hospital or even the starship. The show evolves and continues and it's a journey. So even though Claire goes back in time and she ends up at Castle Leoch right after the first episode, she's not there that long. She's only there for a little while. Then she leaves and she's pretty much on the road and going to different places. So it's not like each show is similar to the one before [Prudom, "Ron Moore"].

Claire and Jamie wander about Scotland and France, fighting and negotiating, camping rough or staying as the guests of others. Before this, Jamie was a mercenary in France, and had been since Randall's soldiers took him from Lallybroch as a young man. Claire had been a nurse in the war, traveling through Europe with minimal gear. But before this she hadn't had a home either. As she notes:

Orphaned at five, I had lived the life of an academic vagabond with my uncle Lamb for the next thirteen years. ... The roving life had continued with Frank, though with a shift from field to universities, as the digging of a historian is usually conducted within walls. So, when the war came in 1939, it was less a disruption to me than to most. I had moved from our latest hired flat into the junior nurses' quarters at Pembroke Hospital, and from there to a field station in France, and back again to Pembroke before war's end [*Dragonfly in Amber,* ch. 31].

When they're wed, Jamie warns Claire that he has little to offer her, as he's afraid to go home with a price on his head and has only a soldier's pay. After their wedding, they stay in inns or camp rough, finally getting upgraded to a nicer room in Castle Leoch, but still not one that's theirs. In all this time, only their short visits to Lallybroch truly feel like a home. After her long homelessness, "It was strange, then, and rather wonderful, to wake in the upper bedroom at Lallybroch, next to Jamie, and realize, as I watched the dawn touch his sleeping face, that he had been born in this bed." Outside are Jamie's mother's rosebushes that seem to touch Claire and Jamie "in welcome" (*Dragonfly in Amber,* ch. 31).

Lallybroch is a beautiful place, a refuge except when the British soldiers invade. (The family keeps one of the British sword marks on a panel so they can remember—the house has been invaded and though it still stands, it remains scarred forever). The kitchen is described as the heart of the house, and the study or speak-a-word room its brain (*An Echo in the Bone,* ch. 26). As such, it's another character, a friend and protector to the protagonists.

As the story continues, Claire finds more homes: the house in Boston and several in North Carolina. Repeatedly she leaves all of it behind: every possession, every precious gift, document, or memory, and sets off with only what's in her pockets and knapsack to begin a new adventure ... and she often loses the knapsack. While there's a longing for home and brief moments of respite, her natural state seems to be adventuring without ties to possessions, if necessary.

Name Meanings

> I turned to Jamie in sudden panic. "I can't marry you! I don't even know your last name!"
> He looked down at me and cocked a ruddy eyebrow. "Oh. It's Fraser. James Alexander Malcolm MacKenzie Fraser." He pronounced it formally, each name slow and distinct.—*Outlander*, ch. 14

While Jamie is named for the Highlander companion Jamie from *Doctor Who,* some associations work quite well. James, originally a disciple of Jesus, means "he who supplants," he who takes another's place. In fact, Jamie was born the second son in his family, and only his brother's childhood death made him a lord. Known for his fiery temper, St. James is traditionally believed to be the first of the twelve apostles martyred for his faith, a parallel for Jamie's constant self-sacrifice.

In Greek legend, the first Alexander was Paris, the romantic hero who stole Helen of Troy from her rightful husband in a parallel to Jamie's life with Claire. The most famous Alexander was a conqueror and great general. It's a Greek name, "Defender of Men," linking to Jamie's classical education and showing his family to be worldly beyond the Scottish borders. He is of course a constant defender of his own people and commanding leader. Malcolm, a more nationalistic name, means "devotee of St. Columba"—one of the most beloved saints of Scotland and also a tie to Jamie's Catholicism. Malcolm was a name given to four Scottish kings, including the prince of Cumberland in Shakespeare's *Macbeth.* The MacKenzies and Frasers were of course two of the greatest clans in the Inverness area.

Jamie is known by many names through the series. As a child, Jamie's older brother calls him Sawney, the Scottish nickname for his middle name Alexander. His sister still calls him "ruadh," meaning red, for his hair. When Claire meets him, he's "Young Jamie" and "Mr. MacTavish," though no one at Castle Leoch remembers that he's calling himself the latter. (On a previous stay there, he went by his proper name.)

When addressed formally in Gaelic, he's often called Seamus, the Celtic for James. Adventuring in France before the events of the first book, a young lady calls him Diego, the Spanish variant ("Virgins"). His Chinese friend offers another variant—Tsei Mei. These all emphasize his flexibility as others put their perceptions on him and address him in ways they can best understand. He accepts all these nicknames blithely.

In France, Jamie and Claire are Lord and Lady Broch Turach—Northfacing Tower, the official name of Lallybroch (Lazy Tower). In the rebellion after, he earns the label "Red Jamie" for his hair as well as his violence. He also holds various military ranks, though while not in the military he often pointedly insists on "Mr. Fraser" instead. In prison, he's simply Mac Dubh, meaning son of the black one. While his father had black hair, the name also suggests his despair at parting from Claire and gives him an air of anonymous mystery. Paroled in England, he tries to dissociate himself from notorious "Red Jamie," so calls himself the simple Alex MacKenzie or "Mac."

As *Voyager* continues, Jamie tries on a dizzying spectrum of names—one for the respectable print business, one for the disreputable smuggling, and the original one he must keep secret, as he is a traitor and violent criminal. He's Jamie Roy on the docks and in town, Alexander Malcolm or A. Malcolm, printer.

Traveling to the West Indies, he takes on more personas and more false names as the Spanish Captain Alessandro or rich plantation owner Etienne Marcel de Provac Alexandre of Martinique. At last, he and Claire wash up in a new land where no one knows them. With a great air of relief, he introduces them as James Fraser and his wife Claire. They keep these identities for most of the remaining series. Gabaldon adds that as Claire and Roger also change their last names to reflect different sides of the self, "*Voyager* is all 'about' the search for identity, and the ways in which people define themselves, and the name-shifting is a deliberate part of this overall theme" (*Outlandish Companion* 407).

Claire has far fewer aliases. When she first time travels, she identifies herself by her maiden name, Beauchamp. Since the first man she meets is Jack Randall and she wants, most of all to separate herself from him, this is quite logical. However, returning to her maiden name suggests a return to independence as she abandons her marriage to Frank. Only her last names change, as she offers to be "Mrs. Malcolm" as Jamie's wife when he hides under an alias. On the show, she spells her identity out in terms of the men around her: "Last time I was here, I was Claire Randall, then Claire Beauchamp, then Claire Fraser. The question was, who did I want to be?" Claire asks in "Both Sides Now."

Of course, Jamie spends the entire series calling her by his nickname for her, "Sassenach." As she describes it, "He had called me that from the first—the Gaelic word for an outlander, a stranger. An Englishman. First in jest, and then in affection" (*Dragonfly in Amber* ch. 5). Later, Jamie tries another variant though very briefly:

"Sorcha," he whispered, and realized that he had called her so a moment before. Now, that was odd; no wonder she had been surprised. It was her name in the Gaelic, but he never called her by it. He liked the strangeness of her, the Englishness. She was his Claire, his Sassenach" [*The Fiery Cross,* ch. 18].

Jamie calls her Claire when giving her her wedding ring, as he does at the ceremony and after, when he asks her for a marriage of honesty. She notes that his use of her real name is "mostly reserved for occasions of formality or tenderness" (ch. 23).

Claire means clarity, casting her as an otherworldly guide, and in fact, this is a common role for her in the series. Gabaldon explains that she likely named Claire for Isabel Allende's *House of the Spirits,* with Claire the clairvoyant (*Outlandish Companion* XX-XI). There's also a link with Saint Clare of Assisi, who grew up as a noblewoman, then abandoned luxury to live in humble poverty with a rough dress and serve others, all through admiration for the selfless Saint Francis. Claire Randall indeed abandons a life as an Oxford don's wife with hot baths and plenty of food to be Jamie's wife in rural conditions. She also abandons her homemaker role to become a healer.

In French, Beau Champ means "beautiful field." It combines nicely with "Fraser" for "a beautiful field of strawberries." Claire's maiden name "Beauchamp" comes from one of Gabaldon's teachers. Gabaldon adds, "Beauchamp was the name of a math teacher at my high school, and I'd been struck—in high school—by the fact that it was pronounced "Beechum," in spite of the obviously French spelling" (*Outlandish Companion* XX-XI). Thus this name went to the English lady who claimed to have French ties.

By contrast, Ian (a variant of John) and Jenny have "everyman" names, emphasizing their ordinariness as they watch over Lallybroch and tend the animals, rather than embarking on wild adventures. Young Jamie, Jamie's namesake, stays on to inherit Lallybroch and be its lord, while Young Ian, Ian's namesake, shares his uncle's wild streak of adventure. The pair cross, with the next generation revealing that a name need not define a life. Their family tree, printed in *Written in My Own Heart's Blood,* reveals many family names repeated through the years and bestowed on children and distant descendants.

Roger goes on to play with his own identities. In book four, he identifies his personas as "mild-mannered historian Roger Wakefield" and the "dashing" Roger MacKenzie in "secret tartan regalia" (ch. 3). The latter is his birth name and suggests a secret yearning for his family roots and buried magic inheritance. Agreeing with his split perception of himself, Brianna tells him he has more accent in Scotland and far less in England. When he travels back in time, he decides he would rather be a dashing and adventurous Scot than a historian, though his name-switching leads him into more adventure than he planned.

Roger means "famous spear" from the German. His middle name, Jeremiah, evokes the Old Testament prophet that promises doom and retribution from God. Aware as Roger is of the violent future, this name seems appropriate— Jamie himself considers Roger "a particularly evil-minded fortune-teller" and voice of foreboding (*A Breath of Snow and Ashes*, ch. 10). Roger's son is named Jeremiah after Roger's father (and other family members in their genealogy, which proves significant later) though this shortens to the more endearing and matter-of-fact Jem. He's certainly a gem of his family, but one wonders whether the power of prophecy from the second sight or the destiny of the Frasers will prove important as he ages.

Jamie's mother Ellen was named with the medieval English form of Helen (from Helen of Troy). Indeed, the story reveals many suitors for the beautiful woman, who chose an unlikely hero and ran off with him, nearly starting a clan war. Jamie's father Brian and Brianna share name roots: the name comes from *bre* ("hill") or *brig*, "high, noble." The goddess Brigid has a share in these name roots as well. Brian was one of the three chief gods of pagan Ireland, a son of the mother goddess Danu. As such, both are tied to the ancient Celtic world of magic and deep wisdom.

Frank, from Franklin, means "freeman" while Wolverton is an English place name from the Old English personal name *Wulfhere* + -*ing*—denoting association + *tun* "farmstead," "settlement." Frank notes that Jack was given the middle name Wolverton after his mother's uncle, a "minor knight from Sussex" (*Outlander*, ch. 1). Frank's family are men of England, free to do as they like, often, unfortunately, unchecked by anyone.

William Ransom and Frank and Jack Randall all have surnames that adapt the Germanic element *rand* meaning "rim" (of a shield). While these characters are often called on to shield others, one might assume Gabaldon likes the sound of the name. There are also many Williams and Young Willies (meaning protector and also suggesting willpower), so much so that Gabaldon found it necessary to change Lord John's name after he's introduced as William in book two.

Objects of Vertu and Objects of Use

The little objects one keeps close can define a life, and Gabaldon uses this technique several times in the series to emphasize their importance, from sentimental keepsakes to the tools one uses each day. In Frank's lecture within a dream Claire has, he says,

> "For some periods of history," he said, "we have history itself; the written testimony of the people who lived then. For others, we have only the objects of the period, to show us how men lived.... The art, and the objects of vertu"—he waved a hand over the glittering array—"these are what we most often see, the

decorations of a society. And why not? ... These are pretty things, after all." A finger's touch set the swans on the clock revolving, curved necks stately in two-fold procession. "Worth preserving. But who'd bother keeping an old, patched tea cozy, or a worn-out automobile-tire?" [*Dragonfly in Amber*, ch. 10].

However, as Frank concludes, "It's the useful object, the things that aren't noted in documents, which are used and broken and discarded without a second thought, that tell you how the common man lived" (*Dragonfly in Amber*, ch. 10). Indeed, they do. On the show, in "Both Sides Now," Frank investigates Claire's suitcase with her neatly folded clothes and gloves and their wedding photo. In his time, this is all that remains of her, and he discards it, too traumatized to think of keeping her last possessions.

In the first book, Claire comments in amusement about all the clutter inside Jamie's sporran. Later, she's presented with a box containing all of Jamie's possessions. "A small, light box, to hold the remains of a man's life," as she thinks.

> I knew the things it held. Three fishing lines, neatly coiled; a cork stuck with fishhooks; a flint and steel; a small piece of broken glass, edges blunt with wear; various small stones that looked interesting or had a good feel between the fingers; a dried mole's foot, carried as a charm against rheumatism. A Bible—or perhaps they had let him keep that? I hoped so. A ruby ring, if it hadn't been stolen. And a small wooden snake, carved of cherry wood, with the name SAWNY scratched on its underside [*Outlander*, ch. 35].

This last was carved by Jamie's brother, dead in childhood.

In *The Scottish Prisoner*, Jamie has lost nearly everything, except for his sister's rosary, which he keeps in prison and beyond. Nonetheless, at Helwater, he accumulates a box of belongings with a statue of the Virgin from his sister, a dried mole's foot, pencil, tinderbox, candlestick, and one pretty colored stone for every person he loves (ch. 38).

Voyager follows Claire and Jamie, who are often left with only the contents of their pockets—pictures of family, Claire's medicines, or sometimes not even those. In later books, they make themselves a house, filled with bookshelves and a desk for Jamie and a well-stocked surgery for Claire. Nonetheless, the small items they carry still indicate much about their priorities and daily life: Jamie has a special saddlebag:

> Brianna had remade it for him, stitching in loops of leather that presented his pistols, hilt up, ready to be seized in an emergency, and a clever arrangement of compartments that held handy his shot pouch, powder horn, a spare knife, a coil of fishing line, a roll of twine for a snare, a hussif with pins, needles, and thread, a packet of food, a bottle of beer, and a neatly rolled clean shirt [*A Breath of Snow and Ashes*, ch. 25].

He carefully discards the soap and other less-useful items she's included.

In the 1960s, Roger enters the series while sorting through the Reverend Wakefield's numerous possessions, from his beloved peacock-printed dressing gown to crates of books and the possessions of Roger's parents. Later, Brianna sends Roger "the objects of vertu and objects of use that comprised [her] history," as he thinks, and asks him to keep her most precious possessions safe for her. There's an emphasis especially in this scene on the history of a person being documented through their possessions as Roger unwraps Brianna's package, calling it "Museum quality, by the way you packed it" (*The Drums of Autumn*, ch. 30). It contains her childhood treasures, from a Raggedy Ann to a Mickey Mouse hat, clothes of her parents, and the family silver, given to her parents for their wedding.

Scars

There are many scars in the series, internal and external. The most blatant are the ones on Jamie's back. Caitriona Balfe describes her character's first sight of them:

> She sees his back for the first time, and that's quite a moment. When you see someone very scarred by war—and this is again where her experience comes into play. She has treated men like him, but never the same kind of situation. The story of what happens to his sister and also the way he tells it. Obviously there's a deep pain there, but he makes light of it. He really opens up to her in such an honest way, but it's without any self-pity.
>
> These are things that attract her to him. Here's a person who's endured so much pain but doesn't seem to have that bitterness or poison. His soul and spirit doesn't seem to be poisoned, and I think that's something that really intrigues her. It makes him a different type of person who's not hardened by what's happened to him [Ng, "Caitriona Balfe on Claire"].

In fact, both characters are psychologically scarred—Claire by the recent war, as she hears the Allies have won and silently chugs at a bottle of champagne. Jamie is scarred by his encounter with Randall—since then, he has been a starving outlaw and an exile in France. He's terrified to go home and face the sister he could not protect, so he exists day to day without his estate or even his real name. The hideous marks on his back are only an outward showing of the inner damage.

Other scars appear later. Jamie is whipped again repeatedly and has his right hand permanently damaged. Psychological scars far deeper accompany this, until Claire feels she can only help him by forcing him to face the trauma and battle through it. As with Jamie's eventual visit to Lallybroch, her support helps him to heal. She in turn discovers true love in an equal partnership, with someone who admires her forthrightness and courage. Thus she heals as well.

Several amputees appear: Ian, Fergus, Duncan Innes, Hugh Munro. Their injuries emphasize the horrors of war and medical care at the time, but also

Jamie's compassion. Jamie keeps these men on as friends, useful partners, and long-term employees despite their disabilities. By emphasizing their usefulness, he demonstrates the heartbreaking care he takes of "his" men as he allows them to lead full lives.

More positive scars exist in later books: Jamie and Claire mark each other's hands with initials and gaze at them to remember when separated. On reuniting, Jamie professes admiration for Claire's "battle scars" rather than revulsion. Wounded in the Battle of Saratoga, Jamie points out philosophically that a sacrifice to save ten good men is worth making, an attitude of compassion and self-sacrifice that clearly defines him.

Literature and Music

LITERATURE

In 2001, Diana Gabaldon wrote an introduction for Modern Library's paperback edition of the classic *Ivanhoe*, by Sir Walter Scott. In 2004, she wrote one to the Bantam Classic printing of *Common Sense* by Thomas Paine. Both are related works to her own books. Indeed, the *Outlander* series celebrates literature throughout.

The story's heroes are very literate. Roger is known for collecting ballads and folksongs. Brianna keeps sketchbooks with family drawings and engineering sketches as well as a dream journal. Fergus invents the newspaper *The Onion,* or rather *L'Oignon.* Benedict Arnold calls it "A Patriot periodical, I gather, and somewhat given to satire" (*Written in My Own Heart's Blood*, ch. 22). As such, it appears to parallel or perhaps even be *The Onion* available today. Jamie not only becomes a printer in book three but names his press Bonnie and regards it with a great deal of affection. "The English took my sword and dirk away," he said softly. His finger touched the slugs that lay in my palm. "But Tom Gage put a weapon into my hands again, and I think I shall not lay it down" (*Voyager,* ch. 27).

Eventually Claire and Jamie each write books: Jamie's is *Grandfather Tales,* a collection of folktales dedicated to his grandchildren. Claire's book is medical advice by "C.E.B.F. Fraser, M.D., with a masculinized portrait of her inside (*An Echo in the Bone,* ch. 26). Jenny loves books as well: she insists on staying up late to read, even if she's too tired to absorb the volume, as she can ponder it the next day over her very manual work. Claire thinks to herself, "Alone among the Highland farms, I was sure, the women of Lallybroch waulked their wool not only to the old traditional chants but also to the rhythms of Molière and Piron" (*Dragonfly in Amber,* ch. 34).

Of course, Frank is a scholar. Claire describes *The Collected Works of Frank*

Randall as five hardbound volumes of 500–600 pages each, excluding index and illustrations (*Dragonfly in Amber*, ch. 1). Several other history professors' works come up in the series. Reverend Wakefield checks in Cameron to verify whether the Duke of Sandringham was a Jacobite, as Claire recalls in a flashback (*Outlander*, ch. 12). Claire dreams about one of Frank's lectures, with portraits of herself and Jamie as exhibits and he references the *Diary of Samuel Pepys*, a famous diary of daily life and observation in 17th century London (*Dragonfly in Amber*, ch. 10).

There's a great celebration of literature and libraries through the series. The monks at the Abbey of Ste. Anne de Beaupre have a great library, where Brother Anselm is doing a translation project. There, Claire believes "the library held a hushed exultation, as though the cherished volumes were all singing soundlessly within their covers." Jamie notes, upon visiting a monastery's private library:

> You could tell from the books whether a library was meant for show or not. Books that were used had an open, interested feel to them, even if closed and neatly lined up on a shelf in strict order with their fellows. You felt as though the book took as much interest in you as you did in it and was willing to help when you reached for it.... Jamie felt a strong desire to go across and see what the open books were, to go to the shelves and run his knuckles gently over the leather and wood and buckrum of the bindings until a book should speak to him and come willingly into his hand [*The Scottish Prisoner*, ch. 19].

Gabaldon has fun creating historical fiction Easter eggs in the second book: Claire thinks she recognizes the Duchess of Claymore at Versailles (*Dragonfly in Amber*, ch. 9). This is the heroines' hereditary title in Judith McNaught's *Westmoreland Dynasty Saga* series—*Whitney, My Love* and *A Kingdom of Dreams*. In the same chapter, Jamie writes something on the back of a broadsheet describing the scurrilous affair between the Comte de Sevigny and the wife of the Minister of Agriculture. The Comte de Sevigny is the main character in Dorothy Dunnett's *Lymond Chronicles* series.

When he has the opportunity, Jamie can often be seen reading beloved classics of his time. Jamie reads Lord John's copy of *Nouvelle Héloïse* in prison and comments that he's been telling the story to the other Highlanders, while pompous Lord John is shocked that any of them can understand it (*Voyager*, ch. 10). Jamie quips to John that he wishes the enormous eighteenth century *Pamela* had been longer, as he was reading it in hiding at the time (*Voyager*, ch. 11). Jamie also reads to the men from *The Adventures of Rodrick Random, The History of Tom Jones,* and *Robinson Crusoe* (everyone's favorite).

Jamie says, "A little learning is a dangerous thing" and Roger surprises him by finishing the quotation (*The Fiery Cross*, ch. 86). While Roger went to Oxford, then taught there, Claire didn't have a great deal of formal education and Brianna presumably knows little about British literature. Roger notes later that Jamie seems surprised anyone in the future knows the classics. Meanwhile, people in his time have read many, as he, Ian, and the young neighbor Malva Christie compare the merits of Henry Fielding, Tobias Smollett, and Ovid (*A Breath of Snow and Ashes,* ch. 35). The bondmaid Lizzie reads De Foe's *The Pirate Gow* to the Beardsley twins (ch. 6), and others in North Carolina quote the pieces of their day.

In the battles of the American Revolution, Jamie finds an abandoned copy of *Tristam Shandy* and brings it to Claire as a gift. He silently recites "Hell hath no fury..." while riding with an angry Isobel Dunsany (*The Scottish Prisoner,* ch. 5). In a more comical scene, Jamie stumbles across the racy book *Fanny Hill: Memoir of a Woman of Pleasure* in the stables at Helwater and smirks at some of the description while in the future Claire does something similar with *The Impetuous Pirate.*

Jamie's own library does much to emphasize his personality:

> There was a small, three-shelf bookcase in Jamie's study, which held the entire library of Fraser's Ridge. The serious works occupied the top shelf: a volume of Latin poetry, Caesar's *Commentaries,* the *Meditations of Marcus Aurelius,* a few other classic works, Dr. Brickell's *Natural History of North Carolina,* lent by the Governor and never returned [*The Fiery Cross,* ch. 38].

The middle shelf has lighter "romances" (modern readers would call them novels): *Robinson Crusoe; Tom Jones, Roderick Random, Pamela.* Most of these are lengthy multivolume epics, and *Pamela* has multiple bookmarks, indicating where their many readers have given up. There's also *Don Quixote* in the more esoteric Spanish.

Historically, Samuel Johnson, traveling through Scotland, noted, "I never was in any house ... where I did not find books in more languages than one, if I stayed long enough to want them" (Morison). Jamie indeed keeps an assortment of books close by. As the books put it, he could acquire languages quite easily as a "natural polygogue" and, after learning classics at the university in Paris, "regarded both Homer and Virgil as personal friends" (*The Drums of Autumn,* ch. 8).

He knows more esoteric languages and their classics as well, speaking with Hugh Munro in sign language and John Grey in German. He also (for reasons unclear) knows Spanish—at one point he tells Claire he's familiar with *Don Quixote* and she calls him quixotic (*Dragonfly in Amber,* ch. 36). At university, he studied the Jewish philosopher Maimonides, and he understands and speaks Biblical Hebrew ("Virgins"). He's picked up Chinese in the third book, enough to communicate with Mr. Willoughby. And he begins to master the slave-talk of the West Indies and some Native American dialects.

Greek and Latin

Eighteenth century men were judged on their education and knowledge of the classics. Thus Jamie has an impressive education in Greek and Latin, quite unlike modern traditions. He's seen reading Tacitus at the Abbey of Ste. Anne de Beaupre, and he quotes the *Odyssey* in Greek upon his first return to Lallybroch, when his dog recognizes him (*Outlander*, ch. 26). While chopping wood, Jamie recites from the "Meditations" of Marcus Aurelius Antonius on "body, soul, and mind" (*The Drums of Autumn*, ch. 20). He trains Young Ian in the *Odyssey* as they journey in a foreign land in "the rudiments of Greek and Latin grammar, and to improve his mathematics and conversational French" (*The Drums of Autumn,* ch. 8). By contrast, Claire says, "All I remember is Arma virumque cano.... My arm got bit off by a dog" (*The Drums of Autumn,* ch. 8) though she occasionally reads simple Latin like the clan mottos.

The most famous Latin of the series is likely the inscription on Claire's ring (in the books anyway), first quoted to her and Jamie by his beggar friend Hugh Munro just after the wedding:

> "Then let amourous kisses dwell
> On our lips, begin and tell
> A Thousand and a Hundred score
> A Hundred and a Thousand more"
> "Da mi basia mille," he whispered, smiling. Give me a thousand kisses. It was the inscription inside my ring, a brief quotation from a love song by Catullus. I bent and gave him one back. "Dien mille altera," I said. Then a thousand more [*The Drums of Autumn,* ch. 10].

Gabaldon describes having Janet McConnaughey, an online friend from the CompuServe Literary Forum, suggest this work as an inscription in the wedding ring (*Outlandish Companion* 524). Longer pieces of the poem appear in the series as well.

LESBIA

> —Catullus (84?—54 BC)
> Come and let us live my Deare,
> Let us love and never feare,
> What the sow rest Fathers say:
> Brightest Sol that dyes today
> Lives againe as blith tomorrow,
> But if we darke sons of sorrow
> Set; o then, how long a Night
> Shuts the eye of our short light!
> Then let amorous kisses dwell
> On our lips, begin and tell
> A Thousand, and a Hundred, score

An Hundred, and a Thousand more,
Till another Thousand smother
That, and that wipe of another.
Thus at last when we have numbred
Many a Thousand, many a Hundred;
Wee'l confound the reckoning quite,
And lose our selves in wild delight:
While our joyes so multiply,
As shall mocke the envious eye.
—translation by Richard Crashaw
(1612?—1649)

Jamie teaches Latin to young Ian using the more instructive "Vertue" by Plautus from about 200 BC. Jamie also quotes the silly Latin-English "macaronic" (playful poems fashionable for showing off multilingual education), "Amo, amas, I love a lass, As cedar tall and slender..." Gabaldon notes, "Several members of the Literary Forum discovered or recalled bits of macaronics, which they helpfully quoted to me; this one was both complete, and most apropos, so I chose it for Jamie" (*Outlandish Companion* 533).

A chapter title for *Written in My Own Heart's Blood* is "Brought to you by the Letters Q E and D," while Jamie carries those typeset letters with him in Edinburgh to remind himself that his printing press is a powerful tool with which he can influence the world. Q.E.D. is short for the Latin *quod erat demonstrandum*, meaning "which had to be demonstrated" or sometimes "the thing proves itself." In *Voyager's* chapter "Q.E.D.," Claire discovers Jamie's whereabouts in the past through hard evidence (ironically, the works of his printing press). There's also an *Echo in the Bone* chapter called "Sic Transit Gloria Mundi"—so goes the glory of the world. In *Written in My Own Heart's Blood,* another chapter is titled with the Hippocrates quote *"Homo est Obligamus Aerobe"* (Man is an obligate aerobe).

Gabaldon adds that she's weaker in Greek and the letters are a pain for typesetters, so she mostly sticks with Latin. She notes: "For the sake of accurate representation, though, I did include one brief exchange in Greek, between Jamie and Lord John Grey, during the Incident of the Snake in the Privy" (*Outlandish Companion* 526). With his son covered in muck, John smirkingly asks for news from the underworld and calls him Persephone. Jamie instantly understands:

> "Epicharmus," he explained. "At the Oracle of Delphi, seekers after enlightenment would throw down a dead python into the pit, and then hang about, breathing in the fumes as it decayed."
> Lord John declaimed, gesturing grandly. "'The spirit toward the heavens, the body to the earth'" [*The Drums of Autumn*, ch. 25].

Jamie recalls "trading bits of Aristophanes" in Greek with Lord John at Ardsmuir (*The Scottish Prisoner,* ch. 24) and reads *The Iliad* in Greek while poised on the edge of his own revolution.

References to Greek myth are common. With her new wedding ring and her old one, Claire feels as if she is held in bondage like Prometheus on his rock (*Outlander,* ch. 23). Asked to give Jenny advice of the future, she understands why Cassandra is so unpopular (*Outlander,* ch. 33). Jamie believes he sees Jack Randall and stands frozen "silent as a statue of Mars" (*Dragonfly in Amber,* ch. 9). In a more whimsical moment, Claire tells Jamie his ears are slightly pointed at the tips like a faun's (*Dragonfly in Amber,* ch. 6). She later jokes that they're married "before God, man, Neptune, or what-have-you" (*Voyager,* ch. 39) and she and Jamie sail onboard the Artemis.

Paris has many tributes to the Greek gods from the Salon of Apollo in the Palace of Versailles to the Judgment of Paris stained glass window in Jared Fraser's townhouse. Claire mistakes a statue of the Four Humors of Man in the gardens of the Palace of Versailles for a statue of Pan (*Dragonfly in Amber,* ch. 9) and Jamie smirks because as a healer she should know better, he believes. In *Voyager,* Claire details the Hippocratic Oath for Jamie with its phrase, "I swear by Apollo the physician, and Aesculapius the surgeon, likewise Hygeia and Panacea, and call all the gods and goddesses to witness." He considers it woefully pagan.

Bible

Bible quotes are frequent: Claire quotes from the Song of Solomon to Jamie or while teasing Philip Wylie, and Roger quotes it to Brianna. Gabaldon notes, "I also used frequent Biblical quotation and allusion, because of the common usage of such allusion in the eighteenth century style, because it was suited to the metaphysical and spiritual concerns of the books—and because it's beautiful" (*Outlandish Companion* 523).

When Dougal's men comment about Claire's foul language as she attempts to bandage Jamie's shoulder, one of them comments "Your husband should tan ye, woman.... St. Paul says 'Let a woman be silent, and –'" To which Claire remarks, "You can mind your own bloody business ... and so can St. Paul (ch. 3). On several occasions she mentions the uselessness of the misogynist Biblical figure. Jamie also quotes Paul's "'Tis better to marry than burn" from 1 Corinthians 7:9. to describe why he kissed Laoghaire in the alcove (*Outlander,* ch. 22). Once again, Saint Paul has brought Claire only misery.

Frank's favorite saying is "Sufficient unto the day is the evil thereof" (Matthew 6:34), which Claire and Brianna repeat on occasion. Seeking divine guidance to help Jamie after Wentworth, Claire finds several passages including the inspiring "But be not thou far from me, O Lord: O my strength, haste thee to help me. Deliver my soul from the sword; my darling from the power of the dog" from Psalm 22 (*Outlander,* ch. 39). In this instance, God does appear to show mercy and deliver her lover.

"Thou shalt not suffer a witch to live," from Exodus 22:18 and the title of chapter 25 in *Outlander,* is a favorite quote of those who murdered women and seized their property through the Middle Ages. The title of part one of *Dragonfly in Amber* references "For now we see through a glass, darkly" from 1 Corinthians 13:12, while the prologue of *A Breath of Snow and Ashes* riffs on the Bible with "Ashes to ashes, dust to dust. Remember, man, that thou art dust; and unto dust thou shalt return."

Claire, a Catholic herself, as Gabaldon is, has brief Bible analogies flash through her head on occasion. Claire holds herself "stiff as Lot's wife," a pillar of salt, while telling Frank she never had an affair (*Outlander,* ch. 1). When Jamie holds Claire's hand on their wedding night, she notices his reddish hairs contrast with Frank's smooth hands and thinks of Jacob and Esau. On her return to Castle Leoch after marrying Jamie, she is so tired she thinks the only thing she would get up for is Gabriel's trump (*Outlander,* ch. 23). When Claire gives Jenny advice to help Lallybroch prepare for the coming Rising and tells Michael about the French Revolution, she recalls Jeremiah the gloomy prophet. Claire also marvels that Brother Anselm doesn't consider her the Whore of Babylon telling lies about her past. She describes Mother Hildegarde as standing "tall and stern as the angel at the gates of Eden" (*Dragonfly in Amber,* ch. 26) and a large horse skull in Master Raymond's collection as "looking eminently suitable for flattening platoons of Philistines" (*Dragonfly in Amber,* ch. 16) (Sampson did this originally with a donkey's jawbone).

Jamie and Claire use the Bible to define their relationship on occasion, following their traditional marriage ceremony by a priest. Jamie asks Claire if she believes "Who looks on a woman with lust in his heart hath committed adultery with her already" from Matthew 5:28 (*Dragonfly in Amber,* ch. 17), while Claire insists Jamie not kill Frank's ancestor with the words, "The sins of the fathers shall not be visited upon the children" (*Dragonfly in Amber,* ch. 21). This appears a paraphrase of Ezekiel 18:20—"The son shall not bear the iniquity of the father." She repeats the Book of Ruth and its "whither thou goest, I will go" to say she won't leave him.

Jamie quotes Ecclesiastes 3:1, "To everything there is a season and a time for every purpose under heaven" when it's time for supper (*Outlander,* ch. 27) and "Put not your trust in princes" from Psalm 146:3, describing why he hesitates to meet Charles Stuart (*Dragonfly in Amber,* chapter 6). Jamie quotes from Psalm 103 as the days race by: "Man is like the grass of the field. ... Today it blooms;

tomorrow it withers and is cast into the oven" (*The Drums of Autumn,* ch.16). *The Drums of Autumn* has chapter titles "A Hanging in Eden" and "Away in a Manger." (Brianna discusses pregnancy in the latter).

Finally, there's a large Jamie-as-Christ analogy in the first book as he's betrayed, nailed through the hand, and nearly killed, only to escape and find safety on Christmas Day. Meanwhile, Master Raymond calls Claire 'Madonna' because her blue aura reminds him of the Virgin's cloak (*Dragonfly in Amber,* ch. 25). Sir Marcus MacRannoch sends her a pearl bracelet and a note saying "For a virtuous woman is a pearl of great price, and her value is greater than rubies" from Proverbs 31:10 (*Outlander,* ch. 41).

The wilderness of unsettled America echoes Eden for the characters. In *The Drums of Autumn,* Claire protests, "When God threw Adam out of Paradise, at least Eve went with him," worried she'll lose Jamie (*The Drums of Autumn,* ch.16). Roger sees Claire and Jamie after an ordeal as "a blood-soaked Adam, a battered Eve, looking upon the knowledge of good and evil" (*A Breath of Snow and Ashes,* ch. 29). In a happier moment, Claire constructs a similar metaphor:

> "I feel like Eve," I said softly, watching the moon set behind him, over the dark of the forest. "Just on the edge of the Garden of Eden."
> There was a snort of laughter from the vicinity of my navel.
> "Aye, and I suppose I'm Adam," Jamie said. "In the gateway to Paradise" [*The Drums of Autumn,* ch. 2].

In the chapter "Serpent in Eden" in *A Breath of Snow and Ashes* Brianna and Roger stand naked and banter about Adam and Eve. However, this chapter is sandwiched between two about murders in their rural community—there is indeed a serpent in Eden. In the New World, as the settlers create a community and explore the virgin forest, they are indeed pioneers, mostly freed from the laws of civilization, for good or ill.

Roger trains as a minister and finds himself dispensing advice to credulous people—beginning with exorcising a devil from a bucket of milk. Following this, he tells bullying children that a boy has been reserved for the Lord and must not be harmed. He also must lead services and give sermons. At a funeral in *A Breath of Snow and Ashes* (ch.2), Roger quotes words of anger and despair from Job 19:7, though more often he quotes the uplifting words and hymns.

The prologue of *Written in My Own Heart's Blood* sounds quite Biblical, with direct quotes from Joel 2:28–29:

> In the light of eternity, time casts no shadow.
> Your old men shall dream dreams, your young men shall see visions. But what is it that the old women see?
> We see necessity, and we do the things that must be done.

Shakespeare

"Alas, Poor Yorick" and "For Many Men Who Stumble at the Threshold Well Foretold that Danger Lurks Within" (*Henry VI*) are chapter titles in *Written in My Own Heart's Blood*. Before that, many other Shakespeare quotes dot the series. Claire quotes *The Merchant of Venice* when she forgives Frank for implying that she had affairs during the war, noting, "The quality of mercy is not strained. It droppeth as the gentle rain from heaven..." (*Outlander*, ch. 1). When she first meets Auld Alec she quotes, "An eye like Mars, to threaten or command" from *Hamlet* (*Outlander*, ch. 7). When Claire wakes Jamie suddenly, she notes that his hair is standing on end like quills and tells him he looks like a 'fretful porpentine' (*Outlander*, ch. 23). This is from *Hamlet* Act I, Scene V— the ghost of Hamlet's father tells Hamlet that he could tell him tales that would make "Thy knotted and combined locks to part, And each particular hair to stand on end, Like quills upon the fretful porpentine." "By the pricking of my thumbs," the title of chapter 24 of *Outlander* is a line from *Macbeth*. Claire quotes "There are more things in heaven and earth than are dreamt of in your philosophy" from *Hamlet* to Sister Angelique at L'Hopital des Anges about her own medical knowledge. She and Jamie continue to quote the bard, as he's a reference from a century past that both have encountered.

WRITING ON WRITING

Gabaldon plays repeatedly with the concept of fiction, breaking down the fourth wall. Jamie and Lord John debate literature in *Voyager*, Chapter 10:

> "Or do you not think that the character of an author shows in the construction of his work?"
>
> "Given some of the characters that I have seen appear in plays and novels, Major, I should think the author a bit depraved who drew them entirely from himself, no?"

Jamie adds a quote that appears to come from Gabaldon herself, introduced into her story as the lady novelist: "It was not Monsieur Arouet, but a colleague of his—a lady novelist—who remarked to me once that writing novels was a cannibal's art, in which one often mixed small portions of one's friends and one's enemies together, seasoned them with imagination, and allowed the whole to stew together into a savory concoction." Jamie notes in *An Echo in the Bone* that if his other occupations fail, he's such a creative storyteller that he might "find useful Employment as a scribbler of Romances" (ch. 89). His completely fictitious story of adventure in the New World is not much more outlandish than Gabaldon's own tales.

Several times, characters pretend they are in romance novels in a twist on self-aware metafiction. Claire notes that "Black Jack" is "A common name for rogues and scoundrels in the eighteenth century. A staple of romantic fiction, the name conjured up charming highwaymen, dashing blades in plumed hats." In chapter 35 of *Outlander,* she thinks, "One never stops to think what underlies romance. Tragedy and terror, transmuted by time. Add a little art in the telling, and voila! a stirring romance, to make the blood run fast and maidens sigh. My blood was running fast, all right, and never maiden sighed like Jamie." She adds in the second book, "Lying on the floor, with the carved panels of the ceiling flickering dimly above, I found myself thinking that I had always heretofore assumed that the tendency of eighteenth-century ladies to swoon was due to tight stays; now I rather thought it might be due to the idiocy of eighteenth-century men" (*Dragonfly in Amber,* ch. 24). As the book ends, Claire complains about all the fiction and history that has romanticized Bonnie Prince Charlie— Gabaldon's book does not do so: "The fault lies with the artists," Claire says. "The writers, the singers, the tellers of tales. It's them that take the past and re-create it to their liking. Them that could take a fool and give you back a hero, take a sot and make him a king" (*Dragonfly in Amber,* ch. 47).

Hal, Lord John's older brother, regards reading novels as "a form of moral weakness, forgivable, and in fact, quite understandable in their mother, who was, after all, a woman. That his younger brother should share in this vice was somewhat less acceptable" (*Brotherhood of the Blade,* ch. 1). Gabaldon's works has been called "women's fiction" and shelved with romances, while she tries to have it put in the mainstream section.

In *A Breath of Snow and Ashes,* Brianna imagines she's in a romance novel and her true love will ride up on a stallion to rescue her. Then, defying the convention, she escapes on her own by knocking a hole in the ceiling. Trying to write about a sexual experience in her dream journal, Brianna finally crosses it out and writes, "Well, none of the books I've ever read could describe it, either!" (ch.38). Gabaldon, of course, writes sex scenes and occasionally deals with criticism about them.

"*Fuirich agus chi thu,*" Gaelic for "Wait and see" appears in *An Echo in the Bone* (ch. 98). This is an inside joke for Gabaldon's fans, as "Wait and see" is her most common response to questions. Eventually the forum discussions switched to the Gaelic phrase instead.

LITERARY ANACHRONISMS

Americana

"I regret only that I have but one life to give to my country," Claire says ironically to Geillis after Geillis reveals that she is a Jacobite when they are in the thieves hole (*Outlander*, ch. 25). These words are reported to be the last words of Nathan Hale, a Captain in the Continental Army during the American Revolution. Geillis doesn't seem to have heard them, but then, she's British, not American.

Claire has many literary references that bewilder Jamie (to say nothing of nods to television, Monopoly, and American history). She calls him a sadist when he threatens to beat her, though the Marquis de Sade (2 June 1740–2 December 1814) hadn't yet written the novels that inspired the word. She jokes that she doesn't have a scarlet A on her chest and Jamie looks confused (*Voyager*, ch. 39). (While *The Scarlet Letter* takes place in Puritan times, Nathaniel Hawthorne wrote it centuries later). Claire goes sailing and quotes Longfellow's "The Building of the Ship": "She moves! She stirs! She seems to feel/The thrill of life along her keel!" (*Voyager*, ch. 41) and also "Home is the place where, when you have to go there/They have to take you in" from "The Death of the Hired Man," by Robert Frost (1874–1963).

In something that appears more of an author joke, the slave Ishmael introduces himself with "Call me Ishmael" in "Lord John and the Plague of Zombies" (358). Geillis says she named him that after hearing of his suffering at sea. Claire attends the Governor's Ball with Jamie in the chapter "Masque of the Red Death" and indeed the ball turns violent. The *Dragonfly* chapter "The Postman Always Rings Twice" is a novel and several noir films. *The Drums of Autumn* has "O Brave New World" and "Strawberry Fields Forever." "Return of the Native" is a title in *A Breath of Snow and Ashes*. *The Fiery Cross* offers chapters "A Hard Day's Night" and "A Whiter Shade of Pale." *Written in My Own Heart's Blood* has "The Body Electric"—in which Brianna thinks of Walt Whitman and also electric currents as ley lines.

In *The Drums of Autumn*, Roger says, "Eat your heart out, Tom Wolfe" upon returning to his adopted father's manor. Gabaldon notes, "He's referring (obliquely) to Thomas Wolfe's (not Tom Wolfe; the earlier one) work, with its reiterated theme of 'You can't go home again.' I.e., Roger is sardonically recognizing both the truth of that statement—and the contradictory fact that the manse under Fiona's management seems just as it did when it *was* his home" (*Outlandish Companion* 381–382).

Later, Claire quotes "early to bed and early to rise," only to realize Ben Franklin said it (*Voyager*, ch. 26). In book four, Claire hears men singing the drinking song "The Anacreontic Song" from the Anacreontic Society, an 18th-century London gentlemen's club. This tune was later used for "The Star-Spangled Banner," and Claire sings these lyrics to it under her breath. As the American Revolution begins, Brianna recites "The Ballad of Paul Revere," realizing that it's happening as she speaks. Jamie likes the rhythm and the stirring words. Claire soon notices that Jamie's been quoting Briana who's been quoting John Adams, and he's been publishing his letters in the newspaper (*A Breath of Snow and Ashes,* ch. 76). In the war, Lord John hears various people singing "Yankee Doodle" and reflects that the Americans have likely never seen the dandy fashion called Macaroni (*Written in My Own Heart's Blood,* ch. 51). Meanwhile Claire wraps his head in a bandage and decides he resembles *The Spirit of '76* (ch. 63).

The show has its own unique collection of anachronisms. Claire teaches Laoghaire a spell from *The Wizard of Oz* (Episode 104) and calls Jamie a "regular Bob Hope" in the wedding episode. He misunderstands Claire's question about hanging stockings for Yuletide in "Both Sides Now." Joining in supplying urine for the waulking, Claire squats over the kettle and says, "Geronimo!" (Episode 105). In the 1940s, Reverend Wakefield references Sherlock Holmes with "When you have eliminated the impossible, whatever remains, however improbable, must be the truth" (Episode 108). This last is perfectly proper for his time, though it's worth mentioning that Doyle was Scottish.

Doctor Who

In the eighth book, Brianna jokes with family friend Joe Abernathy about how much she wishes she had a TARDIS instead of the standing stones (*Written in My Own Heart's Blood,* ch. 97). While it's unlikely she watched this British science fiction show as a child in America, new episodes would have been available in 1980s Scotland. More importantly, this is a nod to the creation of the books as a whole, along with their hero, Jamie Fraser. Diana Gabaldon writes about her first attempt to write a novel in 1988:

> I was casting about for an appealing time and place—American Civil War, Italian Renaissance, medieval Poland...? And while in this malleable frame of mind, I happened to see a Dr. Who rerun on PBS.
>
> This was a really old re-run; one of the Patrick Troughton episodes (for those with a taste for trivia, it was "War Games"). And one of the Doctor's companions in this episode was a young Scotsman from 1745. Maybe 18 or 19 ... and he appeared in his kilt.
>
> "Hm," I said. "That's fetching."
>
> Well, so. I found myself still thinking about this the next day—in church—and said to myself, "You want to write a book; it doesn't matter where you set it; the important thing to pick a place and get started. OK, fine—Scotland, eighteenth century."
>
> So that's where I started. Knowing nothing about Scotland or the eighteenth century, and having no plot, no outline, and no characters—nothing save the rather vague images conjured up by thought of a man in a kilt. (Very powerful and compelling image, that.)
>
> Now, despite the Dr. Who connection, the book actually began as a perfectly straightforward historical novel. The time-travel came in later, when I thought

it would be interesting to have an Englishwoman to play off all these kilted Scotsmen, and she refused to shut up and talk like an 18th century person. She just kept making smart-ass modern remarks about everything she saw—and she also took over and started telling the story [DeLuca].

Jamie's first name came from this character, along with the brash, friendly, kind personality. *Doctor Who*'s Jamie McCrimmon is a twenty-two year old piper, fighting with Clan McLaren at the famous Battle of Culloden Claire fears is coming. When the Doctor arrives in his time travel device, the TARDIS, Jamie and his fellow Highlanders are facing being hanged for treason or transported to the West Indies. As the Highlanders huddle in a ruined cottage, they discuss the needless slaughter after the battle, along with other issues explored in *Outlander*. Meanwhile, the Doctor saves the local laird (ironically, named Colum) with anachronistic actual medical knowledge as Laird McLaren insists on bloodletting, a circumstance Claire must often battle. After besting the Recoats, Jamie joins the Doctor on his time travel adventures.

Very much an action hero, Jamie is friendly and adaptable, though also a product of his time. Gabaldon explains: "Jamie McCrimmon, from the eighteenth century and a culture in which women were respected, but not considered men's physical equals ... he can't help it; he has to try to protect [a woman], even though he accepts her as his intellectual and social equal" ("The Doctor's Balls" Kindle Locations 334–349).

The episode Gabaldon watched was Jamie McCrimmon's last (excepting later guest appearances). It features Jamie's meeting with assertive World War I Nurse Jennifer Buckingham and Captain Ransom, another name Gabaldon was to use later. In this history mash-up, Jamie also encounters a redcoat apparently from the Battle of Culloden, and to his disgust, must ally with him to discover the truth behind the many characters' abductions. As Jamie learns about female competence from a World War II nurse and struggles with English alliances and devil's bargains, he demonstrates his many roots in the episode. Gabaldon comments in her essay for a *Doctor Who* collection that Jamie and Lady Jennifer's disagreements riveted her:

> In this particular scene, Jamie McCrimmon and Lady Jennifer, a World War I ambulance driver (hence demonstrably no one's delicate blossom) are somewhere with the TARDIS, but without the Doctor, who was presumably in considerable danger elsewhere/when. Jamie declares that he must go rescue the Doctor, tells Lady Jennifer to wait there, and heads for the TARDIS—followed closely by Lady Jennifer. When he perceives that she plans to come, too, he insists that she must stay behind, ostensibly because someone needs to tell their other companions what's going on. Lady Jennifer greets this piece of feeble persuasion with the scorn it deserves, demanding, "You just want me to stay behind because I'm a woman, isn't that right?" To which our courageous young Scots-

man (who is considerably shorter than Lady Jennifer) replies, "Well, no, I—that is ... you.... I ... well ... yes!" Now, I found this demonstration of pig-headed male gallantry riveting ["The Doctor's Balls" Kindle Locations 334–349].

While his actor is named Frazer Hines, Jamie's last name appears to be more historical coincidence than homage. Reading *The Prince in the Heather* by Eric Linklater, Gabaldon discovered Culloden had one notable survivor. Linklater writes: "After the final battle at Culloden, eighteen Jacobite officers, all wounded, took refuge in the old house and for two days, their wounds untended, lay in pain; then they were taken out to be shot. One of them, a Fraser of the Master of Lovat's regiment escaped the slaughter; the others were buried at the edge of the domestic park" (14). As Gabaldon explains, "I was thinking that if I expect Jamie to survive Culloden then his last name better be Fraser" (DeLuca). Frazer Hines appears in the second half of the *Outlander* show's first season in another delightful homage to the program that started it all.

Modern English Novels and Poetry

Claire appears to have a love of English literature (no surprise there) and she often quotes pieces from the past. Of course, most of them are from the eighteenth century Romantics or more modern works and thus not actually far back enough.

Claire realizes that reading about child cruelty in Dickens has not prepared her for the reality of ear-nailing (*Outlander,* ch. 9). Trapped together in the snow, Claire tells Jamie the story of *A Christmas Carol,* and recalls another occasion when she and Frank were stuck in their car on another snowy night and they told Brianna the story (*The Drums of Autumn,* ch. 21).

"Water, water, everywhere/Nor any drop to drink" from "The Rime of the Ancient Mariner" by Samuel Coleridge (1772–1834) appears in a book about voyaging. *Written in My Own Heart's Blood* has famous Welsh poem "Do Not Go Gentle into that Good Night" as a chapter title. The *Voyager* chapter title "I Shall Go Down to the Sea" is often attributed to John Masefield (1878–1967). Claire adds that "Kind hearts are more than coronets" (*Dragonfly in Amber,* ch. 24) from "Lady Clara Vere de Vere" by Tennyson.

She quotes Alfred Edward Housman (1859–1936) quite often:

> The rainy Pleiads wester,
> Orion plunges prone,
> The stroke of midnight ceases
> And I lie down alone.
>
> The rainy Pleiads wester,
> And seek beyond the sea
> The head that I shall dream of
> That will not dream of me [*Voyager,* ch. 42].

Off to the Governor's Ball with Jamie, Claire quotes:

> Oh who is that young sinner with the handcuffs on his wrists?
> And what has he been after that they groan and shake their fists?
> And wherefore is he wearing such a conscience-stricken air?
> Oh they're taking him to prison for the color of his hair.
>
> 'Tis a shame to human nature, such a head of hair as his;
> In the good old time 'twas hanging for the color that it is;
> Though hanging isn't bad enough and flaying would be fair
> For the nameless and abominable color of his hair.
>
> Oh a deal of pains he's taken and a pretty price he's paid
> To hide his poll or dye it of a mentionable shade;
> But they've pulled the beggar's hat off for the world to see and stare,
> And they're taking him to justice for the color of his hair.
>
> Now 'tis oakum for his fingers and the treadmill for his feet,
> And the quarry-gang on Portland in the cold and in the heat,
> And between his spells of labor in the time he has to spare
> He can curse the God that made him for the color of his hair.

In this scene, Jamie must disguise his hair with a wig so he isn't recognized (*Voyager*, ch. 58). Later, she quotes from the poem "Because I Liked You": "Halt by the headstone naming/The heart no longer stirred/And say the lad that loved you/Was one that kept his word." Jamie also mentions that Claire sometimes says, "Malt does more than Milton can to justify God's ways to man" (*A Breath of Snow and Ashes*, ch. 51). As Claire spreads anachronisms around Jacobite Scotland and the colonies, she shows her heedless modern color, much like her unladylike swearing and independence.

Apparently, Frank is a fan of the Yeats poem "The Lake Isle of Innisfree," about a beautiful cabin and garden he'll build, far from civilization. Claire and Brianna mention this in *Drums*, as the family does just that. *Drums* has several Keats and Shelley lines in pages 430–431: "Forever wilt thou love, and she be fair!" from "Ode on a Grecian Urn," "Make me thy lyre..." from "Ode to the West Wind," and Keats's "Sonnet Written in Disgust of Vulgar Superstition." "Fiend, I defy thee! with a calm, fixed mind" is from Shelley's *Prometheus Unbound*.

Likewise, Claire hears of a man who leaves his home after crudely painting the word "Rache."

> "That means 'revenge,'" Lord John translated for me.
> "I know," I said, my mouth so dry I could barely speak. "I've read Sherlock Holmes" [*The Drums of Autumn*, ch. 28].

Claire tells Jamie "a man's reach must exceed his grasp—or what's a heaven for" (*An Echo in the Bone*, ch. 64). After Jamie quotes it, Claire hopes "Robert Browning and I hadn't just landed Jamie in the middle of something." Claire also quotes T.S. Elliot (1888–1965) in his "Whispers of Immortality": "And saw the skull beneath the skin/and breastless creatures underground leaned backwards with a lipless grin" while transporting a corpse in *An Echo in the Bone* (ch. 74).

From *Alice in Wonderland,* Claire reminds herself to "Begin at the Beginning and go on till you come to the end: then stop" while writing a letter (*An Echo in the Bone,* ch. 74).

Part one of *Dragonfly in Amber* is entitled "Through a looking glass, darkly," which references both Carroll's second book *Through the Looking Glass* and the biblical passage from 1 Corinthians 13:12. Chapter titles for *Written in My Own Heart's Blood* include "Of Cabbages and Kings." Of course, Claire is journeying through a fantastical new world, much like Alice herself.

Some of Claire's references are actually fitting for the times, and Jamie can join her in discussing them. When Claire sees the highhanded entitled behavior of the Vicomtesse de Rambeau she realizes the woman will likely be executed in the French Revolution and quotes, 'Ask not for whom the tumbril [cart used to take aristocrats to their deaths] calls, it calls for thee,' from Donne's "No Man is an Island" (*Dragonfly in Amber*, ch. 8). Claire and Jamie also debate "No Man is an Island" in *An Echo in the Bone.*

When Claire explains the finer points of lovemaking to Jamie, she feels like the Wife of Bath, a character from twelfth-century *Canterbury Tales* by Geoffrey Chaucer (*Outlander*, ch. 15). In episode five, Claire and Ned Gowan quote "Absence, Hear Thou my Protestation" by John Moses Hoskyns (died 1638):

> Absence, hear thou my protestation
> Against thy strength,
> Distance and length:
> Do what thou canst for alteration;
> For hearts of truest mettle
> Absence doth join, and time doth settle.

Scots

If asked to list the greatest Scottish writers, many would list Robbie Burns, Robert Louis Stevenson, and Sir Walter Scott (to say nothing of Sir Arthur Conan Doyle and J.K. Rowling). However, all of these authors were published long after Claire and Jamie's adventures in the 1740s. Despite this, Claire quotes them all with astonishing frequency. It's unclear whether Gabaldon wanted to drop these authors in as homage to Scottish culture or whether Claire (who's generally uncertain of dates and far from a literary scholar) feels inspired by Scotland and its way of life. Either way, many anachronisms spring up as Jamie requotes the pieces Claire has said to him.

Robbie Burns (1759–1796)

Burns has been considered Scotland's national bard and the voice of Scotland itself. Along with his many original works such as the epic poem "Tam O'Shanter," he attempted to collect and publish the words and music of all Scottish songs, published thereafter in many volumes.

Claire tells Jamie the line "Freedom and whisky gang tegither" from "The Author's Earnest Cry and Prayer" (*Dragonfly in Amber*, ch. 24). Jamie quotes this in a newspaper article he writes, enabling Claire to find him as she and her friends note the paradox—Robbie Burns had barely been born at the time (*Voyager,* ch. 21). Burns' "Auld Lang Syne" is a chapter title in *The Fiery Cross,* though no one sings the song until future decades. On the show, "The Highland Widow's Lament," with lyrics by Burns, plays when Claire sees Highlanders killed by the Black Watch in "Rent." When she and Frank visit Culloden in a flashback, "Ye Jacobites by Name," with lyrics by Burns, plays.

Later, Roger discusses the first Jacobite rising with Brian Fraser and admires the fact that Brian fought at Sheriffmuir. Roger explains his knowledge by saying, "I heard a song about it. 'Twas two shepherds met on a hillside, talking about the great fight—and arguing who'd won it." At Brian's insistence, Roger sings him the song, then writes it down for him, thinking, "Well, what harm could it do to let Robert Burns's poem loose in the world some years in advance of Burns himself?"

> O cam ye here the fight to shun,
> Or herd the sheep wi' me, man?
> Or were ye at the Sherra-moor,
> Or did the battle see, man?"
> I saw the battle, sair and teugh,
> And reekin-red ran mony a sheugh;
> My heart, for fear, gaed sough for sough,
> To hear the thuds, and see the cluds
> O' clans frae woods, in tartan duds,
> Wha glaum'd at kingdoms three, man
> [*Written in My Own Heart's Blood*, ch. 31].

In *Outlander,* young Hamish MacKenzie, Colum's son, solemnly recites the classic Selkirk Grace, attributed to Burns: "Some hae meat that canna eat, And some could eat that want it. But we hae meat and we can eat, And so may God be thankit." Gabaldon included the prayer when she found it attributed to "Anonymous" rather than the more accurate Burns. Nonetheless, Dr. Sheila Brock, curator of the new Museum of Scotland, advised her that "the Selkirk Grace is only *attributed* to Burns; there's no actual proof he wrote it. I should think your best defense is to claim that Burns might have taken it from an existing bit of folk verse." As Gabaldon concludes, "That seemed good advice to me, so I'm sticking with it" (*Outlandish Companion* 502).

In a subtler homage, "The best laid plans of mice and men" is the title of chapter 23 of *Dragonfly in Amber.* This comes from "The best laid schemes o' mice an' men gang aft agley" in the poem "To a Mouse."

Walter Scott (1771–1832)

Sir Walter Scott trained as a lawyer but gave it up after the success of his historical novel *Waverley.* Following this, he produced *Rob Roy, Guy Mannering, Ivanhoe, Old Mortality*, and *The Talisman.* He was knighted in 1820 and organized the visit of King George IV to Scotland in 1822. More importantly, he did much to re-invent Highland society and clan tartans for the visit, leading to the current well-known Scottish culture and tourism.

In *Voyager,* Claire quotes from "Marmion," with "Oh, what a tangled web we weave/ When first we practice to deceive!" These two phrases are also chapter titles in *Lord John and the Private Matter.* Jamie tells Claire she should be nice to him, quoting her own "Marmion" phrase back to her: "When pain and anguish wring the brow, A ministering angel thou!"

Robert Louis Stevenson (1850–1894)

Dealing with pirates and shipwreck in *Voyager,* Claire recites, "Fifteen men on a Dead Man's Chest—Yo-ho-ho, and a bottle of rum!" from Stevenson's *Treasure Island* (*Voyager,* ch. 40). In *Dragonfly,* she quotes his famous "Requiem": "Home is the sailor, home from the sea, And the hunter home from the hill" (ch. 31). His "Sing me a Song of a Lad that is Gone" is discussed in the next section.

MUSIC

The Credits

The opening credits offer a collage of images from the first few episodes: a deer, horses, the stitching of the wound, muddy shoes running, the dragging of the whip, a grasped dirk, running to battle, Frank driving, Frank and Claire sitting on the dock, bare skin and a blanket grasped in passion, and finally the rolling green land of Scotland. This is Claire's life as snapshots—all the impressions and memories she gains, past and future as she struggles to find her place in a new world and say farewell to the old. These images are intercut with the circle dancers—the force of magic and power that carried Claire away on her adventure.

Also striking is the music chosen for the credits. Composer Bear McCreary explains that the team used "The Skye Boat Song," one of the most famous Scottish folk tunes and also a link to the Jacobite uprising. "The lyrics are taken from the lesser-known Robert Louis Stevenson text, with one alteration in the gender of the speaker, which helps the song relate to Claire's character" ("Comic Con 2014 Highlights").

Since Stevenson was born in 1850, this is an anachronism, but the song is certainly known to be associated with Bonnie Prince Charlie. While the tune predates the lyrics, it probably doesn't go back as far as 1740. The original lyrics by Sir Harold Boulton, 2nd Baronet, from 1884 describe the prince's defeat at Culloden, followed by his boat escape with Flora MacDonald "over the sea to Skye." Stevenson's version is vaguer and more romantic in language:

> Sing me a Song of a Lad that is Gone
> Robert Louis Stevenson 1850–1894
> Sing me a song of a lad that is gone,
> Say, could that lad be I?
> Merry of soul he sailed on a day
> Over the sea to Skye.
> Mull was astern, Rum on the port,
> Eigg on the starboard bow;
> Glory of youth glowed in his soul;
> Where is that glory now?
> Sing me a song of a lad that is gone,
> Say, could that lad be I?
> Merry of soul he sailed on a day
> Over the sea to Skye.
> Give me again all that was there,
> Give me the sun that shone!
> Give me the eyes, give me the soul,
> Give me the lad that's gone!
> Sing me a song of a lad that is gone,
> Say, could that lad be I?
> Merry of soul he sailed on a day
> Over the sea to Skye.
> Billow and breeze, islands and seas,
> Mountains of rain and sun,
> All that was good, all that was fair,
> All that was me is gone.

The *Outlander* theme tune is a shorter excerpt of this:

> Sing me a song of a lass that is gone,
> Say, could that lass be I?
> Merry of soul she sailed on a day
> Over the sea to Skye.
> Billow and breeze, islands and seas,
> Mountains of rain and sun,

All that was good, all that was fair,
All that was me is gone.
Sing me a song of a lass that is gone,
Say, could that lass be I?
Merry of soul she sailed on a day
Over the sea to Skye.

McCreary adds that "The Main Title builds energy, until at last it bursts into a rousing march of Great Highland Bagpipes and signature Scottish snare drums" ("Comic Con 2014 Highlights"). The song also reappears as Claire and Frank discuss the Rising in a flashback.

This poem describes a journey to a far-off land but also a romanticized lost time, now gone forever. Certainly, many idealize Bonnie Prince Charlie and his Jacobite cause as symbols of great possibility, a chance for nationalism and rebellion that vanished too quickly, much like the American South's portrayal in *Gone with the Wind*.

The description of a lost person who sailed away certainly alludes to Claire. The ending of the tune, focusing on her journey rather than her loss, suggests continuing adventures in the fairytale-sounding land of "Skye" (though Claire does not in fact visit the actual isle). Nonetheless, the Gaelic name for the Isle of Skye, *An t-Eilean Sgitheanach,* meaning the Winged Isle, and its Gaelic nickname, *Eilean a' Cheo,* or Island of Mist, both cast it as a place of mystery and romance. In English, the sky signifies enlightenment and spiritual ascension, something Claire cannot find as the housewife of an Oxford don, but only as a fighting, healing heroine far in the past.

The credits offer a link to nature as the circle dancers spin and twirl, and Claire travels through the magic of sun festival and ancient stone. The second stanza teams with images of natural wonder, tying them to Claire in a way that suggests her own inner wildness; the "billow and breeze, islands and seas," seem to be part of her. The demanding nature of the song ("Sing me a song") and the search for identity ("All that was me is gone") suggest Claire's own personality as she tries to decide where she belongs and how she's meant to spend her life.

The Television Score

Scottish instruments dominate the score as Claire is surrounded by Scots in 1746. Audible are a Scottish fiddle, bodhrán, fiddle, Uilleann pipes, accordion, viola da gamba and many different-sounding bagpipes, even in the sex scenes. Jamie and Claire's theme plays often, haunting and wistful on a single penny whistle. Every episode has a new end credits piece, allowing viewers to savor the mood of the final scene.

By contrast, scenes in the 1940s with Frank have very different music. Bear McCreary, explains, on a theme music blog about crafting all the pieces for the show:

> I found the clarinet remarkably effective at signifying our jump in time, every bit as useful as the saturated color scheme and the sounds of cars and telephones. Because we would never otherwise hear a clarinet in the score, its presence announces to our subconscious minds that the narrative is leaping back to where we began. In the first episode, Frank's Theme was wistful, nostalgic and romantic. In "Both Sides Now," I altered the harmonic progression beneath the clarinet to highlight Frank's sullen despair and loneliness; however, the melody remains the same ["Outlander: The Garrison Commander, The Wedding, Both Sides Now"].

Specific 1940s songs also set the scene. The first episode features "I'm Gonna Get Lit Up (When The Lights Go On In London)" as recorded by Carroll Gibbons & Savoy Hotel Orpheans and "Shuffle Rhythm" as recorded by Jan Savitt & His Top Hatters on the radio as Claire and Frank go driving together. In the Reverend's library, "Beneath The Lights Of Home" plays, recorded by Geraldo & His Orchestra. Moore adds that he wanted forties music "that wasn't instantly recognizable" rather than doing the "best of" hits (Episode Podcasts 101). "Run Rabbit Run," recorded by Harry Roy & His Band sets the scene as Claire reads the botanical book in her room, then again as she outraces British soldiers in the past, providing an ironic contrast. '40s music in the past helps to emphasize Claire's point of view, as the songs live on within her.

Ballads and Sea Chanties

Poems, ditties, ballads, and songs of the sea all incorporate the larger culture around the characters. Claire cleans out the surgery to "Coming through the Rye." "The Gathering" features folksongs "The Haughs o' Cromdale," and "Clean Pease Strae," (the latter during the shinty game). "Rent" has many songs: "To the Begging I Will Go" as Dougal collects funds, the actual waulking song "Mo Nighean Donn" (chosen for Jamie's common endearment to Claire), "The Skye Boat Song" when Claire understands Dougal's true intentions and "Ye Jacobites by Name" as Claire remembers Culloden Field. These last two, both well-known Jacobite anthems, contain a vital message—that Dougal supports the rebellion and that the cause will end in defeat. As if these weren't enough, "The Highland Widow's Lament" sounds plaintively when Highlanders are seen crucified, and "The High Road to Linton" plays jauntily during the bar brawl. These folksongs help to set the mood authentically and powerfully for viewers.

The books also offer this scene-setting, though rarely with lyrics and obviously not with tunes. Some people in a tavern sing a "blatantly anti–Catholic version" of "Down Among the Dead Men," to Jamie's displeasure (*The Scottish Prisoner*, ch. 18). Murtagh teaches Claire to sing the border ballad "The Dowie Dens of Yarrow" when they travel together looking for Jamie (*Outlander*, ch. 34). Even Jamie sings "Up among the Heather" while happily married to Claire at Leoch (*Outlander*, ch. 24) and recites an old Scottish love song to Claire the day after their wedding.

Through his adventures, Roger collects ballads including "Jamie Telfer of the Fair Dodhead," which he compiles in a book. *Drums* has "How many strawberries grow in the salt sea; how many ships sail in the forest?" from "The Fause Bride," a medieval Scottish ballad. Gabaldon comments, "My friend Jack Whyte (my authority on Scottish ballads) tells me that this particular line rates as perhaps the oldest riddle in Scottish literature, and is from the Northeast of Scotland—'Fraser territory,' he says" (*Outlandish Companion* 533).

Jack Randall asks Corporal Hawkins to recite something to reveal his accent; he recites a short ditty which starts, "Buxom Meg, she washed my clothes" (*Outlander*, ch. 12). In *A Breath of Snow and Ashes*, Roger seduces Brianna while singing her "The Maid Gaed to the Mill," which is "a very bawdy Scottish song, about a miller who is pestered by a young woman wanting him to grind her corn. Whereupon he does" (ch. 6). The men sing this song in the rent-collecting episode of the show. The Ned and the Prostitutes scene in the wedding episode features the popular tune from the time period called "Celia Learning on the Spinnet," another dirty song (McCreary, "Outlander: The Garrison Commander, The Wedding, Both Sides Now").

Composer Bear McCreary explains the folksongs incorporated into the show such as "Loch Lomond," adding:

> The first episode of *Outlander* introduces the fundamental themes that will provide the building blocks for the score: the Claire and Jamie Theme, the Frank Theme and the Stones Theme. Other themes will weave their way into the score in upcoming episodes, but the biggest shift in the music coming will be my emphasis on Scottish folk tunes and other eighteenth century music. Each episode henceforth features new folk tunes in the score, offering us a glimpse into the world. Some will be familiar, and others will be more obscure. My hope is that the score lives up to and enhances the authenticity of the writing, costumes and immaculate production design ["Outlander, Sassenach"].

As characters journey far from Scotland, songs of the sea multiply through the story. *The Drums of Autumn* offers traditional sea-chanties like "From Ushant to Scilly is thirty-five leagues" and "Farewell to you all, ye fair Spanish ladies" (ch. 59). Claire cares for an ill visitor by singing a sea chantie to him, as they don't share a language. She notes, "I poured a small bit of lavender oil into my hand, dipped the feather in it, and anointed his temples and throat, while singing "Blow the Man Down," in a low, sinister voice. It might help the headache" (*The Drums of Autumn*, ch. 26). Claire says that Jamie is a landlubber and "not one of the hardy, seafaring Scots who hunted whales from Tarwathie," a reference to the whaling ballad "Farewell to Tarwathie" (*Dragonfly in Amber*, ch. 6).

Many of these songs still exist today. In the future, Roger sings many popular airs at the Celtic festival in New England—"The Road to the Isles," "The Gallowa' Hills" "The Lewis Bridal Song" "Vair Me O," "MacPherson's Lament," "The Bonnie Banks o' Loch Lomond," and "Hey, Johnnie Cope, Are Ye Waking Yet?" The last of these also appears in the American Revolution in the series. He also sings "The Sherramuir Fight" about the rising of 1715, which featured Bonnie Prince Charlie's father (*The Drums of Autumn*, ch. 4). This scene offers a modern view of the Scottish bard, as Roger exaggerates his accent and wears a kilt, even while appalled by the food truck haggis and tacky Scottish souvenirs for sale. This scene contrasts with his rabble-rousing in the past, when Jamie asks him to sing at a gathering for a more political purpose.

In *The Fiery Cross*, Jamie asks him to inspire their people before the upcoming war. Brianna tells Roger, "He wants you to do 'Ho Ro!' and 'Birniebouzle,' and 'The Great Silkie'—you can do other stuff in between, he said, but he wants those—and then get into the warmongering stuff" (ch. 23). In an anachronism, Roger also sings Scotland's "unofficial national anthem," written by Roy Williamson of the Corries in 1967:

> It was a solemn song, that one, and melancholy. But not a song of grief, for all that; one of remembrance, of pride and determination. It wasn't even a legitimately ancient song—Roger knew the man who'd written it, in his own time—but Jamie had heard it, and knowing the history of Stirling and Bannockburn, strongly approved the sentiment [ch. 24].

The old Scottish ballad "Eppie Morrie" (Child Ballad No. 223) appears in *A Breath of Snow and Ashes*, as Ian and Roger joke about the lyrics:

> "And put a pistol to his breest, his breest," Young Ian chanted, "Marry me, marry me, minister, or else I'll be your priest, your priest—or else I'll be your priest!"
> "Of course," Roger said, dropping the song, in which a bold young man named Willie rides with his friends to abduct and forcibly marry a young woman who proves bolder yet, "we'll hope ye prove a wee bit more capable than Willie upon the night, aye, Joseph?" [ch. 85]

Jamie thinks of the same song on a mission to rescue a young woman from a seducer in *The Scottish Prisoner*. In fact, this is the story of an empowered young woman who refuses to submit to a forced marriage, beginning by saying "There's not a man in a' Strathdon/Shall wedded be with me," then wrestling with him all night with the words, "Ere I lose my maidenhead/I'll fight with you till day."

In the morning, she demands the man provide her a horse so she can return to her mother "virgin as I came." A few chapters after the scene above, Brianna, also abducted by a man, resists him by sharpening one of her stays into a knife and smashing an escape hole in the roof. She defends herself as fervently as the ballad's heroine, striking several blows for feminism.

Myth

MYTH AND THE STANDING STONES

Circle Dancers and Stone Circles

Claire first sees the standing stones with the dancers weaving among them. Their ritual links the story to older times and emphasizes a pagan magic present still. Mrs. Graham is their leader, she who inherited palm and tea reading from an older time and offers the ancient magic of the women (notably no men perform the ritual). In the book, Frank notes that the dance words are ancient Norse but the dance is "very much older." He speculates it's from the Beaker Folk. The vanished culture of the Picts was matrilineal, and the Beaker culture, 2800–1800 BC, stretches back even earlier, following the Neolithic culture that built the megalithic passage tombs.

Circle dances are the most ancient, evoking magic circles and fairy rings. They are egalitarian—meant for all, with no special training for participants. Around the world, they are often danced around a central figure, such as a standing stone or altar. On the show, the scene is filmed to be eerie, beautiful, and magical. Moore calls it "tribal, paganistic, primitive" (Episode Podcasts 101). As Claire describes it:

> They should have been ridiculous. And perhaps they were. Parading in circles on top of a hill. But the hairs on the back of my neck prickled at the sight. And some small voice inside warned me, I wasn't supposed to be here. That I was an unwelcome voyeur to something ancient and powerful [Episode 101].

The scene fills with unearthly chanting and vague ghostly shapes of women, grey on grey, with only the lights truly visible. Faces are not discernable, only shawls and long hair. The gauzy tunics suggest a *Mists of Avalon* culture of women's mysteries from pre–Roman times. When the sun rises, the light makes everything even more blinding—golden light with only silhouettes before it and lamps held like prehistoric torches. All the spinning foreshadows Claire's twisting, disorienting journey as the circle dance continues through the opening credits.

Composer Bear McCreary explains creating the music for this scene with a Celtic harp and twined female voices:

> No music from the Druids survives today, and much of the music people associate with Druids today is based on mythology built up from pop culture, about as historically accurate as Spinal Tap. With no true piece to draw upon, I decided instead to adapt the oldest lyric from the region that I could. Adam found a number of contenders and I chose the one I felt matched the scene the best, the first stanza of a poem called "Duan Na Muthairn," or "Rune of the Muthairn." These were drawn from a collection by Alexander Carmichael called *Carmina Gadelica,* published in 1900, that was at the forefront of the Gaelic revival movement of that time period. Translated into English, the text reads:
>
>> Thou King of the moon,
>> Thou King of the sun,
>> Thou King of the planets,
>> Thou King of the stars,
>> Thou King of the globe,
>> Thou King of the sky,
>> Oh! lovely Thy countenance,
>> Thou beauteous Beam.
>
> For the music, I composed an original theme, setting this text. I wrote it in the Dorian Mode, a scale I employ frequently for this show for its "old world" flavor, and elegant implied harmonies. Underneath the melody, I composed a distinctly modern harmonic progression to give the theme an other-worldly quality. Listen for the interaction between the F# in the melody and F natural in the bass line. Historically speaking, these scale tones would rarely if ever both appear in a folk song in A minor. With that, I had composed the Stones Theme.

In book four, Mrs. Graham's granddaughter explains a bit: Her grandmother was a Caller, "The one who calls down the sun." As she adds, "It's one of the auld tongues, the sun-song; some of the words are a bit like the Gaelic, but not all of it. First we dance, in the circle, then the caller stops and faces the split stone" and chants until the sun peeps through (*The Drums of Autumn,* ch. 87).

Roger uncovers this spell in Geillis's notes:

> I raise my athame to the North,
> where is the home of my power,
> To the West,
> where is the hearth of my soul,
> To the South,
> where is the seat of friendship and refuge,

To the East,
from whence rises the sun.

...

My left hand is wreathed in gold,
and holds the power of the sun.
My right hand is sheathed in silver,
and the moon reigns serene.
I begin.

Garnets rest in love about my neck.
I will be faithful [*The Drums of Autumn,* ch. 40].

Roger notes that the four directions are traditional Celtic. "As for the blade, the altar, and the flames, it's straight witchcraft" (*The Drums of Autumn,* ch. 40). Nonetheless, the mention of silver, gold, and gemstones also seems significant for travel. There are other ties to modern witchcraft. The reference to "three flames" echoes the magician's Triangle of Manifestation, while the four cardinal points are also important to spellcasting. Five is the points of the pentagram, protective as well as mystical. Jewelry is also common in ceremonies, and jewels are revealed to be important for travelers. Garnets, however, ominously suggest drops of blood.

There are several rules governing time travel, though Claire is slow to piece them together. Two hundred years appears to be the standard journey, but in the *Outlander* world "It could be changed by use of gemstones, or of blood" as with the ritual ("The Space Between" 234). Gemstones protect travelers; so do silver and gold. Focusing on a loved one as anchor also helps, though a person cannot enter a time when his or her younger self lives.

Only a few people are sensitive to the stones and can pass through—to everyone else, they are inert. It's established in the first book that Jamie can't travel—Claire hears the stones singing and feels their power, but he does not. Metaphorically, he's a character of the romantic past and he's tied there, as much as Bonnie Prince Charlie is. This also gives Claire more agency as Jamie cannot come to the future seeking her or offer to accompany her if she goes back—it's her choice whether to stay or return.

Clava Cairns

Jamie and Claire travel to Corrimony Cairn in Invernesshire to bury General Simon Fraser in *An Echo in the Bone.* As Claire describes it:

I had drawn closer, along with the other women, and found I was now standing within a foot or two of one of the standing stones that ringed the cairn. These were smaller than the stones on Craigh na Dun—no more than two or three feet high. Moved by sudden impulse, I reached out and touched it.

I hadn't expected anything to happen, and it very luckily didn't. Though had I suddenly vanished in the midst of the burial, it would have substantially enlivened the event [ch.75].

The general is buried in a clava cairn, an ancient passage tomb where great chieftains were placed in ancient times. These are scattered through Britain. The cairn is believed to have been built 4000 years ago as a burial place for someone noteworthy. Claire notes that, like the standing stones, "the passage was meant to orient with some astrological object on some significant date" (ch.75). Many cairns had passageways aligned to the Midwinter sunset, as this was an important time of rebirth in the ancient calendar.

Legends of Traveling

Gwyllyn the bard tells the story of the wife of the Laird of Balnain whose wife was stolen by fairies then returned through rocks on a fairy hill. The show's version is even more blatant, with the woman finding a lover in a different time, then returning to her man at home. As Jamie translates for Claire:

> Now this one is about a man out late on a fairy hill on the eve of Samhain who hears the sound of a woman singing sad and plaintive from the very rocks of the hill. "I am a woman of Balnain. The folk have stolen me over again," the stones seemed to say. "I stood upon the hill, and wind did rise, and the sound of thunder rolled across the land. I placed my hands upon the tallest stone and traveled to a far, distant land where I lived for a time among strangers who became lovers and friends. But one day, I saw the moon came out and the wind rose once more. So I touched the stones and traveled back to my own land and took up again with the man I had left behind" [Episode 103].

In the books, Gwyllyn tells two significant tales, first of the Wee Folk who tried to steal Ewan MacDonald's wife to be a wet-nurse to their own fairy children when she's staying at Castle Leoch. This scene emphasizes how Claire has tumbled into Scottish folklore, as the story takes place "Two hundred years ago." Following this comes the tale of the wife of the Laird of Balnain. A man wandering late at night hears a woman singing "sad and plaintive" from the rocks of a fairy hill. He hears the words: "I am the wife of the Laird of Balnain, The Folk have stolen me over again." He hurries to Balnain and finds the owner gone and his wife and baby missing. Dragging a priest to the fairy knoll, he and the priest consecrate the ground and the wife of Balnain appears, exhausted on the grass with her child beside her. "The woman was tired, as though she had traveled far, but could not tell where she had been, nor how she had come there" (*Outlander,* ch. 8).

In book and show, the story is meant to parallel Claire's own situation and also provide her with hope—after their travels, the women usually return home.

Returning through the stones, Brianna also quotes, "I am the wife of the laird of Balnain. The fairies have stolen me over again" (*A Breath of Snow and Ashes,* ch. 120).

In a similar tale from folklore, a man discovers his own wife has been taken:

> In the olden times, when it was the fashion for gentlemen to wear swords, the Laird of Balmachie went one day to Dundee, leaving his wife at home ill in bed. Riding home in the twilight, he had occasion to leave the high road, and when crossing between some little romantic knolls, called the Cur-hills, in the neighbourhood of Carlungy, he encountered a troop of fairies supporting a kind of litter, upon which some person seemed to be borne. Being a man of dauntless courage, and, as he said, impelled by some internal impulse, he pushed his horse close to the litter, drew his sword, laid it across the vehicle, and in a firm tone exclaimed—
> "In the name of God, release your captive."
> The tiny troop immediately disappeared, dropping the litter on the ground. The laird dismounted, and found that it contained his own wife, dressed in her bedclothes. Wrapping his coat around her, he placed her on the horse before him, and, having only a short distance to ride, arrived safely at home.

He discovers, however, that he's brought home a changeling by mistake, and must use some violence to make her fly away.

> He then brought in his own wife, a little recovered from her alarm, who said, that sometime after sunset, the nurse having left her for the purpose of preparing a little candle, a multitude of elves came in at the window, thronging like bees from a hive. They filled the room, and having lifted her from the bed carried her through the window, after which she recollected nothing further, till she saw her husband standing over her on the Cur-hills, at the back of Carlungy. The hole in the roof, by which the female fairy made her escape, was mended, but could never be kept in repair, as a tempest of wind happened always once a year, which uncovered that particular spot, without injuring any other part of the roof [*Folk-Lore and Legends*].

Scottish tales often take place in a particular century, rather than a nebulous "Once Upon a Time." However, in examining folklore, two hundred years is not a particular staple. (The only place where this appears prominently in a Scottish time travel or otherworld tale is the popular fifties musical *Brigadoon*). In Gabaldon's work, the two hundred years seems to be common knowledge to the Scots. As Joan MacKimmie describes tiny fairies, "They give you food and drink…. But if you take any, you lose time … there's music and feasting and dancing. But in the morning, when he goes back it's two hundred years later" ("The Space Between" 234).

In fact, stolen children may be boys but stolen adults are often young women, taken as brides or wet-nurses for the fairies. (The woman in the tale of Ewan MacDonald of Dundreggan is given the latter job. The wife of the Laird of Balnain may be on a mission to save her child, another common staple of fairy kidnapping tales.) Some young men are stolen as well, to become great poets or musicians like Thomas the Rhymer. He is famously snatched under the hill for seven years. John Gregorson Campbell explains in *Superstitions of the Highlands & Islands of Scotland:*

> The Elfin Queen met Thomas of Ercil-doune by the Eildon tree, and took him to her enchanted realm, where he was kept for seven years. She gave him the power of foretelling the future, "the tongue that never lied."...In Gaelic tales seven years is a common period of detention among the Fairies, the leannansith [fairie] communicates to her lover the knowledge of future events, and in the end is looked upon by him with aversion....True Thomas, who is as well known in Highland lore as he is in the Lowlands, is said to be still among the Fairies, and to attend every market on the look-out for suitable horses. When he has made up his complement he will appear again among men, and a great battle will be fought on the Clyde [45–46].

Brianna and Roger visit the past for seven years precisely, a possible homage to famous tales like this one. However, Claire visits for half that, and the various journeys in *Written in My Own Heart's Blood* seem to last weeks, not years. Geillis's time in the past is varyingly described as five or ten years before she meets Claire.

Ley Lines

> A ley line is an observed alignment between two geographical features of interest, usually an ancient monument or megalith. There are a number of theories about ley lines and considerable controversy as to whether they actually exist as a phenomenon, and not only as an artifact....What people usually have in mind when using this term is an ancient pathway that leads, say, from a standing stone to an ancient abbey, which is itself likely built on a spot of much older worship.—*An Echo in the Bone,* ch. 46

Energy lines exist around the world, known as "Holy Lines" to the Germans, "Spirit Lines" to Incas and Mayans, "Dragon Lines" to the Chinese, and "Song Paths" to the Australian Aborigines. In his celebrated *The Fairy-Faith in Celtic Countries,* W. Y. Evans-Wentz calls them "fairy paths" or "fairy passes" of Ireland—"actual magnetic arteries, so to speak, through which circulates the earth's magnetism" (33). Amateur archaeologist Alfred Watkins named them ley lines in 1921, with his book *The Old Straight Track,* which brought the concept to the attention of the wider public. He charted mounds, long-barrows, cairns, dolmens, standing stones, mark-stones, stone circles, henges, water-markers (moats, ponds, springs, fords, wells), castles, beacon-hills, churches, cross-roads, notches in hills, and hill-forts, only to find they were laid out in straight lines. True leys according to his theories have a start (or finish) point in the shape of a hill (4).

Straight roads, often attributed to the Romans, in fact appear to predate them back to Neolithic times, as Romans record discovering them in Europe, North Africa, Crete, and the regions of ancient Babylon and Nineveh. These often lie along the ley lines, connecting the sacred sites. Gabaldon adds:

> There are lines of geomagnetic force running through the Earth's crust, and most of the time these run in opposing directions—forward and backward. In some places they deviate and will cross each other, and when that happens, you kind of get a geomagnetic mess going in all different directions. I call these vertices.
>
> Essentially, it could be possible to have something like this nexus of crossing lines to create a little time vortex. And if you could have a person whose sensibility to geomagnetism is sufficiently advanced so that they can not only detect this but enter into it in some way, then you have a plausible way of time travel.
>
> So if prehistoric people noticed that every so often when people crossed that particular patch of grass, they disappeared, it would cause considerable consternation, and they might think it worthwhile marking that spot. So that might be the reason why the stones are there, and why they're set up the way they are, as in, "People tended to disappear on the winter solstice when they step over here, so don't do that!" [DeLuca].

Many ley lines are constructed to match astronomical events. One of the largest in England, St. Michael's Ley, is aligned along the path of the sun on the 8th of May (St. Michael's Day). This line passes through Great Yarmouth and several megalithic sites before it reaches Glastonbury, the artificial hill known from Arthurian legend, and then on to the stone circle at Avebury, all the way to Penzance on the coast. While Stonehenge is not on the line, it aligns with Glastonbury and Avebury to create a perfect right-angled triangle, accurate to within 1/1000th part.

Roger tries to write a book about how the standing stones work, and he writes a chapter on ley lines. He relates them to dowsing, explaining both may work because of magnetic currents. (A significant dowsing scene appears in the same book, emphasizing a tie between the magics.) As Roger adds, "Another interesting bit of information is that homing pigeons (and quite possibly other sorts of birds) demonstrably do sense these geomagnetic lines, and use them to navigate by, though no one yet has figured out quite how they do it." He concludes: "The basic point is that the ability to time-travel may be dependent on a genetic sensitivity to these ... convergences? vortices? ... of ley lines" (*An Echo in the Bone,* ch. 46).

Claire and Roger speculate that the solar festivals may correspond with ley lines and earth's orbit, providing a link with the stone circles that only open at certain times. Roger writes that this may "have something to do with the grav-itational pull of the sun and moon. This seems reasonable, given that those bod-ies really do affect the behavior of the earth with respect to tides, weather, and the like—why not time vortices, too, after all?" (*An Echo in the Bone,* ch. 46). Mrs. Graham on the show adds, "The stones gather the powers and give it focus like a glass" in the proper times of year ("Both Sides Now").

Gabaldon explains, "If the passage through the stones stands widest open on sun feasts and fire feasts, it is presumably more or less 'closed' in the periods between. As Geillis/Gillian's notes indicate, an attempted passage at the wrong time can be fatal" (*Outlandish Companion* 368). At one point, Claire approaches the standing stones but cannot feel them—it's not a sun feast yet. Count St. Ger-main notes, "The stones. They make a buzzing sound, most of the time. If it's close to a fire-feast or sun-feast, though, they begin to sing" ("The Space Between" 237).

Jewel Magic

There is some logic in gold, silver and gems, products of the earth, pro-tecting travelers from the magical might of the stone circles. Raymond notes of jewels, "They have no more—and surely no less—magic than the skulls. Call them the bones of the earth. They hold the essence of the matrix in which they grew, and whatever powers that held, you may find them here as well" (*Dragonfly in Amber,* ch. 16). St. Germain adds in his thoughts, "Everyone knew that gem-stones had a specific vibration that corresponded to the heavenly spheres, and the spheres themselves of course affected the earth—'As above, so below'" ("The Space Between" 190).

Geillis believes faceted gemstones provide the most control and protection, and Gabaldon explains that her theory comes "presumably on the basis of ancient writings she later discovered" (*Outlandish Companion* 333). She shows an increasing obsession with gemstone magic, to the point of madness. Nonethe-less, there are traces of method therein. For her ritual, Geillis makes a pentacle of protective diamond dust with five specific gems at the points and quicksilver for the lines. Mercury, or quicksilver, was beloved of alchemists. As it tran-scended the liquid and solid states, it was believed to transcend life/death and heaven/earth. Diamond was defensive, for its hardness. As Young Ian tells Claire, Geillis "said the stone grew in a lad's innards—the one she wanted. She said it must be a laddie who'd never gone wi' a lass, though, that was important. If he had, the stone wouldna be right, somehow. (*The Drums of Autumn,* ch. 28)

She grinds up amethysts in wine and burns powdered emeralds in the flames. While these uses are rather exotic, gemstones as protection are nothing new: Geillis insists on using "Stones of protection; amethyst, emerald, turquoise, lapis lazuli, and a male ruby" for travel through the stones (*Voyager,* ch. 60).

(Theophrastus, a disciple of Aristotle decided all gems had gender.) Indeed, all the stones she mentions have lore of protection for their bearers.

Medieval jewelry was meant to guard its wearer, though it generally did its job through inscriptions of "Jesus Nazarenus Rex Judeorum," and "Ave Maria Gracia Plena." Bacon in his "Sylva Sylvarum" says that gems have "fine spirits, as appears by their splendor, and therefore may operate, by consent, on the spirits of men, to strengthen and exhilarate them. The best stones for this purpose are the diamond, the emerald, the hyacinth, and the yellow topaz" (qtd. in Jones 131). "Elf arrows," old flint arrowheads, were sometimes mounted in silver to be used as amulets. Master Raymond gives Claire a crystal that will change color if dipped in poison, another kind of talisman. He also sends her small shaped stones with carving on one side when she's at Lallybroch. She gives a patient one as a placebo, but otherwise their use is not clear. With ancient runes or protective symbols, Raymond may have sent them to keep her safe, even possibly while she's traveling the stones. Claire says she sometimes carries these stones in her pocket—it's even possible she carries them to battle or on her second journey.

"White quartz pebbles (called fairy firestones) were offered to quell storms at sea and to bring home the sailors" (Williams). There is also a tradition in the Celtic lands of white stones that offer healing. As Jamie says of St. Bride's shrine:

> The shrine itself is a small stone in the shape of an ancient cross, so weathered that the markings scarce show on it. It stands above a small pool, half-buried in the heather. Ye can find small white stones in the pool, tangled among the roots of the heather that grows on the bank. The stones are thought to have great powers.... But only when used by a white lady [*Voyager,* ch. 10].

George Henderson writes:

> Psychic suggestion associated with stones and wells is very prominent in folk-belief. Thus, when Burns's Highland Mary (Mary Campbell) fell ill, her friends at Greenock supposed, it is said, that she had come under the malign power of the evil-eye. To avert this, seven smooth stones were procured from the junction of two streams. These were placed in milk, which, after being boiled, was administered, but without success. There are many still living who have heard mention at some time or other of a pebble or crystal (*griogag*) and of witch-stones (*clachan buitseachd*), to which various virtues were ascribed in the Highlands [308].

In a famous story, Columba offered a white pebble to the king's druid Broichan, foster-father of King Brude. He promised, "If Broichan shall ... at once immerse this little stone in water and let him drink from it, and he shall be instantly cured." The stone succeeded and was afterwards preserved among the treasures of the king, where it continued to cure those who used it. (G. Henderson 309).

The importance of facets is less clear, though they appear to channel power as they increase the stone's brilliance and shine. Speculating, Brianna writes:

> Joe Abernathy told me about one of his patients, an archaeologist who told him about some study done on standing stones up in Orkney, where they discovered that the stones have interesting tonal qualities; if you strike them with wooden sticks or other stones, you get a kind of musical note. Any kind of crystal—and all gems have a crystalline interior structure—has a characteristic vibration when struck; that's how quartz watches work.
>
> So what if the crystal you carry has vibrations that respond to—or stimulate, for that matter—vibrations in the standing stones nearby? And if they did what might be the physical effect? [*Written in My Own Heart's Blood*, ch. 96]

Jewels are lovely and rare, but that alone doesn't explain people's desperation for them and the high cost they are prepared to pay. In fact, jewels have often been suspected of strange attributes and mystic powers. The folktale collector Andrew Lang recorded divining stones used throughout the world—"usually crystals or black stones, I have found among Australians, Tonkaways, Aztecs, Incas, Samoyeds, Polynesians, Maoris, Greeks, Egyptians, in Fez" (qtd. in Sutherland 129). Gabaldon adds, "We can only speculate as to the nature of these; however, [Geillis] did, when talking to Claire about gemstones, refer to them as bhasmas and nagina stones, which are terms from Ayurvedic texts. All ancient cultures have mysterious sites—and all involve stone" (*Outlandish Companion* 333).

Geillis's carefully-selected "amethyst, emerald, turquoise, lapis lazuli, and a male ruby" fit smoothly into gem lore. In Asia, the emerald represented "hope in immortality, courage and exalted faith, and protection from pestilence.... The Romans believed that nothing evil could remain in the presence of this gem which discovered falsehood and treachery by changing colour and turning pale, and when powerless to avert misfortune would fall from its setting, giving rise to the belief that the falling of this gem is a bad omen" (Thomas and Pavitt 180–181).

Lapis lazuli is an opaque blue stone from the Near East. It is the stone of the Virgin Mary, used by the Greeks and Romans to cure apoplexy, epilepsy, diseases of the spleen, and all skin ailments and blood disorders. The stones could inspire courage and cure depression as well (Thomas and Pavitt 223). Egyptians buried it with mummies to replace the heart and bring about regeneration in the Underworld (Walker 515). It was sometimes confused with turquoise in ancient writings, which failed to discriminate between types of blue stones. Both had connections with the heavens and the goddess Isis; miracles could be worked with a single grain of the stone (Walker 525).

> The Turquoise is more frequently used for Amulets than any other stone, as much for its mystic virtues as for its beauty, particularly in the East, where sen-

tences from the Koran are engraved upon it and the characters gilded. Amongst its many virtues it was believed to warn of poison by becoming moist and changing colour.... This gem has always been regarded as a pledge of true affections, and is also credited with the power of drawing upon itself the evil that threatens its wearer; but this quality belongs only to the Turquoise that has been given, and not purchased [Thomas and Pavitt 158].

The ruby was said to "protect the body from plague, poison, and fevers, and to secure love and friendship, preserve health, vitality, and cheerfulness, against disorders of the liver and spleen, and to drive away evil dreams and spirit" (Thomas and Pavitt 253). Throughout the east, it guarded wearers from attack and attracted friends and fortune.

In China and Japan it is also worn to confer long life, health, and happiness. Pliny describes it as the Lychnis, and says the Star Rubies were considered by the Chaldeans to be most powerful in protecting from evil and attracting the favour of those in authority. Throughout the whole of the Orient the Ruby was believed to possess the power of foretelling danger by a loss of brilliancy and colour, a belief also common throughout Europe as confirmed by Wolfgangus Gabelschoverus, who writing in the year 1600, says, whilst travelling with his wife: "I observed by the way that a very fine Ruby (which she had given me) lost repeatedly and each time almost completely its splendid colour and assumed a blackish hue." He goes on to tell that the threatened evil was fulfilled by the loss of his wife, and that after her death the stone regained its colour and brilliancy [Thomas and Pavitt 252].

Geillis's journal adds, "Garnets rest in love about my neck. I will be faithful" (*The Drums of Autumn*, ch. 40). "By the rules of sympathetic magic, garnet has always been associated with blood, bleeding, wounds, diseases of the blood, and blood bonds" because of its deep red color (Walker 511). Thus it disturbingly foreshadows Geillis's death as she puts them on her neck like a slit throat. Garnets were an amulet against poison and the plague in the East. "During the Middle Ages it was used as a remedy for inflammatory diseases, and to confer constancy, fidelity, and cheerfulness to its rightful wearers, but was said to cause discord amongst those having no right to it by birth" (Thomas and Pavitt 264). The concept of a right to it by birth is intriguing—Roger specifically uses his mother's garnets to protect himself. The word "garnet" comes from granatum, the pomegranate, symbol of the womb. As such, they are a women's stone (Walker 511). With his mother's blessing on him, Roger attempts to go quest for his lover.

In fact, Brianna, Roger, and their family travel with diamonds, rubies, garnets, a sapphire, and a chrysoberyl. Several times the gems offered have sentimental value: John's sapphire ring, Fiona's engagement ring, Roger's mother's garnet brooch. Brianna finds an old diamond brooch of her family's and cuts it in half. Jamie and Claire gather stones for Brianna's family, and Jem's school principal offers his Masonic ring. The "golden sherry" color of the chrysoberyl suggests Claire's eyes and thus Claire's protection over little Mandy. As such, there's a repeated emphasis on guardianship from loved ones in the stones.

Chrysoberyl and other golden stones protected their wearers from evil dreams and the assaults of demons (Thomas and Pavitt 173). The sapphire was also protective: "During the Middle Ages the qualities attributed to the Sapphire were that it preserved Chastity, discovered Fraud and Treachery, protected from Poison, Plague, Fever, and Skin Diseases, and had great power in resisting black magic and ill-wishing" (Thomas and Pavitt 156). The Tuscarora call it a "fearless stone" that strengthens people's spirits so they can recover from illness (*The Drums of Autumn,* ch. 20).

> The diamond is the hardest stone known, hence the name of Adamas, meaning 'the Indomitable.' It was believed by the old writers to be the most powerful of all precious stones in its influence and effect upon humanity both spiritually and physically, and it is connected with marvellous records of adventure and enterprise, as well as representing Purity, Innocence, and protection from witch-craft and evil.... Bestowing fortitude, strength of mind, and constancy in wedded love, it repelled sorcery, poison, and nightmares, calmed anger, and strengthened friendship [Thomas and Pavitt 140–141].

Standing Stones

The Standing Stones are of course central to the story. The book describes them as foreign stone that has been transported some distance, like the stones of Stonehenge. One is cleft, with the sides pulled apart, and it's through this that Claire travels.

While stone circles appear across Britain and beyond, Craigh na Dun itself is fictional. Gabaldon comments that after she finally visited Scotland, she found a stone circle much like Craigh na Dun at Castlerigg. As she adds, "There is also a place near Inverness called the Clava Cairns, which has a stone circle, and another place called Tomnahurich, which is supposed to be a fairy's hill" (*Outlandish Companion* 373).

Scotland has many stone circles, while over 900 remain today across the British landscape (Varner 108). Old Keig is the largest recumbent stone circle in Scotland. The Callanish-I stone-circle, built in the shape of a Celtic cross, was built to incorporate the moon's rising and setting. This is just one of over twenty megalithic sites on the Isle of Lewis. Scottish stone circles include Balfarg Henge and Bilbirnie Stone Circle, now in the midst of a housing estate near Perth. The Isle of Arran, off the West Coast of Scotland, has many stone circles dating from the Neolithic period and the early Bronze Age.

There are several prominent megalithic sites on the Orkney Islands. Maes Howe, the largest passage-mound in Scotland, was constructed to allow the winter solstice sunlight to enter the passage, entering the inner chamber for several minutes only each year. The overall layout of Skara Brae has many rooms with hordes of treasure—one find alone revealed 2,400 inscribed beads and pendants. Kilmartin Valley is home to one of the most varied collections of prehistoric sites in the whole of Scotland. Bronze Age cairns, Neolithic chambered tombs, and enigmatic rock carvings, can all be found within a two-mile radius from Kilmartin village.

Some standing stones were said to dance or move about the land, while others made noise, much like the roaring Claire hears each time. Old Irish and Welsh tales describe stones that could speak or move, especially at the Fire Feasts and Solstices. The *Lia Fáil*, or "Stone of Destiny" was said to emit a loud cry when the rightful ruler sat upon it (British monarchs today are still crowned upon this stone). Likewise, "ringing" and "humming" sounds are sometimes heard at Stonehenge and ancient cairns in the Wicklow Hills, Ireland. The Blind Fiddler standing stone near Penzance is said to emit a thunderclap (Varner 49).

To the South of course lies Stonehenge. Claire and Frank visited Stonehenge soon after they were married, and she emphasizes the human sacrifices there, foreshadowing what Geillis will do. Geillis notes that "The auld ones— they always used the blood. That and the fire. They built great wicker cages, filled wi' their captives, and set them alight in the circles" (*Voyager*, ch. 60). The stones' purpose is something of a mystery. Gabaldon adds:

> I was doing a lot of research on Scotland at that point because I'd never been there and kept coming across the standing stone circles. Every time I'd read about the stone circles, it would describe how they worked as an astronomical observance. For example, some of the circles are oriented so that at the winter solstice the sun will strike a standing stone. But all the texts speculate that nobody knows what the actual function of these stone circles was. And so I began thinking, Well, I bet I can think of one [Laughs] [DeLuca].

Around the world, people would walk through the stones seeking healing or regeneration. "Passing through large, pierced stones is a ritual commonly seen throughout the world's folk medicine traditions. In Greece and Scotland, women desiring children would wade into the sea and then pass through large waterworn holes in nearby rocks" (Varner 14). Lover's vows were considered permanent if uttered while clasping hands through a stone's opening. In Saintongue, France, women "passed their newborn infants through holes in dolmens to guard them against evil, present and future" (Varner 15). George Henderson adds in his studies of Celtic lands:

> On the west side of the same island there is a rock with a hole in it, through which children are passed when suffering from whooping-cough or other complaints. On the point of Oa, Islay, there is a small arch formed in a huge boul-

der, which had been resorted to by invalids for ages. Any person who passed through it was supposed to have left his malady behind him, whatever it was. The transit was a cure for all diseases. Within the last twenty years a poor man carried his sickly wife on his back for miles to give her the benefit of the charm [338].

Claire refers to the stones at Craigh na Dun as Merlin's stones (*Outlander,* ch. 25), and in fact Geoffrey of Monmouth credits Merlin with transporting the stones of Stonehenge from Ireland to England. Frank notes in the first episode, "According to local folklore, these stones were carried here from Africa by a race of Celtic giants." These legends are common—at Machrie the double circle, *Suide Choir Fhionn,* or Fingal's Cauldron Seat, is named after the legendary warrior Fingal (Fionn Mac Cumhaill).

Cairney in his ethnography calls the tales of a great leader, such as Arthur or Fionn, who sleeps under a fairy hill until needed, "recurrent archetypal themes" and "an outgrowth of the pre–Christian religion of the Germanic and Celtic peoples." This pre–Christian "dawn religion" originated with the pre–Celtic Western-European peoples, the builders of the ancient stone circles. "Thus, one way or another the 'dawn religion' seems to ultimately descend from the ancient fertility cults of Neolithic Europe (associated with the famous Cro-Magnon 'mother-goddess' or 'Venus' figures)," adding Pictish matrilineality, druidic "second sight," folk-medicine and ancient fertility rites into the Gaelic culture (12–13).

Standing Stones aren't unique to Britain. Legends of magical standing stones appear in France, Borneo, Central America, and elsewhere (Hill 2489). Greeks believed the center of the world was at Delphi, marked by the conical "naval stone" called omphalos. The Babylonians used stones as boundary-markers, often with mystical attributes around them. In Gabaldon's world, more working portals, with stone circles, appear under Paris and in the cave of Aban-dawe on Hispaniola. Roger finds another in the Adirondack Mountains. In the New World, Claire and her friends meet another Traveler, who reveals there are many more sacred places including a portal at "Ocracoke ... the northmost portal in the Bermuda Triangle group." They tend to appear in groups, with more in the Caribbean, near the Canadian border, from Arizona to Mexico, in Northern Britain and from France to Spain. Those marked with stone circles appear in areas of long human habitation and are deemed "safer" (*A Breath of Snow and Ashes,* ch. 55).

Tall standing stones have masculine symbolism, while passages, especially underground ones, represent the feminine. As such, Claire travels through a unity of male and female, a cleft stone in a ring of standing ones, seeking her true love and the union of marriage.

Menhirs, another term for standing stones, have come to be seen as symbols of the masculine creative force. The dolmen, on the other hand, is the feminine gateway to the Earth Mother's womb—the underworld. A dolmen is a megalithic (large-stone) slab placed across a number of upright stones, like a table; often, dolmens were covered by earth to create a small hill, or barrow. While the menhir represents the world's axis, the dolmen symbolizes rebirth and the beyond. Together they represent the yin and yang of nature, and all complementary forces [Varner 85–86].

SUN FEASTS AND FIRE FEASTS

Frank in book one, describes "the ancient feasts.... Hogmanay, that's New Year's, Midsummer Day, Beltane, and All Hallows. Druids, Beaker Folk, early Picts, everybody kept the sun feats and the fire feasts" (I.12). He notes on the show that Yule and Halloween come from the earlier Pagan festivals, appropriated by the church.

Here are the pagan festivals, still celebrated in some cultures today:

Imbolc ~ Spring Festival of the Goddess Brigit, held on Feb 1st or 2nd
Alban Eilir ~ Spring Equinox also known as The Light of the Earth or
    Ostara, Mar 21st/22nd
Beltane ~ Celtic Fertility and Fire Festival observed on May 1st
Litha or Midsummer's Eve ~ Summer Solstice on or around June
    21st/22nd
Lughnassadh or Lammas ~ First Harvest, July 31st/Aug 1st
Alban Elfed or Mabon ~ Autumn Equinox and Second Harvest, Sept
    21st/22nd
Samhain ~ Day of the Dead, October 31st /November 1st
Alban Arthuan or Yule ~ Winter Solstice and Festival of Light, December 21st

In the books, Claire passes through the stones on Beltane the first time, going to her "summer romance" in the youth of the world, when she and Jamie are youths themselves and the world post–World-War is filled with promise. Beltane was a festival of young love and fertility, leaving civilization for the woods and fields, much as Claire does in a more pastoral time.

On the show it's changed to Samhain. Part of the decision was because filming had to take place in winter, but also Samhain and its creepiness can be incorporated as the locals spill cockerel blood and dance among the stones (Episode Podcasts 101). Later this became All Hallow's Eve/Hallowe'en, and All Saints Day, a time of ghosts, hauntings, and the supernatural. The second time Claire travels is in April, around the Spring Equinox. She's going to the time of her youth, brimming with new life and possibility, though also sorrow. Most of all, this is Easter, a time of sacrifice and resurrection for both Claire and Jamie. She travels again on Samhain, the first of November, this time much older and in the autumn of her life. She's spent her life haunted by the past.

Brianna, herself a young woman, travels on Beltane for her own summer adventure as she thinks. Roger follows her on Midsummer's Eve, the Summer Solstice. Both characters, notably, are in the summer of their lives. In a time of danger, Roger travels again, this time on Samhain, as spooky people prey upon him.

Four of these days, solstices and equinoxes, logically split the year by the season mid-points. Unsurprisingly, these nearly correspond with the "quarter days": Lady Day (March 25th), Midsummer (June 24th), Michaelmas (September 29th) and Christmas (December 25th). These were the four dates on which servants were hired, rents due or leases begun. Claire and Jamie celebrate one of these at Lallybroch in the first book.

The other times, midpoints within those, were particular harvests and celebrations of the natural world. "In druidical times four great fire-festivals were held at different periods of the year; namely, on the eve of May day, or Spring; on Midsummer's eve; on Hallowe'en, hence our Hallowe'en bonfires; and at Yule, the mid-winter feast" (Guthrie, ch. 1). Particular superstitions attached to these days, all linked with fire:

> On the first day of every quarter of the year—New-Year day, St Bride's Day.
> Beltane, and Lammas—no fire should be given out of the house. On the two
> last days especially it should not be given, even to a neighbour whose fire had
> gone out. It would give him the means of taking the substance or benefit
> (toradh) from the cows. If given, after the person who had come for it left, a
> piece of burning peat (ceann fbid) should be thrown into a tub of water, to
> keep him from doing harm. It will also prevent his coming again. On New-
> Year's day fire should not be given out of the house on any consideration to a
> doubtful person. If he is evil-disposed, not a beast will be alive next New Year.
> A suspected witch came on this day to a neighbour's house for fire, her own hav-
> ing gone out, and got it. When she went away a burning peat was thrown into a
> tub of water. She came a second time and the precaution was again taken. The
> mistress of the house came in, and on looking in the tub found it full of butter
> [J.G. Campbell 234–235].

Imbolc

This is the festival of the lactating sheep, derived from the Gaelic "oimelc" meaning "ewes' milk." Herd animals have lately given birth and have milk to feed the babies. It is the festival of the Maiden, for from this day to March 21st, it is her season to prepare for growth and renewal. It marks the center point of the dark half of the year. Brigid's snake emerges from the womb of the Earth Mother to test the weather, (the origin of Groundhog Day), and in many places the first crocus flowers begin to spring forth from the frozen earth. Young girls then carry the *Brídeóg*as door to door, and gifts are bestowed upon the image from each household. Folk put out and re-light home hearth fires, and a besom by the front door symbolizes sweeping out the old and welcoming the new. Candles glow in each room of the house to honor the rebirth of the Sun. Candlemas is the Catholic holiday of the season, also honoring motherhood as the Feast of the Purification of the Blessed Virgin. As this holiday has merged into Saint Brigid's Day, and the goddess Brigid into Jesus's midwife, girls celebrate with corn dollies called *Brídeóg*as.

> On Bride's Eve, the girls fashion a woman out of corn called "Bride," "Brideag," Bride, Little Bride, and drape her with primroses, snowdrops, shells, and crystals, with an especially bright stone over the heart of the figure. This is called "reul-iuil Bride," the guiding star of Bride, representing the guiding star over the stable door of Bethlehem. Gowned in white with their hair down, symbolizing purity and youth, the girls carry the figure, singing the song of "Bride bhoidheach oigh nam mile beus," Beauteous Bride, virgin of a thousand charms. They visit every house, so everyone can greet the Bride and give her gifts of decorations. Mothers, however, give "bonnach Bride," a Bride bannock, "cabag Bride," a Bride cheese, or "rolag Bride," a Bride roll of butter. At last, the girls reach their special house where they will have a Bride feast together, with the figure watching them in a place of honor, until the young men arrive and ask to come in. After a night of celebration and dance, the young people greet the dawn with a hymn to Bride [Carmichael 168].

Spring Equinox

Easter "is a relic of the old heathen feasts to celebrate the return of the spring" from the Saxon goddess Ostarra or Estre, the personification of east and the spring (Daniels and Stevens 1521).

Rabbits, flowers, and dyed eggs all are part of the festival. In Scotland, people also watched in a pool of water for the sun to whirl round like a millwheel and give three leaps (Daniels and Stevens 1522). Many invocations and special rites surrounded the annual marking of the lambs, an occasion considered fraught with potential danger.

In Celtic lands, St. Columba's Day (*Diardaoin Chaluim-Chille*) is celebrated on Maundy Thursday, the Thursday before Easter. Children would divide a special bannock baked on a fire of sacred wood (oak, yew or rowan) to find the silver coin hidden within. The lucky finder received the major share of the crop of lambs for the year. Libations of ale were made to a mysterious sea god named Shony on this date.

Beltane

Beltane, is the first day of May, still celebrated today as May Day. Rituals and practices varied through Britain, but it was mainly a pagan holiday of fertility and blessing, a relic of ancient times. Joyous bonfires were meant to reignite the sun above and celebrate its warmth at this, the beginning of the summer half of the year.

> The Beltane or Bel tein (Bel, in Gaelic, signifies sun; and teirt, fire) customs are believed to have had their origin in those heathen times, when our ancestors worshipped Baal the Sun god, and Ashtoreth, "Astarte, queen of heaven," with certain mystic observances chiefly connected with fire…. It was a day set apart by the herdsmen and others of the Scottish peasantry, for the celebration of such time-honoured observances as were deemed suitable to the occasion, such as digging a hole on a hill top and lighting a fire therein; then lots are cast, and he on whom the lot falls, must leap seven times over the fire, while the young folks dance round in a circle. Then they cook their eggs and cakes, and all sit down to eat and drink and rise up to play [Guthrie, ch. 1].

It's also notable that Gabaldon gives Jamie's birthday as May 1, 1721. There were many traditions given ritual form for the holiday. At Callander, James Robertson, minister of the parish, reports:

> The people of this district have two customs, which are fast wearing out, not only here, but all over the Highlands, and therefore ought to be taken notice of while they remain. Upon the first day of May, which is called *Bel-tan*, or *Baltein* day, all the boys in a township or hamlet meet in the moors. They cut a table in the green sod, of a round figure, by casting a trench in the ground, of such circumference as to hold the whole company. They kindle a fire, and dress a repast of eggs and milk in the consistence of a custard. They knead a cake of oatmeal, which is toasted at the embers against a stone. After the custard is eaten up, they divide the cake into so many portions, as similar as possible to one another in size and shape, as there are persons in the company. They daub one of these portions all over with charcoal, until it be perfectly black. They put all the bits of cake in a bonnet. Every one, blindfold, draws out a portion. He who holds the bonnet is entitled to the last bit. Whoever draws the black bit is the *devoted* person who is to be sacrificed to *Baal*, whose favour they mean to implore in rendering the year productive of the sustenance of man and beast. There is little doubt of these inhuman sacrifices having been once offered in this country, as well as in the east, although they now pass from the act of sacrificing, and only compel the *devoted* person to leap three times through the flames; with which the ceremonies of this festival are closed [H. Henderson 260–261].

Some believe the word "bonfires" comes from bone-fires—for human sacrifices (H. Henderson 84). Here is a traditional blessing for the season:

> BLESS, O Threefold true and bountiful,
> Myself, my spouse, and my children,
> My tender children and their beloved mother at their head.
> On the fragrant plain, on the gay mountain sheiling,
> On the fragrant plain, on the gay mountain sheiling.
> Everything within my dwelling or in my possession,

All kine and crops, all flocks and corn,
From Hallow Eve to Beltane Eve,
With goodly progress and gentle blessing,
From sea to sea, and every river mouth,
From wave to wave, and base of waterfall.
Be the Three Persons taking possession of all to me belonging,
Be the sure Trinity protecting me in truth;
Oh! satisfy my soul in the words of Paul,
And shield my loved ones beneath the wing of Thy glory,
Shield my loved ones beneath the wing of Thy glory.
Bless everything and every one,
Of this little household by my side;

Place the cross of Christ on us with the power of love,
Till we see the land of joy,
Till we see the land of joy,
What time the kine shall forsake the stalls,
What time the sheep shall forsake the folds,
What time the goats shall ascend to the mount of mist,
May the tending of the Triune follow them,
May the tending of the Triune follow them.
Thou Being who didst create me at the beginning,
Listen and attend me as I bend the knee to Thee,
Morning and evening as is becoming in me,
In Thine own presence, O God of life,
In Thine own presence, O God of life [Carmichael 183–185].

Midsummer

Summer solstice is the longest day of the year, a time of warmth and growth as well as celebration. The word "solstice" comes from the Latin words, sol sistere—"sun stand still." Indeed the sun does seem to stand still in the sky at this time. The series notes, "On Midsummer's Eve in Scotland, the sun hangs in the sky with the moon. Summer solstice, the feast of Litha, Alban Eilir. Nearly midnight, and the light was dim and milky white, but light nonetheless" (*The Drums of Autumn,* ch. 32).

Litha is the Lord of Light, and this holiday is sacred to him. The summer solstice is often the time of the first harvest and hence a celebration of this bounty has been held for hundreds of years. The day is celebrated with dancing, food, mead, wine and merriment. The sun, Sol, is celebrated as well with rituals and herb gathering, for this special day brings extra potency to medicine and spells. The Druids celebrate the "wedding of Heaven and Earth," leading to the present day belief of a "lucky" wedding in June. Brianna, Roger, Jem and Mandy all arrive on the Ridge in mid–June, to the delight of Claire and Jamie. It's a moment of life, warmth and reconnection for all of them.

At the same time, the holiday heralds the fall—after the solstice, days will start growing shorter, so celebrants remember they will need to start the harvest soon. Colder, more difficult times are coming. "Midsummer was the vital, somewhat scary time when the sun reached its turning point and began its slow decline toward another winter" (Walker 187). Thus it is the season of Roger's frightening ordeal as he descends into dark and primitive times seeking his lover.

Lughnassadh or Lammas

This festival from sunset to sunset August first and second was called lamb-mass or loaf-mass by the Christians for the blessings done at church. To the ancient Celts it was named for the ancient sun god Lugh and the Celtic *nasadh,* commemoration. Lugh's light began to dwindle after midsummer, and this was a time of harvest, of taking communion and blessing the bread or for acknowledging the death of the grain and the god of summer. This was a fire-festival, and no one would bathe or fish for three days prior to the grain-king's sacrifice. Grain has always been associated with Dying God, dismembered and then resurrected by the Goddess. Tammuz, Osiris and Adonis particularly fit this pattern. Many believe the Year-King was killed on this date, sacrificed in the time of harvest.

Fall Equinox

For the ancient Druids, the fall equinox was *Alban Elfed.* Many modern pagans celebrate this as a time of balance. In some traditions it was called Mabon for the newborn son stolen by the sidhe who vanished each year from Samhain to spring in a variant of the Persephone tale. Harvest time is celebrated in several books, and *The Drums of Autumn* links symbolically with the midpoint of the year and Jamie and Claire's lives, a time of plenty and flourishing crops, but also the approaching darkness of winter and war.

The Catholic correspondence is Michaelmas, the feast of St. Michael, on September 29. An autumn Thanksgiving was traditional around this time, long before the American custom appeared. Specific practices include eating a goose who has fed on the stubble of the fields following the harvest (called a stubble-goose). There are also St. Michael's bannocks or *Struan Michael*, a special oatcake with more than a small link with older pagan spirits:

> After the cake was cooked, a small piece was broken off and cast into the fire. Why? you will ask. Well, as an offering to the *Donas,* or old Hornie, or whatever may be the correct designation of that presiding genius whom we are led to believe inhabits the fiery regions. The housewife did this in order to safeguard herself and her household against the Evil One. After reserving some of the *Struan* for the use of the household, she went round the neighbours in triumph and gave them a bit each, there being usually a great rivalry as to who should be the first to grind the new meal and get the *Struan* ready. The first to do so was

generally understood to have the best crops through the corning year [G. Henderson 255–256].

Samhain

> The dark came down on All Hallows' Eve. We went to sleep
> to the sound of howling wind and pelting rain, and woke on
> the Feast of All Saints to whiteness and large soft flakes falling
> down and down in absolute silence. There is no more perfect
> stillness than the solitude in the heart of a snowstorm. This
> is the thin time, when the beloved dead draw near—*A Breath
> of Snow and Ashes,* ch. 38

This was a day when the spirits were close: November first. Geillis writes: "This is the first of the feasts of the dead. Long before Christ and his resurrection, on the night of Samhain, the souls of heroes rose from their graves" (*The Drums of Autumn,* ch. 32). She notes that few have the courage to seize their destinies.

Late October was the time the Celts harvested nuts and salted the winter's supply of meat. One of the four greater Sabbats of the pagan year, Samhain was the feast of the dead. Its arrival signaled the close of harvest and the start of the winter season. With a name meaning "summer's end," it marked the dark half of the year. Fairies were imagined as particularly active at this time. One folklorist writes:

> On All-Saints' Even they set up bonfires in every village. When the bonfire is
> consumed, the ashes are carefully collected in the form of a circle. There is a
> stone put in, near the circumference, for every person of the several families
> interested in the bonfire; and whatever stone is moved out of its place, or
> injured before next morning, the person represented by that stone is devoted, or
> *fey,* and is supposed not to live twelve months from that day. The people
> received the consecrated fire from the Druid priests next morning, the virtues of
> which were supposed to continue for a year [H. Henderson 260–261].

This was a time when the barriers between the human and supernatural worlds were broken ... rather than honoring any particular Celtic deity, Samhain acknowledged the entire spectrum of nonhuman forces that were set loose on the earth then. Barrows and mounds would open and the fair folk come out to dance. Spirits and souls of loved ones were said to have more power and the ability to visit, so many would honor their dead with food and wine left out for them. Samhain is also a time for personal reflection and the most powerful night of the year to perform divination.

According to legend, the Celtic great god Dagda would take the Morrigan, shadow queen of the battlefield, as his consort. "She begins the great rite as an old hag but is rejuvenated by the union, regaining her youth and beauty" (Illes

218). This reflects (to some extent) Claire's journey in the third book as she travels at Samhain to find Jamie and resume their marriage after so long apart.

In the books, Claire has her palm and leaves read at Beltane, but on the show, this is at Samhain, the time when a Highland ghost appears outside her window. Frank's ghost appears to visit Claire in late October for Brianna's wedding day (*The Fiery Cross,* ch. 1). Later on, Brianna and Roger return to the future around Samhain, and Jamie dreams of them. He writes to Brianna and asks her to pray for him. She realizes it's All Saint's Day and that "By saying an Our Father, a Hail Mary, and a Glory Be on the Feast of All Saints, you can obtain the release of a soul from purgatory" (*An Echo in the Bone,* ch. 72).

Yule

Brianna, Jem, and Mandy find Roger in the past around this time of year. Yule may come from "Iul" meaning "wheel," as the wheel of the year concludes. While Brianna's desperate journey to flee pursuit takes place at the darkest time of year, there's also a suggestion of hope and faith, so critical in the dark time. The festival was already closely associated with the birth of older Pagan gods like Hercules, Dionysus, Apollo, Mithra, and Horus, just as Brianna abandons predictable life in the future to dive headlong into a primitive time of superstition and find her beloved.

Yule is another fire festival, celebrated by private hearths. It acknowledges the darkness of the world yet hopes for a return of light.

In *The Scottish Prisoner,* the English family at Helwater celebrates Christmas with an enormous Yule Log and branches of pine and fir, emphasizing the connection between pagan and Christian traditions (ch. 43). The episode "Both Sides Now" includes the death of Patton on the radio. This marks the date as December 21, 1945 / 1743, or Yule, a time the stones stand open. Claire and Frank rush towards each other and nearly reunite, but their hope is dashed, and darkness and despair quickly descend. In the past, Jamie also notes the season:

> **JAMIE:** Be yuletide by the time we get back to Leoch.
> **CLAIRE:** Christmas.... I don't suppose you hang stockings by the fire.
> **JAMIE:** To dry them off, you mean?
> **CLAIRE:** Never mind ["Both Sides Now"].

Christmas was virtually banned in Scotland from the end of the seventeenth century to the 1950s: In the Protestant Reformation, the church portrayed Christmas as a Catholic feast, so Protestants avoided it. The winter holiday of choice came at New Year when family and friends gathered to exchange presents and hold a party, which came to be called Hogmanay.

Hogmanay

The Scandinavian word for the feast preceding Yule was "Hoggo-nott" while the Flemish words "hoog min dag" mean "great love day" and the French "Homme est né" mean "Man is born" One of these, or perhaps "Haleg monath," Holy Month, inspired the name for the New Year celebration. Traditions include cleaning the house and clearing all debts on December 31st before "the bells" at midnight.

> When the Highland home was cleaned out at Hogmanay—and the cleaning at that season can only be compared to a good modern Spring cleaning—the ill-luck of the past year was supposed to be driven out, and everything was ready for a fresh start; and to prevent the powers of evil again entering, first the Bible was placed above the door during the last hours of the year, and the cat kept inside, so that if by any mishap an unlucky first-foot should dare to enter in spite of this, the evil could be got rid of by throwing out the cat, for poor pussy was supposed to be able to carry out with it all the mischief which such a person was supposed to bring in [Poison].

Immediately after midnight it is traditional to sing Robert Burns' "For Auld Lang Syne," published in 1788. "Auld Lang Syne" is also a chapter title in *The Fiery Cross*. Traditional Hogmanay visitors might chant:

> We are come to the door,
> To see if we be the better of our visit,
> To tell the generous women of the townland
> That to-morrow is Calendae Day.

After being entertained, the visitors circle round the fire sunwise, singing—

> May God bless the dwelling,
> Each stone, and beam, and stave,
> All food, and drink, and clothing,
> May health of men be always there [Carmichael 156–157].

In the books, the household celebrates with dancing and music, then with a brief ceremony. In *Voyager*, Jamie and Laoghaire have an interlude at Jenny's New Year party and she convinces him to come dance. On the ridge, the ceremony is central. "First footing" (that is, the "first foot" in the house after midnight) is still celebrated a bit in Scotland. The luckiest possible first foot should be male and dark (possibly a throwback to the Viking days when blond strangers meant trouble) and should bring symbolic coal, shortbread, salt, black bun and whisky. As Claire tells it:

> Custom held that the most fortunate "firstfoot" on a Hogmanay was a tall and handsome dark-haired man; to welcome one as the first visitor across the threshold after midnight brought good fortune to the house for the coming

year. ...A red-haired man, though, was frightful ill luck as a firstfoot, and Jamie had been consigned to his study.

...

A firstfoot was to bring gifts to the house: an egg, a faggot of wood, a bit of salt—and a bit of whisky, thus insuring that the household would not lack for necessities during the coming year.

There is nothing special about January the first, save the meaning we give to it. The ancients celebrated a new year at Imbolc, at the beginning of February, when the winter slackens and the light begins to come back—or the date of the spring equinox, when the world lies in balance between the powers of dark and light. And yet I stood there in the dark, listening to the sound of the cat chewing and slobbering in the cupboard, and felt the power of the earth shift and stir beneath my feet as the year—or something—prepared to change [*The Fiery Cross*, ch. 35].

Scottish Folklore

INTRODUCTION

Frank tells Claire, "There's no place on earth with more of the old superstitions and magic mixed into its daily life than the Scottish Highlands. Church or no church, Mrs. Baird believes in the Old Folk and so do all her neighbors" (*Outlander* ch. 1). Her pagan circle dances come from an older tradition, but have their place in Scottish mysticism:

> The otherworld of faerie-maidens (Gaelic "sidhe," pronounced "shee") was part of a dawn or pre–Christian religion that included sacral kings, sun gods and ancestor worship, "gessa" or taboos, moon goddesses, fertility cults, divine heroes, nature worship, druidic oak groves, and goddesses presiding over rivers and lakes. Other aspects included head-hunting and the cult of the head (the Gaelic sun-god, the god of wisdom, is named after the head in its capacity as the seat of reason), ritual triads (things done three times: St. Patrick railed against sun-worship and made use of the three-leaf clover to demonstrate the trinity for his pagan Irish audience), sacred tribal animal totems and shape-changing (werewolves count here, as does the raven, in which form Odin presided over battles), votive offerings in wells (holy wells are still associated with healing and prophecy), burnt offerings and human sacrifice [Cairney 27].

"The whole island of mainland Britain had an aura of the supernatural for both Greek and Roman. To the latter, it was known as *Insula Sacra* (The Sacred Isle)" (Williams). On Claire's journeys, she hears the Gaelic storyteller in Castle Leoch and also stories told by the fire while collecting rents. In later books, Jamie tells Brianna "tales of silkies and seal-catchers, of pipers and elves, of the great giants of Fingal's cave, and the Devil's black horse that passes through the air faster than the thought between a man and a maid" (*The Drums of Autumn*, ch. 64). Scotland has always teamed with memorable folktales: of kelpies, selkies, and of course, the Loch Ness Monster. Beyond these are the Old Ones of Fair Folk—the fairie people dwelling under the hills.

Hill spirits, kirk spirits, and water spirits, were held responsible for sickness and divers other misfortunes. "Trows" inhabited Trolhouland—the hill of demons or Trows and within its recesses had their abodes, whose walls were dazzling with gold and silver. Brownies were the inmates of houses, and at night had tables placed for them in the barn where they slept, covered with bread, butter, cheese, and ale, while charms for killing sparrows that destroyed the early corn, expelling rats and mice from houses, for success in brewing and churning, procuring good luck, curing diseases of cattle and human beings, were in constant use [Guthrie, ch. 1].

Jamie emphasizes the growing conflict between rationalism and the old myths when he tells Claire on the show: "I'm an educated man, mistress, if I may be so bold. Maybe not as educated as you, but I had a tutor, a good one. He taught me Latin and Greek and such, not childhood stories of fairies, devils, waterhorses in lochs. But I am also a Highlander, born and bred, and I dinna believe in tempting fate by making light of Old Nick in his very own kirkyard" (Episode 103). After he hunts, he faithfully says the gralloch prayer, "so old that some of the words were no longer in common use," for any animal killed that was larger than a hare (*The Drums of Autumn,* ch. 15).

As Roger notes, most of the history of the Highlands is oral, up to the mid-nineteenth century or so. "That means there wasn't a great distinction made between stories about real people, stories of historical figures, and the stories about mythical things like water horses and ghosts and the doings of the Auld Folk" (*Voyager,* ch. 3). Gabaldon adds, "Whether Highlands or Lowlands ... they're storytelling cultures, both in terms of the Highlands' rich oral tradition, and the Lowlands' remarkable literary heritage of the 19th and 20th centuries" (Brittain).

Writing was considered a sacred act by many early people including the Celts. It is for this reason that the Celts had a strong bardic tradition, even among their magical folk, as very little was believed safe to commit to paper.

Gaelic bards and historians prided themselves in the cultivation of memory for the oral transmission of information and records, a task which they accomplished with the aid of poetic conventions, thematic paraphrase and aphoristic formulas of stock idiomatic cultural meaning (the phrase "be literal" had no meaning prior to the coming of the literate Christians). The spoken ire of a poet would maim a king through sympathetic magic, while his blessing could bring prosperity [Cairney 7].

While modern Scots are less likely to uphold the ancient beliefs, traces remain. Mrs. Graham in the books leads women to dance at the standing stones in a pre–Christian cult and she tells fortunes as well. Jamie recalls the tales of his childhood and collects them. Even sensible Roger invents a rat satire to drive rats from his house. For as Geillis reminds Claire on the show, there are things in the world that rationalism can't explain.

FAIRIES AND THEIR KIN

Bean Sidhe

Jamie insists that if he dies, Claire should return to the future. He tells Roger, "She is an Old One. They will kill her if they know" (*The Fiery Cross*, ch. 94). Roger reflects later that if Jamie had said this in Gaelic, he'd know whether Jamie "truly thought his wife was one of the fairy-folk, or only a thoroughly human wisewoman," as the English words might suggest either. While Jamie accepts the truth of Claire's origins, he must be discomposed as she knows the future of those around him and creates truly miraculous inventions like ether. Moreover, she can hear the singing of the stones and travel through them, as most people cannot. The books may finally reveal that a fairy ancestor is the key to this hereditary ability. In *An Echo in the Bone*, Jamie notes that at Lallybroch, the locals called Claire a witch "frequently to your face, Sassenach.... But ye didna have enough Gaelic then to know it" (ch. 76). He adds that it wasn't meant as an insult, "Only that Highlanders call a thing as they see it."

Claire is called a "Bean Sidhe" (good fairy), from which the word banshee is derived. Its roots, however, are older: "The Banshi is, without doubt, the original of the Queen of Elfland, mentioned in ballads of the South of Scotland" (J.G. Campbell 45). "Banshee" (in Gaelic *bean sidhe*) originally meant a "woman of the fairies." In old Irish folklore, banshees were grieving women keening for the deaths they foresaw. The banshee was attached to a single family and would escort them to the realm of the dead, mourning stridently ... although sometimes her wail could be heard before death (Illes 441). Only in the world of film did they become vampiric monsters who *caused* that death.

> In Mull and Tiree she is said to have preternaturally long breasts, which are in the way as she stoops at her washing. She throws them over her shoulders, and they hang down her back. Whoever sees her must not turn away, but steal up behind and endeavour to approach her unawares. When he is near enough he is to catch one of her breasts, and, putting it to his mouth, call herself to witness that he is his first nursing or foster-mother (jnuime ciche). She answers that he has need of that being the case, and will then communicate whatever knowledge he desires. If she says the shirt she is washing is that of an enemy he allows the washing to go on, and that man's death follows; if it be that of her captor or any of his friends, she is put a stop to.
>
> In Skye the Bean-nighe is said to be squat in figure (tiugkiosal), or not unlike a "small pitiful child, (J)aisde beag brhnach." If a person caught her she told all that would befall him in after life. She answered all his questions, but he must answer hers. Men did not like to tell what she said. Women dying in child-bed were looked upon as dying prematurely, and it was believed that unless all the clothes left by them were washed they would have to wash them themselves till the natural period of their death. It was women "dreeing this weird" who were

the washing women. If the person hearing them at work beating their clothes (slacartaick) caught them before being observed, he could not be heard by them; but if they saw him first, he lost the power of his limbs [J.G. Campbell 42–43].

Another possibility for the Scots (and one closer to the truth) is that Claire is a Glaistig "a woman of human race, who has been put under enchantments, and to whom a Fairy nature has been given" (J.G. Campbell 45). The fairies were known for stealing humans to be midwives and brides, and one who returned maintained a supernatural side. Whether living in future or past, Claire is marked by knowledge beyond her ordinary life, knowledge that impresses those around her with her otherworldly presence.

Changelings

Claire discovers a changeling child in *Outlander,* a sickly baby abandoned on a fairy hill with a bouquet and bowl of milk for the fairies. Geillis defines a changeling, saying, "When the fairies steal a human child away, they leave one of their own in its place ... you know it's a changeling because it cries and fusses all the time and doesn't thrive" (ch. 24). Geillis adds that if the changeling is left on their hill the fairies must take back the babies. Jamie points out to Claire that the parents take some comfort believing their child is alive and well in fairyland. These beliefs long existed in Invernesshire and other areas of the Celtic world, and were actually put into practice:

> About 1730, it is said, a man of the name of Munro had a sickly attenuated child, which he and his neighbours considered to be a changeling, substituted by the sportive elves, at an unguarded moment, in place of his own. There is a conical knoll in the carse called Tom Earnais, or Henry's Knoll, which was famed as the scene of the moonlight revels of Titania and her court; and it was believed, that if the changeling were left overnight on the hillock, the real child would be found in its stead in the morning. The infatuated father actually subjected his ailing offspring to this ordeal, and in the morning found it a corpse [Guthrie, ch. 9].

Changelings were a staple of folklore. In one tale (J.F. Campbell II 58–60), a teenage boy was looking sickly and strange. He weakened further and further until he lay close to death. A traveling old man told the worried father, "It is not your son you have got. The boy has been carried away by the *Daoine Sith,* and they have left a *Sibhreach* in his place." He advised the father to draw water with empty eggshells, where the boy could see him.

Upon viewing this strange sight, the boy burst out, "I am now 800 years of age, and I have never seen the like of that before."

With this proof, the old man confirmed that the son was a changeling. The only remedy however was to pick up the changeling and throw him into the fire.

The old man added, "If it is your own son you have got, he will call out to save him; but if not, this thing will fly through the roof." This the father did, and the changeling flew off and vanished.

With the changeling gone, the father hiked to the round green fairy hill with a Bible, a dirk, and a crowing cock. There he found light where light was seldom seen before and the sounds of piping and merriment.

> Overcoming every impulse to fear, the smith approached the threshold steadily, stuck the dirk into it as directed, and entered. Protected by the bible he carried on his breast, the fairies could not touch him; but they asked him, with a good deal of displeasure, what he wanted there. He answered, "I want my son, whom I see down there, and I will not go without him."
>
> Upon hearing this, the whole company before him gave a loud laugh, which wakened up the cock he carried dozing in his arms, who at once leaped up on his shoulders, clapped his wings lustily, and crowed loud and long.

The angry fairies seized the smith and his son, and hurled them both out of the hill. For a year and a day the boy was silent and still, but he recovered in time and became a maker of fabulous crafts and tools.

In later books, Roger thinks of William Buccleigh MacKenzie as a "changeling," since he's the son of Geillis, but given to another family to raise. Symbolically, a changeling might represent a father's fears the child wasn't his, or a mother's postpartum depression. People who acted strangely or babies who didn't thrive were thought to be fairy replacements for beloved family members. At one point, Lizzie notes, "her gentle, kindly mistress had vanished like smoke, taken over by a *deamhan*, a she-devil" (*The Drums of Autumn*, ch. 40). She worries that next her mistress will become an *ursiq*, a werewolf. While the first book regards the changeling lesson as foolish superstition for Claire to debunk, these later emotions focus on the real transformation characters often undergo.

Demons

Demons were a very real presence for the Highlanders. While many were thought to work for the devil, they originally came from the darker aspects of the fairyfolk. Evil fairies include the vampiric *baobhan sith*. A *brollacan* is a shapeless shady thing and night demon. In Scottish lore, *Ly Erg*, with a bloodstained right hand, lurked on roads near water. The *bodach* was an elderly bogeyman who slipped down the chimney to frighten children. The *Fachen* or *Direach*, with one leg and one arm, haunts the glens. *Powries* or red caps killed travelers and splashed themselves with blood. The *Slaugh*, Host of the Unforgiven Dead or Unseelie Court of evil fairies, were believed to be the Fallen Angels that roam the midnight skies of the earth searching for lost souls.

Animal spirits included *crodh mara*, Highland fairy water cattle. The *cait sith* was a cat fairy, completely black apart from one white spot on its breast. The *boobrie,* a giant black bird, ate entire cows. The *cu sith* were fairy dogs.

Water spirits were generally called *fuath.* The *cuachag,* a dangerous river sprite who haunts Glen Cuaich in Invernesshire, had many cousins: the sea ghosts called *ashrays,* as well as the *fideal,* goat-bodied *glastigs. peallaidh, nuggies, tangies, shellycoats,* the *loireag,* an aquatic fairy from the Hebrides and the *luideag* who haunted the loch of the Black Trout. The *shony* from the Isle of Lewis and the *morool,* a Shetland monster with many eyes. *Caoineag* (the weeper) wailed at the bottoms of waterfalls to presage deaths. *Selkies* transformed from seal to human on the shore. *Kelpies, noggles, nucklavees, shoopiltees* and the *each uisge* were water-horses. *Peallaidh* was a shaggy beast living near water. The *Cirein Croin,* or Sea Serpent, was said to be the largest animal in the world, as a popular Caithness rhyme describes it:

> Seven herring are a salmon's fill,
> Seven salmon are a seal's fill,
> Seven seals are a whale's fill,
> And seven whales the fill of a Cirein Croin [J.G. Campbell 220].

Shapeshifters (some of which were also water spirits) include the *glastig, tangie, doonie, kelpie,* and the *Baisd Bheulach.* The *buachaillen*—shapeshifters in pointed red hats—resembled tiny, young men.

Even the cruelest creatures were cowed by holy protection from iron or cross, Bible, bell, or cockcrow. Generally in the tales, simple cleverness would suffice:

> Off the Rhinns of Islay is a small island formerly used for grazing cattle. A strong tide sweeps past the island, making the crossing of the Sound dangerous. A story, related by Mr. Campbell, tells that on a certain boisterous night a woman was left in charge of a large herd of cattle on the island. She was sitting in her cabin, when all at once she heard strange noises outside, and, looking up, saw a pair of large eyes gazing in at her through the window. The door opened, and a strange creature strode in. He was tall and hairy, with a livid covering on his face instead of skin. He advanced towards the woman and asked her name. She replied in Gaelic, "Mise mi Fhin." "Me myself." He then seized her.
>
> In her terror she threw a ladleful of boiling water on the intruder. Yelling with pain he bounded out of the hut. These unearthly voices asked what was the matter, and who had hurt him? "Mise mi Fhin"—"Me myself," replied the creature. The answer was received with a shout of laughter from his mysterious companions. The woman rushed out of the hut, and dislodging one of the cows lay down on the spot, at the same time making a magical circle round her on the ground. All night she heard terrible sounds mingling with the roaring of the wind. In the morning the supernatural manifestations disappeared, and she felt herself safe. It had not fared, however, so well with the cow, for, when found, it was dead [Mackinlay, ch. 10].

The Fair Folk

Even in recent times, scholars gathering folktales discovered a reluctance to discuss the fair folk and especially to describe them by name. These were not the tiny Tinkerbells of children's stories, but creatures unnaturally *other* who might help or cause vicious harm. As Young Ian tells Brianna: "Ye call them *sidhe* in the Gaelic. The Cherokee call them the Nunnahee. And the Mohawk have names for them, too—more than one." He explains that to him, they much like vitamins are for his modern friends:

> "Ye canna see the vitamins, but you and Auntie Claire ken weel that they're there, and Uncle Jamie and I must take it on faith that ye're right about it. I ken as much about the—the Old Ones. Can ye no believe me about *that*?"
>
> "Well, I—" She had begun to agree, for the sake of peace between them—but a feeling swept over her, sudden and cold as a cloud-shadow, that she wished to say nothing to acknowledge the notion. Not out loud. And not here.
>
> "Oh," he said, catching sight of her face. "So ye *do* know" [*A Breath of Snow and Ashes,* ch. 69].

This is how Highlanders have always seen them, as an otherworldly presence, the power and force of nature and old things. Claire has a similar moment to Brianna's, not believing, and yet feeling the sacred serenity of the forest around her. "Perhaps the legends of green men and the myths of transformed nymphs began this way," she thinks, "not with trees come alive and walking, nor yet with women turned to wood—but with submersion of warm human flesh into the colder sensations of the plants, chilled to slow awareness" (*The Drums of Autumn,* ch. 25).

The Ballad of Thomas the Rhymer follows a singer kidnapped by the fairy queen and force to serve her for seven years. It explains that there are three paths: one to heaven, one to hell and one to fairyland. Thus the otherworld evolved alongside the Christian path, neither good nor evil but set apart. Reverend Kirk explains:

> The Siths, or Fairies, they call *Sluagh Maith*, or the Good people, it would seem, to prevent the dint of their ill attempts (for the Irish used to bless all they fear harm of), and are said to be of a middle nature betwixt man and angel, as were demons thought to be of old, of intelligent studious spirits, and light change-able bodies (like those called astral), somewhat of the nature of a condensed cloud, and best seen in twilight [Kirk].

A *booman, bwca, grogan,* or *brownie* cared for the house in Shetland and Orkney. A solitary Scottish elf called the *urisk* was quite friendly, half-human and half-goat. The *Ghillie dhu* were solitary tree nymphs with black hair. A Shetland supernatural creature with the body of man and a wolf's head was the *wulver.* All were benevolent. Above them all were the *Sidhe* (pronounced shee), the High Fairies or fairy court with their fabled queen.

Possibly a memory of Bronze Age folk, vulnerable to iron, possibly a vision of ancestors dwelling under the hill, the Others were deeply ingrained in the culture. In the deep forests, when a trickling pool or darting shadow suddenly appeared, it became easy to believe in more than the human world.

Fairy Hills

"Some say the hill is enchanted, others say it is cursed. Both are right," Claire notes in the prologue to *Dragonfly in Amber.* In folklore, the fairies live under the artificial hills that are manmade cairns or burial chambers from the ancient peoples of the land—many believe the tiny folk who could not abide iron are in fact memories of primitive civilizations. *Sidhe* is also the Gaelic word for the treasure-filled barrow-mounds, as fairies are said to live "under the hill." Prehistoric flint arrowheads scattered throughout Scotland were always known as elf-shot—proof of the primitive fay who refused to use iron. Exploring the land around Lallybroch, Roger discovers an ancient chapel and feels the presence of its ancient builders.

> Wiping sweat from the back of his neck, he stooped and picked up the statue's head. Very old. Celtic, Pictish? Not enough left to tell even the statue's intended gender.
> He passed a thumb gently over the statue's sightless eyes, then set the head carefully atop the half wall; there was a depression there, as though there might once have been a niche in the wall.
> "Okay," he said, feeling awkward. "See you later, then." And, turning, made his way down the rough hill toward home, still with that odd sense of being accompanied on his way [*An Echo in the Bone,* ch. 28].

Tomnahurich Hill on the outskirts of Inverness is famed as an abode of the fairies. (A modern cemetery now stands there.) According to legend, two travelling fiddlers were lured into playing for a fairy revel that emerged after one night beneath the hill to find that hundreds of years had passed in their own world. In other legends of Tomnahurich Hill, Thomas the Rhymer is said to be buried beneath it, waiting to lead an army in Scotland's hour of need. In Celtic myth, Fionn Mac Cumhaill trained his dog to lead two of every species of animal around the hill in pairs to unravel enchantment by an Irish enemy.

Reverend Kirk made a special study of the fairies and their homes, explaining:

> There be many places called fairy-hills, which the mountain people think impious and dangerous to peel or discover, by taking earth or wood from them, superstitiously believing the souls of their predecessors to dwell there. And for that end (say they) a mole or mound was dedicate beside every churchyard to receive the souls till their adjacent bodies arise, and so became as a fairy-hill; they using bodies of air when called abroad.

A seventh son of a seventh son, he was finally stolen away by the fairies after he examined them too closely, or so the legend goes.

W. Y. Evans-Wentz, a folklore scholar, describes being told by the locals at Aberfoyle, "where the Highlands and the Lowlands meet, and in the very place where Robert Kirk, the minister of Aberfoyle, was taken by them, in the year 1692," that it was well-known that the fairies lived in caverns nearby. As he adds:

> Kirk was taken into the Fairy Knoll, which she pointed to just across a little val-
> ley in front of us, and is there yet, for the hill is full of caverns, and in them the
> "good people" have their homes. And she added that Kirk appeared to a relative
> of his after he was taken, and said that he was in the power of the "good peo-
> ple," and couldn't get away. "But," says he, "I can be set free if you will have my
> cousin do what I tell him when I appear again at the christening of my child in
> the parsonage." According to Mr. Andrew Lang, who reports the same tradition
> in more detail in his admirable Introduction to The Secret Commonwealth, the
> cousin was Grahame of Duchray, and the thing he was to do was to throw a
> dagger over Kirk's head. Grahame was at hand at the christening of the posthu-
> mous child, but was so astonished to see Kirk appear as Kirk said he would, that
> he did not throw the dagger, and so Kirk became a perpetual prisoner of the
> "good people" [89].

Ghosts

The first book begins with Frank encountering a spirit of a Highlander and fearing he's Claire's love interest in a foreshadowing moment. The description of a "big chap" in Highland dress with a running stag brooch suggests Jamie. He gazes at Claire's window and looks unhappy—at being parted from her or at the ordeal she will undergo.

"It was thought that ghosts appeared in Scotland according to some previous engagement made in life with a friend, to appear if they could" (Daniels and Stevens 1205). This is a strong possibility, as Gabaldon has promised the final Jamie and Claire book will explain the ghostly appearance. They will likely part with a promise to meet again.

Claire's comments through the series also allude to this future moment. "I thought that was perhaps how some ghosts were made; where a will and a purpose had survived, heedless of the frail flesh that fell by the wayside, unable to sustain life long enough" she says in *Dragonfly in Amber* (ch. 45). Jamie certainly has a will and a purpose, especially for Claire.

Ghosts are central to the story, as the narrative splits between two times when everyone is dead or at least "not alive." Jamie and Claire speak to Frank's ghost on occasion, as Claire speaks to Jamie's. Jamie tells Claire of his dead brother and adds, "I talk to Willie sometimes, in my mind ... does that sound daft?" (*Dragonfly in Amber* ch. 31). Claire tells him she does the same with her uncle and her parents. He finishes by saying, "I think sometimes the dead cherish us, as we do them" (437).

Ghosts emphasize that loved ones never truly leave, but linger to protect those still living. Jamie's mother's rosebush, planted by the door of Lallybroch, suggests her protection over the house. When Jamie is near drowning on the selkies' isle, he imagines he hears his mother calling him to swim to her and he survives. He also believes Murtagh comes to keep him company on the night of battle—Jamie finds his presence a comfort, though Claire fears Murtagh has come to take him to heaven (*A Breath of Snow and Ashes,* ch. 112). In the Battle of Saratoga, young Ian feels his father protecting him and hears the older man shout a warning, so that an arrow takes him in the shoulder not the chest (*Written in My Own Heart's Blood,* ch. 79).

When Roger bungles the attempt to use the stones, he sees his father, at least for a moment. Fiona, who's with him, carefully avoids saying the names of his parents, noting, "Ye dinna call something unless you want it to come." By thinking of his father, Roger invokes him, however unconsciously. Ian echoes this with warnings of seeing a fetch, which he defines as "the sight of a person when the person himself is far awa'" (*The Drums of Autumn,* ch. 34). Seeing one is unlucky, but seeing one's own image is a premonition of death. While no one yet has done this last, it may be coming.

William describes hearing ghosts as a small child. As he notes, "He'd heard the rocks talking to themselves on the fells at Helwater. The Lake District, his maternal grandparents' home. In the fog. He hadn't told anyone that." He goes on to describe the presence of the dead:

> He'd heard his mother—his real mother—whisper to him, too. That was why he'd gone into the fog.
>
> ...
>
> She'd answered him, he'd swear she'd answered him—but in a voice with no words. He'd felt the caress of cool fingers on his face, and he'd wandered on, entranced [*An Echo in the Bone,* ch. 36].

Symbolically, mist and fog suggest the Veil between life and death. Mist blurs and distorts one's vision and perception, shielding him from what lies behind it. This, the world of death, is often not meant to be experienced by the rational mind. The fog blankets the person, representing confusion that exists before enlightenment.

Scotland was known for its ghosts, and beyond the presence of family, there are more menacing figures. Even clan ghosts could be disturbing, if benevolent:

> Almost every Highland and Lowland family possessing any claims to distinction had in former times its spirit or demon with its own peculiar attributes. Thus the family of Rothiomurchus had the Bodach-an-dun or ghost of the hill; Kincardine's, the spectre of the bloody hand; Gartinberg House was haunted by

Bodaoh Garten; Tulloch Gorm by Mang Mulloch, or the girl with the hairy left hand. The little spectres called Tarans, or the souls of unbaptised infants, were, it is said, often seen flitting among woods and secluded dells, lamenting in soft voices their hard fate. The Macleans of Lochbuv had their headless horseman, who has been heard in the silence of the night careering on horseback round the castle ringing his bridle-rein; the Ogilvies of Airlie, fairy music; Kincardine Castle had its lady in green, who-sat weeping beneath a particular tree when the dark shadow of death hovered near the family of Graham; the house of Forbes of Balmano, their Lady Green Sleeves, and so on [Guthrie, ch. 18].

In Scottish Gaelic spirits are often called *spiorad*, in Irish Gaelic, *anam, intinn,* or *aigne. Dunters,* which were once sacrificed to guard building foundations, haunt castles with a constant sound of beating flax. There are traditions of ghost sightings at Culloden Field, especially on April 16. In addition, in Invernesshire, a spectral army is said to appear on the shores of Loch Ashie at dawn on Beltane, traditionally the mythic Fionn Mac Cumhaill and his warriors.

In one book, Jamie tells the story of a *tannagach*, or spirit, that his friend met once. Seeking a cow, he discovered a cairn in a circle of trees "laid wi' slabs of rock, all heaped round with stones, and he could see before him the black opening of the tomb" (*The Drums of Autumn,* ch. 1). As he walked away, he heard footsteps following. When he finally looked back with a great cry, gripping his crucifix, he saw a figure made of mist with great black empty holes where the eyes belonged. He ran home and his wife threw him "a twig of myrtle bound wi' red thread and black, that she'd made to bless the cows." Thus they managed to drive off the unholy spirit (*The Drums of Autumn,* ch. 1). In a later book, Roger's companion suspects a *tannasg*, a similar spirit, when a light approaches. Roger realizes that it's near Samhain ("All Hallows" 461).

In book four, a ghost appears to Claire and saves her life. She discovers it was a man from the future, who traveled through the stones and tried to save the Iroquois, urging them to attack the French and English instead of being used by both. He failed to change the future. However, in sympathy for a fellow traveler, or perhaps reconciliation for how events turned out, he guides Jamie to Claire when she's hurt and lost. He also leaves her the spiral-marked opal he once called his "ticket home." This is a moment of mentoring and blessing as Claire decides on the eve of war how far to interfere.

Bonnet calls Jamie an *asgina ageli* in the fourth book—a Cherokee term for one who was condemned to death but still lives. He adds:

> It means "half-ghost," one who should have died by right, but yet remains on the earth; a woman who survives a mortal illness, a man fallen into his enemies' hands who escapes. They say an *asgina ageli* has one foot on the earth and the other in the spirit world. He can talk to the spirits, and see the Nunnahee—the Little People [*The Drums of Autumn,* ch. 2].

This suggests guilt and trauma as well as the mystical. Ghosts continue to symbolically haunt the characters. After Jamie confronts a tenant's death, Jenny orders him to go out and "piss on the doorposts" to keep the ghost from returning (*Dragonfly in Amber,* ch. 30). When she's troubled by flashbacks, Jamie brings Claire a pinch of salt, and she is oddly comforted, thinking, "Salt, they said, kept a ghost in its grave" (*A Breath of Snow and Ashes,* ch. 54).

Some moments only appear to be ghost stories, though they continue to emphasize the motif even as it calls it into doubt: The corpse from the beginning of book four comes to life in the chapter "In Which We Meet a Ghost," but it's really a criminal escapee taking his place. The "hollow, sepulchral voice from the flue" in Paris (*Dragonfly in Amber,* ch. 11) is a nighttime visitor escaping an assignation.

Kelpies and Waterhorses

In the Highlands and Lowlands alike, the spirit inhabiting rivers and lakes was commonly known as the water-kelpy. As Claire observes, "These beings, I was given to understand, inhabited almost all bodies of water, being especially common at fords and crossings, though many lived in the depths of the lochs" (*Outlander,* ch. 18). Water horses were sometimes considered monsters and sometimes more of a *genius loci,* a place guardian and the spirit of the local loch or river. There were also water-cows and water-bulls in folklore, which the Manx called *tarroo-ushtey.* The Reverend Stewart describes water-horses and water-bulls in his "Twixt Ben Nevis and Glencoe."

> [They are thought of] as, upon the whole, of the same shape and form as the more kindly quadrupeds after whom they have been named, but larger, fiercer, and with an amount of "devilment" and cunning about them, of which the latter, fortunately, manifest no trace. They are always fat and sleek, and so full of strength and spirit and life that the neighing of the one and the bellowing of the other frequently awake the mountain echoes to their inmost recesses for miles and miles around [qtd. in Mackinlay, ch. 11].

The lochs of Llundavra, and Achtriachtan, in Glencoe, were at one time famous for their water-bulls; and Loch Treig for its water-horses, believed to be the fiercest specimens of that breed in the world. If anyone suggested to a Lochaber or Rannoch Highlander that the cleverest horse-tamer could "clap a saddle on one of the demon-steeds of Loch Treig, as he issues in the grey dawn, snorting, from his crystal-paved sub-lacustral stalls, he would answer, with a look of mingled horror and awe, 'Impossible!' The water-horse would tear him into a thousand pieces with his teeth and trample and pound him into pulp with his jet-black, iron-hard, though unshod hoofs!" (Mackinlay, ch. 11).

Waterhorses were most famous in the Highlands. "Lonely lochs were their favourite haunts. In treeless regions, a belief in such creatures would naturally arise. Any ordinary animal in such an environment would appear of a larger size than usual, and the eye of the beholder would transmit the error to his imagination, thereby still further magnifying the creature's bulk" (Mackinlay, ch. 11). When waves inexplicably appeared on a lake, or strange sounds emerged, the waterhorse was blamed. They were famous for luring riders to their doom, though they could be benevolent if they chose, like all the fey.

According to James Mackinlay in *Folklore of Scottish Lochs and Springs* (1893): "The lochs of Llundavra, and Achtriachtan, in Glencoe, were at one time famous for their water-bulls; and Loch Treig [near Fort William] for its water-horses, believed to be the fiercest specimens of that breed in the world." Famously they were impossible to ride, as they would turn on a rider, "tear him into a thousand pieces with his teeth and trample and pound him into pulp with his jet-black, iron-hard, though unshod hoofs!"

Embracing the wild and willful Brianna, Roger thinks, "Once a man has touched the mane of a water horse, it's no simple matter to let go." He pictures the old kelpie rhyme:

> And sit weel, Janetie
> And ride weel, Davie.
> And your first stop will be
> The bottom of Loch Cavie [*The Drums of Autumn*, ch. 19]

In both the book (*Outlander*, ch. 18) and the episode "Both Sides Now," Rupert tells a story about a waterhorse who steals away a human wife, who is cold and unhappy thereafter. As he tells on the show:

> And so the water-horse carries the builder straight into the water, and down through the depths to his own cold, fishy home, then he tells the builder if he would be free, he must build a fine house, and a muckle chimney as well, so that the waterhorse's wife could warm her hands by the fire and fry her fish. And the builder, having little choice, did as he was bid, because the waterhorse's wife was sad, and cold, and hungry in her new home beneath the waves.

This he does, and the waterhorse's wife is warm, happy, and well-fed. As the story concludes, "And the waters of the east end of Loch Garve never freeze over, because the heat from the waterhorse's chimney melts the ice" ("Both Sides Now").

The creepy feel of the underwater legend is juxtaposed against the men's worry as another clan raids them and tries to steal their horses. It's the first menace to break up Claire and Jamie's wedded bliss. In the tale, it's the horse that steals men, but their adventure has men stealing horses, emphasizing the brutality of the men's world in this scene and the one to come, rather than the savagery of the natural world.

The selkie tale seems a better match for Claire, with a magical wife and ordinary Scottish man, rather than a magical husband and human wife. However, there are parallels as Claire's new husband Jamie must struggle to make his wife comfortable in a world without hot baths, chocolate, or the comforts she remembers from her old life. The story also serves to enforce the concept of storytelling and the rich culture surrounding Claire on her travels.

Loch Ness Monster

At the beginning of the book, Claire and Frank visit Loch Ness, and their tour guide tells them vague rumors of the monster there: "Weel, the loch's queer, and no mistake. There's stories, to be sure, of something old and evil that once lived in the depths. Sacrifices were made to it—kine, and sometimes even wee bairns, flung into the water in withy baskets" (*Outlander,* ch. 2). J.F. Campbell tells this origin story of the Loch:

> Where Loch Ness now is, there was long ago a fine glen. A woman went one day to the well to fetch water, and she found the spring flowing so fast that she got frightened, and left her pitcher and ran for her life; she never stopped till she got to the top of a high hill; and when there, she turned about and saw the glen filled with water. Not a house or a field was to be seen! "Aha!" said she, "Tha Loch ann a nis." (Ha Loch an a neesh). There is a lake in it now; and so the lake was called Loch Ness (neesh).

The Gaelic *neesh* means "now," while the old Norse word *nes* means "headland"— either may be the meaning here. Inverness, in turn, means the "mouth of the River Ness."

Of course, the loch is famed for its monster, a rumored shadowy figure with a long neck, gliding through the water. St. Columba was the first to see it, and sightings have appeared in legend through the centuries. In 1934, a London doctor snapped a possible photograph of the creature. In 2009, a newspaper reader claims to have spotted 'Nessie' while browsing Google Earth's satellite photos of Loch Ness.

In the first book, Claire actually sees the monster—likely a plesiosaur from primeval times, and perhaps a time traveler as well if one of the portals lies within the lake. Gabaldon explains:

> Now, if you believe that time-travel is possible–and both Stephen Hawking and I think it is—then you don't have to have either a set quantity of biomass or a breeding population of monsters. All you need is a time-portal under Loch Ness, which would occasionally allow a prehistoric creature to pass through it.
>
> OK, if this is the case, then the monster could quite easily be a plesiosaur, elasmosaur, or any other aquatic prehistoric reptile. Going just on the basis of the most popular published photo of the supposed monster, my guess would be plesiosaur ["FAQ"].

Claire notes, "Oddly enough, I was not really afraid. I felt some kinship with it, a creature farther from its own time than I" (ch. 19). The chapter is titled "The Waterhorse," linking the monster with the kelpie. The tale of the waterhorse in episode eight is meant as a nod on the show to the monster's appearance, though Moore explains he chose not to use the latter. He considers it a step too far into the world of fantasy—this is meant to be a mostly realistic show rather than a fantasy adventure of magical monsters (Podcast, 108). In folklore, the kelpie has some parallels with the monster—Kelpies were said to dwell in Loch Ness as much as anywhere else:

> A noted demon-steed once inhabited Loch Ness, and was a cause of terror to the inhabitants of the neighbourhood. Like other kelpies, he was in the habit of browsing along the roadside, all bridled and saddled, as if waiting for some one to mount him. When any unwary traveller did so, the kelpy took to his heels, and presently plunged into deep water with his victim on his back.
>
> Mr. W. G. Stewart, in his "Highland Superstitions and Amusements," tells a story to show that the kelpy in question did not always have things his own way. A Highlander of the name of MacGrigor resolved to throw himself in the way of the water-horse in the hope of getting the better of him. The meeting took place in the solitary pass of Slochd-Muichd, between Strathspey and Inverness. The kelpy looked as innocent as usual, and was considerably startled when Mac-Grigor, sword in hand, struck him a blow on the nose. The weapon cut through the bridle, and the bit, falling to the ground, was instantly picked up by Mac-Grigor. This was the turning point of the encounter. The kelpy was powerless without his bit, and requested to have it restored. Though a horse, the kelpy had the power of human speech, and conversed, doubtless in excellent Gaelic, with his victor, using various arguments to bring about the restoration of his lost property. Finding that these were unavailing, he prophesied that MacGrigor would never enter his house with the bit in his possession, and when they arrived at the door he planted himself in front of it to block the entrance. The Highlander, however, outwitted the kelpy, for, going round to the back of his house, he called his wife and flung the bit to her through a window. Returning to the kelpy, he told him where the bit was, and assured him that he would never get it back again. As there was a rowan cross above the door the demon-steed could not enter the house, and presently departed uttering certain exclamations not intended for benedictions [Mackinlay, ch. 11].

In Claire's encounter, the river symbolizes creative power, but also Claire's nemesis, "the irreversible passage of time" (Cirlot 274). The Loch Ness monster offers a moment of magic and wonder but also the terror of the Otherworld. The liquid element is a passage between life and death. To the Irish and Bretons, the lake symbolized the underworld as the sun seemed to set into it (Cirlot 175). Thus by the lakeside, Claire finds herself poised between two worlds, in this case solid and magical, as she discovers legends brought to life before her.

Nuckelavee and Piskies

When an alarm clock is dismembered, Jem insists, "We must have got piskies, Mama." Later, Roger tells Brianna, the word "'pisky' is Cornish; they're called pixies in other parts of the West Country, though." As he adds, "Scots tend toward the grimmer manifestations of the supernatural—water horses, ban-sidhe, blue hags, and the Nuckelavee, aye? Piskies are a wee bit frivolous for Scotland" (*An Echo in the Bone,* ch. 21). He warns Brianna the Nuckelavee is nothing she wants to hear about at bedtime.

As the story continues, a frightening figure stalks the family and tells the children he's the Nuckelavee. Horrified, Brianna reads about him in Roger's collection of Scottish folklore, though she assures Jem he was clearly just a "nasty tramp." As Roger's book tells:

> The creature's home was in the sea, but it ventured upon land to feast upon humans. The Nuckelavee rode a horse on land, and its horse was sometimes indistinguishable from its own body. Its head was ten times larger than that of a man, and its mouth thrust out like a pig's, with a wide, gaping maw. The creature had no skin, and its yellow veins, muscle structure, and sinews could clearly be seen, covered in a red slimy film. The creature was armed with venomous breath and great strength. It did, however, have one weakness: an aversion to freshwater. The horse on which it rode is described as having one red eye, a mouth the size of a whale's, and flappers like fins around its forelegs [ch. 21].

While the monster is really a man, its menace as it prowls outside their home reminds Roger and Brianna of the Otherworldly magic of the stones and the fairyfolk ... it's difficult to completely dismiss the possibility of monsters.

Rowan

> I looked down and saw a layer of fallen rowan berries, gleaming red and black among the grass. Very appropriate, I thought, vaguely amused. I had fallen down under a rowan—the Highland protection against witchcraft and enchantment.—*Voyager,* ch. 24

Rowans have long been revered for the mystical powers. "The tree stood for magic and was sacred to the Goddess Brigit. It was thought effacious in breaking evil enchantments" (Walker 470). The berries grow in a pentagram, adding to the lore with the old rhyme: "Rowan tree and red thread / make the witches tine (meaning 'to lose') their speed." The wood was used for divining and for dyeing ritual robes black. While it wasn't often used to fashion everyday objects, a Gaelic threshing tool of rowan called a *buaitean* was used on grain meant for rituals and celebrations. The rowan's white flowers cast it as a fairy or goddess tree. It was said to protect a house or person or even the cow barn from witchcraft. From Scotland to Cornwall, people wore equal-armed crosses of rowan bound with red thread. The plant was very significant in Scottish culture—the Scots Gaelic name is *caorunn,* appearing in Highland place names such as *Beinn Chaorunn* in Invernesshire and *Loch a'chaorun* in Easter Ross. Rowan was also the clan badge of the Malcolms and McLachlans.

Silkies

The selkie legend describes "mythological creatures said to live as seals in the sea but to become humans on land" (*Outlander,* ch. 24). These traditional stories all go the same way: A man steals a selkie's sealskin, and she turns into a woman and weds him. Eventually, however, she discovers the stolen skin and returns to the sea.

> A story is told of an inhabitant of Unst, who, in walking on the sandy margin of a voe, saw a number of mermen and mermaids dancing by moonlight, and several seal-skins strewed beside them on the ground. At his approach they immediately fled to secure their garbs, and, taking upon themselves the form of seals, plunged immediately into the sea. But as the Shetlander perceived that one skin lay close to his feet, he snatched it up, bore it swiftly away, and placed it in concealment. On returning to the shore he met the fairest damsel that was ever gazed upon by mortal eyes, lamenting the robbery, by which she had become an exile from her submarine friends, and a tenant of the upper world.

In love with her, he insisted on marriage, and they lived happily for a time, though she would often gaze to sea, looking for the seal-lover she'd lost. One day, their child discovered the cloak hidden away.

> The husband immediately returned, learned the discovery that had taken place, ran to overtake his wife, but only arrived in time to see her transformation of shape completed—to see her, in the form of a seal, bound from the ledge of a rock into the sea. The large animal of the same kind with whom she had held a secret converse soon appeared, and evidently congratulated her, in the most tender manner, on her escape. But before she dived to unknown depths, she cast a parting glance at the wretched Shetlander, whose despairing looks excited in her breast a few transient feelings of commiseration. "Farewell!" said she to him, "and may all good attend you. I loved you very well when I resided upon earth, but I always loved my first husband much better" [*Folk-Lore and Legends of Scotland*].

This story parallels Claire's own—a magical woman is trapped in Scotland, unable to return to her birthplace and forced to marry a Scottish man of the time. He's able to keep her for a while, but eventually must let her return home. Jamie seems to realize this on some level as he guides Claire to the standing stones in the first book and season. "From the male teller's point of view, this type of romance reflects a desire to connect with the world of nature, and particularly the threshold to the magical world, as heroes court nymphs of the wild feminine oceans, streams, forests and skies"—these semi-divine women offer a bridge from the human world to that of the unconscious (Frankel 306).

These stories appear around the world: "Related tales feature swan maidens in Sweden, frog wives in China and Tibet, porpoise girls in Micronesia, bear women in North America, peries (fairies) in Persian folklore, and aspares (water-bird nymphs) in Hindu myth" (Frankel 305). This universality emphasizes the tale's symbolic meaning.

> The sealskin or swanskin represents the woman's untamable magical nature: When she wears it, she feels completely herself, able to swim and fly as well as tend the fire. Like the animal she imitates, she becomes completely unselfconscious, wholly in tune with the forces around her. Even while she is married, the skin waits in a chest or closet, set aside but awaiting her desire.
>
> ...
>
> This unending cycle of going and returning is natural for the women, a way to feel completely themselves "within their skins." Withdrawal may be a short respite, time taken for herself each day to read the newspaper or do yoga. This may be a vacation, like Aphrodite's annual sacred bath, from which the mother returns, rested and ready to resume her family roles. Or it may be a new career, a return to independence, a seeking of the autonomy she once had before creating a family [Frankel 306].

Claire is given the choice several times—to go or return, to stay in the twentieth century or the eighteenth with either set of family, friends, and husbands. This power she has, to choose which world she will live in, to become a lover then a doctor then make more choices, emphasizes the power of choice and the renewing power of departure from her previous world.

Seal legends appear on coasts around the world, shared among Scots and Inuit, among others. Seals notably resemble humans with their round heads and huge dark eyes. Like wolves, they are nearly human-sized, and as playful mammals and hunters, they evoke some of the personality. They often swim close to fishing boats out of curiosity and their calls, especially echoed by caves, sound oddly human.

Alec McMahon tells Claire the story of Jamie's parents: Brian was black-haired and "folk in the village would tell the tale to each other that Ellen MacKenzie was taken to the sea to live among the seals.... Brian Fraser was said to have hair like a silkie" (*Outlander,* ch. 24). Thus as he crept into Clan MacKenzie and stole away Jamie's mother, many compared him to the magical creature. In the comic, Murtagh sees selkies as he stands on the coast awaiting Jamie's arrival from France. "Is that you, Brian? Come to welcome back your son?" he wonders.

Later on, little Germain notes that some people think Jamie is a silkie and the scars on his back come from someone cutting his skin from him (*A Breath of Snow and Ashes,* ch. 49). A bit amused, Jamie says that's correct.

The Wild Hunt

In *The Scottish Prisoner,* Jamie and Lord John embark to Ireland for an adventure based in ancient lore ... and another plot for Prince Charlie's return. A poem about The Wild Hunt is used as Jacobite code:

> *Listen, you men of the three lands.*
> Listen for the sound of the horns that wail in the wind,
>
> that come out of the night.
> She is coming. The Queen is coming
> and they come following, her great train, her retinue
> wild of hair and eye,
> the volunteers who follow the Queen.
>
> They search out blood, they seek its heat.
> They echo the voice of the king under the hill [ch. 17].

With the return of great royalty surrounded by loyal followers, the poem alludes to Prince Charles—in another section, there's a reference to her people strewing white roses (the Tudor sigil) before their adored and majestic queen.

Father Michael tells Jamie that like the famous poem "Tam Lin," this poem references the fairies' teind to hell—a tithe of a person every seven years. ("Tam Lin" is the ballad of a young man stolen by the fairies, whose pregnant lover must save him before he's chosen for the teind.) The wailing horns and seekers of blood reference darker tales. The Wild Hunt, in folklore, was a team of fairy hunters who rode the skies at night, hunting animals and sometimes people. In parts of Britain, the hunt was thought to be variously King Arthur, the angry dead, or a pack of hell-hounds chasing sinners and the unbaptized. Seeing the Wild Hunt presaged a great catastrophe such as war or plague, or possibly the death of the one who witnessed it. Gabaldon adds in her Author's Notes for the book:

> In some forms of these stories, the horde consists of faeries, in others, the "hunt" consists of the souls of the dead. Either way, it isn't something you want to meet on a dark night—or a moonlit one, either.... The notion of abduction of humans by the hunt is common to almost all hunt tales, though—and it may be this aspect that caused our Irish Jacobite plotters to adopt this *nom de guerre,* as they planned to abduct George II. Then again, it might have been a reference to and natural extension from the older name, "Wild Geese," as the Irish Jacobites of the late seventeenth century called themselves. The idea of the *teind*—the tithe to hell—is from "Tam Lin," and likely a word that would have resonance to people who lived by a code of honor, to whom betrayal and treason would carry a heavy price.

Gabaldon then quotes Yeats' "The Hosting of the Sidhe":

> *The host is riding from Knocknarea*
> *And over the grave of Clooth-na-Bare;*
> *Caoilte tossing his burning hair,*
> *And Niamh calling Away, come away:*
> *Empty your heart of its mortal dream.*
> *The winds awaken, the leaves whirl round,*
> *Our cheeks are pale, our hair is unbound,*
> *Our breasts are heaving our eyes are agleam,*
> *Our arms are waving our lips are apart;*
> *And if any gaze on our rushing band,*
> *We come between him and the deed of his hand,*
> *We come between him and the hope of his heart.*
> *The host is rushing 'twixt night and day,*
> *And where is there hope or deed as fair?*
> *Caoilte tossing his burning hair,*
> *And Niamh calling Away, come away.*

Later in the novel, Jamie admits he once saw the Wild Hunt after he killed a deer but hadn't yet said the prayer. They sensed the blood and came riding up for their share. He jumped in the river and hid, since "Ye dinna want to look upon them.... If ye do, they can call ye to them. Cast their glamour upon you. And then ye're lost" (ch. 28). He adds that sometimes they take people and return them two hundred years later—a clear reference to the tales of the Fair Folk that correspond with Claire's story. He discovered in the morning that someone had taken the head and entrails and a haunch—"the huntsman's share."

At the climax of the story, an Irish Jacobite commits suicide and writes the word *Teind* in his blood on the wall, inviting the fairies to take him down to hell for failing to put Prince Charlie on the throne. As such, he ties himself into the ancient legends as well as offering himself in sacrifice. One must die every few years, like the pattern of Jacobite uprisings that tried over and over and never achieved the throne.

Jamie buries the man who died for the teind and sees the Wild Hunt come. He hears "Horns. Like the blowing of trumpets, but trumpets such as he had never heard, and the hair rippled on his body."

> *They're coming.* He didn't pause to ask himself who it was that was coming but hastily put on his breeks and coat. It didn't occur to him to flee, and for an instant he wondered why not, for the very air around him quivered with strangeness.
> *Because they're not coming for you*, the calm voice within his mind replied. *Stand still.*
> ...
> They were closer now, close enough to make out faces and the details of their clothing. They were dressed plain, for the most part, dressed in drab and home-

spun, save for one woman dressed in white—*why is her skirt no spattered wi' the mud?* And he saw with a little thrill of horror that her feet did not touch the ground; none of them did—who carried in one hand a knife with a long, curved blade and a glinting hilt [*The Scottish Prisoner,* ch. 37].

This plot adds a trace of true magic to the series beyond the Standing Stones. If Jamie's point of view can be trusted here, the *sidhe* are real, and they come for their offerings in the human world. As they float above the land and carry their prey off to hell, they remind Jamie of life's precarious nature.

GODS, SAINTS AND DEVILS

Bride

Jamie tells Lord John about following a cryptic message to find the "white witch." Seeking Claire, he goes to a shrine of St. Bride and finds a hoard of jewels. He notes that "St. Bride was also called 'the white lady'.... Though the shrine has been there a verra long time—since long before St. Bride came to Scotland" (*Voyager* ch. 10).

Many characters swear by "Jesus, Mary and Bride," or give blessings in their name. This Triune, slanted toward the women of the religion, reflects various Celtic trinities as well as Christian ones—Bride is explained as Jesus' midwife, but is probably derived from Brigid, an ancient Celtic goddess.

There were several Brides, Christian and pre–Christian, leading to a confusion of legends as many tales and characters merged. The culmination of these was a Bride who presides over fire, art, and all beauty, *fo cheabhar agus fo chuan,* beneath the sky and beneath the sea. As Christ's midwife, she watches over the birth of man and dedicates each newborn to the trinity. When a woman is in labor, the midwife goes to the door, and standing on the doorstep, with her hands on the jambs, softly beseeches Bride to come:

> Bride! Bride! come in,
> Thy welcome is truly made,
> Give thou relief to the woman,
> And give the conception to the Trinity
> [Carmichael 165–167].

When things go well, it is believed that Bride is blessing the young mother. If she has been offended she will not appear. As the earthly representative of Bride, the midwife dedicates the child to the Trinity by pouring three drops of clear cold water on his forehead, invoking the protection of the Goddess.

Celtic Gods

Bride or Brigit is mentioned constantly in the series. Aside from their link to the Fire Festivals, other gods are not—Bride was adopted into the Catholic saints but many other gods fell behind. Nonetheless, they are included briefly here for their influence on the legends and customs of the Highlands. These gods are shared with Ireland and parts of Western Europe, though some have a particularly Scottish angle.

> It is believed that the Celts started with the concept of a Mother Goddess named Danu (meaning "water from heaven"). The name of the Danube River is derived from Danu, and evidence shows that the Celtic civilization evolved at the headwaters of the Danube River around this time. Water was venerated as the source of life, personified by Danu. Numerous rivers in Europe bear her name, such as the Don Rivers in England, France, Scotland and Russia. The Irish called themselves "Tuatha De Danaan," the people of the goddess Danu [Foubister, Kindle Locations 846–850].

Lugh, the Shining One, is Sun God and God of War and metalwork. His symbols are the white stag and ravens, and he wields a great spear. He is a god of the sun, light, and the grain harvest, who is honored at the Sabbat of Lughnassadh. He is the chief Lord of the Tuatha De Danaan, the Celtic father god.

The Ogham Alphabet was invented by Ogham, patron deity of poets. Grannos is an early god of mineral springs whose shrines have been found from France to Edinburgh. Creator of the Scottish mountains, the Cailleach is the Queen of Winter and the Great Goddess in her Destroyer aspect, the "Veiled One." Her other name, Scota, inspired the name Scotland (which was previously called Caledonia, or land given by Cailleach). Dia Greine, "sun's tear," an ancient Scottish sun goddess, travels to the underworld from which the Cailleach, disguised as a fox, must free her. Her story thus offers a metaphor of reincarnation, like that of Demeter and Persephone.

Epona, "The Great Mare," is the goddess of horses, also concerned with healing and domestic animals. She is arguably the only Celtic goddess to have been worshipped in Rome itself. In Scotland she is referred to as Bubona. Other horse-associated goddesses such as Macha, Edain, Rhiannon, and Maeve may have grown out of her myths.

Cernunnos the horned god appears in all Celtic-inspired pantheons. His symbols are the stag, ram, bull, and horned serpent, making him a god of the woods and of regeneration. He is sometimes associated with the Green Man. Reigning over the battlefield and their warriors' school on the Isle of Shadow, Aoife and Scathach are sister warriors. Their father, Ard Greimme, whose name means "high power" is a sun god. Llyr is the god of the sea and the father of sea god Mannanan. Four of his children (by Aebh) are part of the folk tales known as the "Four Sorrows of Erin."

Celts believed as they engaged in battle, the Morrigan flew shrieking overhead in the form of a raven or carrion crow. Queen of the Fairies in some tales, she is also a dark goddess or crone, the goddess of war, fate and death. With her, Nemain (Venomous), Badb (Fury), and Macha (Battle) encourage fighters to battle madness. Cerridwen is the white, corpse-eating sow representing the Moon. She has a great cauldron of power, in which she brews a great potion of regeneration and wisdom.

Eostre, an Anglo-Saxon Goddess, was eventually adopted into the Celtic pantheon. She is the goddess of spring, rebirth, new beginnings, and fertility, namesake of Easter and the Celtic Spring Equinox. A specifically Scottish goddess of prophecy, Corra often takes the form of a crane. Coventina, a water goddess, is generally pictured as a nymph, pouring water from a vessel. She is the queen of river goddesses, representing abundance, inspiration, and prophecy. Cliodna, a goddess of beauty and the otherworld, often takes the form of a sea bird and rules the waves. According to legend, she rides in every ninth one which breaks on shore.

Christ Allusions

The scene in Wentworth and Jamie's recovery at the Abbey offer many Christ allusions and nods to Biblical sufferers. First, Robbie McNabb betrays Jamie to the English as the Judas of the tale. Undergoing torture, Jamie receives a nail wound through his palm, which leaves a permanent scar. He is also flogged and sentenced to die. Finally, Jamie chooses to give up his life so Claire can live.

Claire and Murtagh plot to rescue Jamie from Wentworth on December 21; this is a moment reflecting Mary and the disciples in hiding "in the upper room" around Pentecost, deliberately added, as the author notes (*Outlander Podcast*). Jamie reaches the Abbey of Ste. Anne de Beaupre and safety on Christmas Eve. The library at the Abbey has a stained-glass window showing Joseph and Mary's Flight into Egypt with Jesus as another nod to the quest for sanctuary (*Outlander*, ch. 38).

The monks at the Abbey of Ste. Anne de Beaupre bring additional references to mind. They hold a nightly vigil called the ritual of Perpetual Adoration, recalling Christ's words at Gethsemane, "Can you not watch with me one hour?" from Matthew 26: 36–46 (*Outlander,* ch. 38). The Abbey itself is named for St. Anne, the mother of the Virgin Mary. Jamie and Claire have symbolically found a safe haven, protected by the grandmother of Christ. St. Anne was also known for protecting sailors at sea, emphasizing her role as a refuge for the hunted travelers.

The chapel at the abbey is named for Saint Giles. Claire finds herself at peace there: "The flames of the white candles before the statues of St. Giles and the Blessed Mother flickered and jumped occasionally.... But the red lamp burned serene, with no unseemly waver to betray its light" (ch. 38). St. Giles was a Greek Christian hermit whose sole companion was a deer (Jamie's symbol, indicated by his brooch.) His right hand pierced by an arrow, Giles is the patron saint against sterility and of cripples and beggars—in the abbey, exiled with nothing but his wits, Jamie discovers he can keep his hand, though it has been pierced and broken as well. Also Claire discovers she isn't barren. Perhaps time in this chapel has helped her.

Jamie mentions his favorite book is Job, and indeed, Jamie has far more than his share of suffering, almost always with a purpose. In despair after Wentworth, Claire opens to the passages "But his flesh upon him shall have pain, and his soul within him shall mourn" (Job 14:22) and "Yea, his soul draweth near unto the grave, and his life to the destroyers" (Job 33:22). She adds to these, "He is chastened also with pain upon his bed, and the multitude of his bones with strong pain.... His flesh is consumed away, that it cannot be seen; and his bones that were not seen stick out" (Job 33:19 and 33:21). Of course, after his suffering, Job finds peace and a wonderful life as a gift from God. She finally reads, "Deliver him from going down to the pit: I have found a ransom. His flesh shall be fresher than a child's: he shall return to the days of his youth" from Job 33:23–25 and sets out to do so in the chapter titled 'To Ransom a Man's Soul' (*Outlander*, ch. 39).

In the next chapter, Claire awakes to find she and Jamie have destroyed the tapestry of a martyr. "From the pattern of indentations impressing itself painfully into my back, I thought I must be lying on the indifferently executed tapestry of St. Sebastian the Human Pincushion; no great loss to the monastery, if so." St. Sebastian was a Roman soldier shot with arrows to a frightening degree of punishment and left for dead. When the widow of St. Castulus went to recover his body, she discovered that he was still alive and was able to nurse him back to health. This echoes Jamie and his recovery on multiple levels. St. Sebastian is the patron saint of athletes because of his endurance and his energetic devotion to spreading and defending the Faith. He is also patron to all soldiers and a suitable guardian for Jamie.

During his recovery, Jamie leaves the building stark naked and when Claire finds him, he insists on walking to the oak tree on his own. "...After a moment, though, I found I couldn't bear to watch his labored progress. When he fell the first time, I clutched the reins tight in my gloved hands, then resolutely turned my back, and waited" (ch. 40). This suggests a second fall, reminiscent of Jesus on his way to the cross.

The Devil

The educated Colum, upon hearing a child has died, notes, "It's Satan's work. The foolish child, he went up to the Black Kirk." He immediately adds, thinking of his own disability, "Sometimes I wonder what I did to make the devil punish me like this" (Episode 103). Claire spends the episode saving a child with medicine while the priest insists the boy is possessed.

The devil was very much a figure of popular life. He was said to appear at card games and witches' meetings, when he was summoned or would come to claim his prey. "He is apt to appear to persons ready to abandon their integrity, and to haunt premises which are soon to be the scene of signal calamities. He sometimes comes in unaccountable shapes and in lonely places for no conceivable purpose but to frighten people" (J.G. Campbell 291). Thanks to medieval art and religious theater, the devil was known to have horns, tail, and cloven hooves, often something of a caricature. Campbell adds:

> In Gaelic the exaggeration is not carried to the same lengths as in English. There is nothing said about the fiend's having horns or tail. He has made his appearance in shape of a he-goat, but his horns have not attracted so much attention, or inspired such terror, as his voice, which bears a horrible resemblance to the bleating of a goat. A native of the Island of Coll is said to have got a good view of him in a hollow, and was positive that he was crop-eared (corc-chluasacfi) He has often a chain clanking after him. In Celtic, as in German superstition, he has usually a horse's hoof, but also sometimes a pig's foot. This latter peculiarity, which evidently had its origin in the incident of the Gadarean swine, and in the pig being unclean under the ceremonial law, explains the cloven hoof always ascribed to him in English popular tales [290–291].

In Gaelic the devil is called many epithets:

> The worthless one (am fear naqh fhiack)
> The one whom I will not mention (am fear nach abair mi)
> Yon one (am fear ud)
> The one big one (an aonfhear mor)
> The one from the abyss (an t-aibhisteir)
> The mean mischievous one (an Rosad)
> The big sorrow (an dblas mbr)
> The son of cursing (Mac-mollachd)
> The big grizzled one (an Riabhach tnor)
> The bad one (an donas)
> The bad spirit (ain-spiorad, droch-spiorad)
> Black Donald (Dbinhnull Du) [291]

Irish Gods

> "The Old Ones thought the number three holy, just as we do."
> Father Michael's words, half-shouted above the wind, drifted

back to him. "They had the three gods—the god of thunder,
him they called Taranis. Then Esus, the god of the underworld—mind, they didn't see the underworld quite the same
way we think of hell, but it wasn't a pleasant place, nonetheless."—*The Scottish Prisoner,* ch. 19

The third is the local god, whoever that may be. Michael FitzGibbons, the
abbot of an ancient Irish church and Murtagh's cousin, adds that men would
sacrifice other men to these gods. "They would take prisoners of war and burn
them in great wicker cages, for Taranis" (*The Scottish Prisoner,* ch. 19). The
ancient bog man Father Michael discovers has been strangled, throat slit, and
head bashed in, as a threefold sacrifice to the three gods.

This scene reminds readers of the older Celtic-Druid culture in Britain—
Ireland in this case. As such, it adds a sense of otherworldliness and spooky mys-
tery to the story. Later, Jamie calls the Wild Hunt by the gods' three names:
Esus, Taranis, Teutates, and banishes them.

This triad may have evolved from the god Zeus, as they share linguistic
similarities and attributes (Mountain 1044). Grimm similarly writes in *Teutonic
Mythology* that "All the Celtic tongues retain the word *taran* for thunder, Irish
toran, with which one may directly connect the ON. form *Thôrr*" (ch. 8). Thus
Taranis, as well as the Irish name for Thursday, *dia Tordain,* may derive from
the Norse tradition and its thunder god Thor.

Taranis was a Gaulish god of thunder and lightning, whose sacrifices were
burned alive in wooden cages. He held a six-spoked wheel and a spiral stick,
emphasizing the cycle of time and heavenly power (Mountain 995). Teutates was
a tribal god of arts trading and fortune, whose sacrifices were typically drowned.
Esus (Celtic for Lord or Master) was He Who Directs Wars, and in token of
this, his sacrifices were hang head down from a tree and beheaded. "The triple
death of stabbing, burning, and drowning (or strangulation) held considerable
significance, involving 3 of the 4 elements" (Mountain 995). The four elements
concept partially comes from the knowledge than bodies might be disposed of
and returned to nature through air, water, earth, or fire, so deaths by these methods, or all of them, held a particular gravity.

Saints' Springs

In the new world, a spring lies near the Big House called White Spring,
"so-called for the big pale boulder that stood guardian over its pool" (*An Echo
in the Bone,* ch. 91). It has a "sense of inviolate peace." Jamie notes that in the
Highlands, these springs are common, and they're called saints' pools. "There's
something there that listens ... folk say the saint lives by the pool and listens to
their prayers."

There were numerous Holy wells in the Highlands and Lowlands of Scotland, which were much resorted to in cases of sickness by the more superstitious of the peasantry, and even yet in certain remote districts the old superstition still lingers. The benefits supposed to be derived from draughts of the sparkling waters varied in character. Certain fountains proved efficacious when the eyesight was affected; others such as St. Fillans and Strathill, Perthshire, were resorted to in cases of insanity; a spring near Ayr cured King Robert Bruce of his leprosy; that of Tobar-na-donhernid was believed to denote whether a sick person would overcome his complaint; one loch in Ross-shire is said to cure deafness, and so on. Water drawn from under a bridge "o'er which the living walked and the dead were carried," as well as south-running water, were reputed to possess wonderful properties. Those pilgrims who frequented wells for healing purposes, made votive-offerings to the guardian spirit of the water, or to the saints to whom they were dedicated. These generally consisted of pieces of cloth, thread, and other such simple materials—occasionally a small coin was deposited in the fountain. If trees and bushes grew in the immediate neighbourhood of these Siloams, to the branches of these the gifts were attached [Guthrie, ch.1].

"Their waters could quiet storms at sea, cure diseases and lameness, help the blind to see, the crippled to walk, aid the lovers in their quest for happiness, curse the enemy or the unwelcome neighbor, cure barrenness or toothache, help ensure a successful harvest" (Williams). Water to ancient peoples was holy as a symbol of life and also mysterious, as it jutted unexpectedly from the earth. "Where rivers flowed, or springs welled up out of the ground, or waterfalls thundered over rocks, there some divine force was felt to have its abode, and was worshipped in fear and hope by all who approached" (Hole 2472). These beliefs were deep-seated and lasted through the introduction of Christianity. Many springs were renamed after saints during the early conversion period, in order to induct pagan traditions into Christian practice. "This is why the first small churches were often built inside or near stone circles, or close to heathen holy springs, and the water of the latter was used for the baptism of converts" (Hole 2473). The Abbey of St. Anne de Beaupre in France has such a spring known for its healing properties. Jamie describes the "spirit of the spring" and points out that it's been there much longer than the monastery (*Outlander,* ch. 41).

St. Ninian's spring features in the first book and the sixth episode. Ninian was an early bringer of Christianity to Scotland. He reportedly arrived in Scotland during the fifth century, and did much missionary work. Bede's *Ecclesiastical History of the English People,* written around the year 730, is the earliest source. According to Bede, Ninian was "a most reverend bishop and holy man of British race, who had been ... instructed in the mysteries of the Christian Faith in Rome. Ninian's own Episcopal see, named after Saint Martin and famous for its stately church, is now held by the English." The place is called the White House because, unusually, he built the church of stone (148). The other two written sources about Ninian are an eighth-century Latin poem and a Saint's Life from the twelfth century. Both texts recount a series of miracles performed by Ninian, including his healing of the sick and his gift of speech to a newborn baby. A series of springs bear his name, even today.

> Sinavey Spring, in Mains parish, near the site of the ancient Castle of Fintry, is believed to represent St. Ninian's name in a corrupted form. His springs are numerous, and have a wide range from the counties of Wigtown and Kirkcudbright to those of Forfar and Kincardine. There is a well to him near Dunnottar Castle, in the last-mentioned county. In the island of Sanda, off the Kintyre coast, is a spring named after him. It had a considerable local celebrity in former times. St. Ninian's Well in Stirling is a familiar spot in the district [MacKinlay, ch. 3].

Dougal takes Claire to drink from the water as he asks whether she's a spy. As he tells her, "The water smells o' the fumes of hell. Anyone who drinks the water and then tells untruth will ha' the gizzard burned out of him" (ch. 13). Later, Joan, who has the Second Sight, meets a young woman here and says she'll have a healthy child ("The Space Between" 221). This is only one of many sacred springs in Scotland.

> St. Mungo's Well in Huntly, St. Fergon's Well near Inverloohy, the well at Metheshirin near Dufftown, the well of Moulblairie in Banffshire, St. Colman's Well in the parish of Killarn. in Ross-shire, Culboakie, also in Ross-shire, St. Mary's Well in the birch wood above Culloderx House, the Craigie Well in the Black Isles opposite Inverness, the Wallaek Well, and the Corsmall Well, at Glass in Banffshire, together with "these superstitious round-earth wells of Menteith," are still resorted to by the common people. Miss Gordon Gumming tells us, that among the various efforts made to check the favourite well worship two centuries ago, was an order from the Privy Council appointing com missioners to wait at Christ's Well in Menteith on the 1st May, and to seize all who might assemble at the spring, and imprison them in Doune Castle [Guthrie, ch.19].

While the church considered reverencing the springs a pagan act, many people continued to visit and still do, praying to the saints and to the older spirits of the sacred places for healing and guidance.

Saints

As her new baby stares into space, Marsali notes, "Oh, the wee ones still see heaven, my Mam said. Maybe there's an angel sitting on your shoulder, aye? Or a saint who stands behind ye" (*A Breath of Snow and Ashes*, ch. 38). Saints were another part of daily life in the Highlands, as everyone seems to swear by "Jesus, Mary, Michael, and Bride," or some combination thereof.

Carmichael notes of those who still practice the Celtic ways:

Roman Catholicism prevails in Benbecula, South Uist, and Barra, and in their dedicatory hymn the people of these islands invoke, besides the Trinity, St. Michael of the three-cornered shield and flaming sword, patron of the horses; St. Columba of the holy deeds, guardian of their cattle; Bride of the clustering hair, the foster-mother of Christ; and the golden-haired Virgin, mother of the White Lamb. As the people intone their prayers on the lonely hill-side, literally in the wilderness, the music of their evensong floats over glen and dell, loch and stream, and is echoed from corrie and cliff till it is lost on the soft evening air [Vol. 1, 192].

Bride, Christ's midwife, was of course mingled with the Christian legend as Brigid transformed from her former status as Celtic goddess. Saints taking on attributes of past gods were quite common, as were churches, statues, and holy sites appropriated from older gods. Visiting the church of St. Kilda and beholding a statue of her, Roger comments, "It was probably one of the pagan gods to start with.... You can see where they added the veil and wimple to the original figure" (*Dragonfly in Amber,* ch. 5).

St. Michael, the patron saint of the sea, is particularly significant to the people of the Highlands. "He seems to have taken over some of the attributes of the earlier pagan protectors; for many centuries, he was spoken of as 'the god Michael,' or even as *brian* Michael (Brian was one of the three chief gods of pagan Ireland, a son of Danu, the mother goddess)" (Williams). His festival, Michaelmas, was marked with horse racing along the sands, with sun-dried seaweed used in place of whips. It was customary (an even legal on this particular holiday) to steal a neighbor's horse for the race, safely returning it later. The old customs appear transplanted onto the new deity in a quiet transition.

St. Andrew is the patron saint of Scotland. One of Jesus's disciples, he roamed far over the earth, possibly even visiting Scotland and building a church in Fife, according to some legends. This, the town of St. Andrews, became a popular spot for British pilgrimages. Other legends have his relics brought here after his death. It is said that he believed himself unworthy to be crucified on a cross like Christ's, so he died on a saltire, or X-shaped cross, today called St. Andrew's Cross, a symbol of Scotland and part of the Union Jack. His feast day is November 30.

In Boston, Claire visits St. Finbar's Roman Catholic Church (one by this name is actually located in Brooklyn, New York).

> "St. Finbar?" Frank had said incredulously. "There isn't such a saint. There can't possibly be."
> "There is," I said, with a trace of smugness. "An Irish bishop, from the twelfth century."
> "Oh, Irish," said Frank dismissively. "That explains it" [*Voyager,* ch. 3].

The Irish St. Finbar, patron saint of the city of Cork, Ireland, actually lived in the sixth century, but Claire is fallible after all. He lived in "an Corcach Mór" (Great Marsh), now the city of Cork, where he gathered many students. University College Cork's motto became "Ionad Bairre Sgoil na Mumhan" ("Where Finbar taught let Munster learn") in his honor.

Describing the Abbey of Ste. Anne de Beaupre's monks to Claire, Jamie calls them "the holy brothers of St. Dominic" (ch. 14). Dominic of course founded the Dominican Order, who are strongly associated with the rosary. In *Voyager*, Jamie is seen wearing a rosary for twenty years. St. Dominic also is the patron saint of falsely accused people.

Brother Anselm at the Abbey is a significant homage. St. Anselm of Canterbury was a philosopher, famous as the originator of the ontological argument for the existence of God—if God can be conceived of, He must exist. His emphasis on free will as a gift of God also connects him with Father Anselm, who advises Claire to use hers. St. Anselm of Canterbury also inspired Claire's friend Mother Hildegarde with his care for people's "temporal needs as well as those of the spirit." After reading of him, Hildegarde wants to follow him in leading "an eminently useful life" (*Dragonfly in Amber*, ch.15).

Meanwhile, Fergus wears a greenish medal of St. Dismas, patron saint of second chances, prisoners, criminals, and reformed thieves. Dismas is the name given for the Penitent Thief, also known as the Thief on the Cross who was crucified alongside Jesus and asked Jesus to remember him in his kingdom. As stated in *The Drums of Autumn*, Fergus leaves his wife under the protection of his medallion. Claire thinks: "I wouldn't myself have thought that mothers and babies fell into the sphere of influence of the patron saint of thieves, but Fergus had lived as a pickpocket for all his early life, and his trust in Dismas was absolute" (ch. 8).

Jamie knows an enormous list of saints and offers Claire a list of patron saints of abducted persons when Claire asks. He says he learned them from Brother Polycarp, at the Abbey of St. Anne, who would tell the stories when Jamie was restless. Jamie adds, "It didna always put me to sleep, but after an hour or so of hearing about holy martyrs having their breasts amputated or being flogged wi' iron hooks, I'd close my eyes and make a decent pretense of it" (*A Breath of Snow and Ashes*, ch. 72). He reads tales of saints and martyrs to little Marsali and Joan, inspiring the latter's vocation as a nun.

Meanwhile, Claire jokes about Saint Ferreolus, the patron saint of sick poultry, demonstrating that her knowledge rivals Jamie's (*The Drums of Autumn*, ch. 65). Even Roger, a Protestant, chimes in, quoting Saint Teresa of Avila and adding, "I take advice where I can get it" (*Written in My Own Heart's Blood*, ch. 44).

Talismans

Catholic talismans included Saints' relics and crucifixes as well as other tokens. A portrait of La Infanta Maria Ana con Sonajeros shows the young Spanish princess decked in a medal of her patron saint, several crucifixes, a malachite lozenge and spring of coral to guard her, and a closed fist carved from jet to protect from the evil eye as well as a mounted animal tooth for luck and pomander with protective spices, as Miranda Bruce-Mitford explains in *The Illustrated Book of Signs and Symbols* (41).

A reliquary of Saint Orgevald is important in "Lord John and the Succubus." According to legend, he stopped people from buying poor children and walling them up in foundations and bridges to guard them from the wicked crossing through (113). Other relics were used as powerful charms across the Highlands: St Drostan's bones were preserved in a stone tomb at Aberdovvyr, where they healed many. Those who drank the water in which St. Marnock's head was washed every Sunday were healed as well. The bell of St. Fillan could cure insanity. The staff of St. Fergus, cast into the waves, caused a storm to cease (Black).

In the books, Colum gives Claire a jet rosary with an inlaid silver crucifix in appreciation for her efforts in helping his mare foal (*Outlander,* ch. 24). The rosary beads suggest the bonds of the community and the diverse skills Claire is using to bond different people at Castle Leoch. Also a religious symbol, it saves Claire during the witch trial—Jamie dramatically tosses it over her head to show she's not a witch, quoting the phrase that "Jet will burn a witch's skin," and showing she's unmarked (*Outlander,* ch. 25). Jet is particularly apt for this. "When in direct contact with the skin, jet was believed to become part of a person's body and soul and to safeguard the wearer" (Bruce-Mitford 38).

The only talisman Jamie keeps during his time in prison and paroled at Helwater is a rosary of ash beads, carved for him by his sister. As he notes, he's only allowed to keep them because they're not worth anything to the English. The name comes from the rose, symbol of Mary, emphasizing its link with the feminine in Jamie's life—only his sister, as he's far from Claire. After wearing it for many years, he passes the rosary on to young Willie as he returns to Lallybroch and Jenny. Later in *Voyager,* he's seen with a replacement rosary. He tells Claire that it looks gnawed because he lets Jenny's grandchildren teethe on it as it provides a further link between him and his family.

LOCAL LEGENDS

Claire hears water dripping and recalls "an old Highland superstition—the 'death drop.' Just before a death occurs, the story goes, the sound of water dripping is heard in the house" (*Voyager,* ch. 36). People's daily lives in the High-lands were filled with such superstitions—one had to get out of bed on the right foot or kneed the last few oats into a special extra cake. Fairies were always present: "Just as it was held highly unlucky for a boy to sweep the floor after a death, some would not have the floor swept after food was cooked or partaken of. The fragments that fell on the floor belonged to the household spirit or *sithich, i.e.* the 'fairy'" (G. Henderson 252). These little stories and bits of folk wisdom fill the books as colorful background.

The Dunbonnet

In *Voyager,* Claire reads of the unusual formation of Leap o' the Cask, named for an incident with a servant and a Jacobite laird in hiding in a cave for seven years after Culloden. He was only known as the "Dunbonnet," to avoid any chance of giving him away to the English patrols.

> *"One day, a boy bringing a cask of ale up the trail to the laird's cave met a group of English dragoons. Bravely refusing either to answer the soldiers' questions, or to give up his burden, the boy was attacked by one of the dragoons, and dropped the cask, which bounded down the steep hill, and into the burn below"* [*Voyager* ch. 3, italics in original].

Brianna points out that this may be Jamie, disguising his red hair under a dun-bonnet or "dull brown bonnet." While this is a local legend, it's based in history rather than myth. As Roger notes, most of the history of the Highlands is oral, up to the mid-nineteenth century or so. "So far as the Scottish Highlands go, scholars who wrote the stories down often didn't know for sure which they were dealing with, either—sometimes it was a combination of fact and myth, and sometimes you could tell that it was a real historical occurrence being described" (*Voyager* ch. 3).

Dun Bonnet is a cave near Foyers on Loch Ness. Gabaldon comments, "Leap o' the Cask is real—so is the story of the laird who hid in the cave for seven years, whose tenants called him the Dunbonnet, and his servant, who brought the ale to him in hiding. His name? Ah ... James Fraser. Really" ("FAQ"). One of the sources is the actual book *History of the Frasers* by Alex MacKenzie. This is an alias of Jamie Fraser, just to add to the blurring of fiction and reality.

Mary Grant

Touring Loch Ness, Frank and Claire learn from their guide of Mary Grant, daughter of the laird of Urquhart Castle, and her lover, Donald Donn, poet son of MacDonald of Bohuntin. As the chronicle of the Invernesshire Parish recounts: Mary, daughter of the Laird of Grant, lived in Urquhart Castle and fell in love with Donald. "But her father refused to have him for his son-in-law, and forbade ail intercourse between them. They, however, found opportunities of meeting secretly on the wooded banks of Loch Ness." When the Laird of Grant discovered Donald and his companions had stolen some of his cattle, he swore, "The Devil may take me out of my shoes, if Donald Donn is not hanged!"

Pursued by soldiers but still desperate to stay by Mary, Donald hid in a near-inaccessible cave in Glaic-Ruidh-Bhacain, still known as Uamh Dhomhnuill Duinn—Donald Donn's Cave. There he composed songs to his lady love. However, his pursuers discovered where he hid. Unable to reach the cave in force themselves, they sent Donald a message that appeared to be from Mary. He went to a nearby house to meet her, but sixty-three of his enemies attacked. He fought his way free and ran for his life. But he slipped and fell, and was dragged to the Castle dungeon. Convicted of cattle-stealing, he begged for one favor before sentence of death was passed upon him—he asked that he should be beheaded like a gentleman, instead of hanged. When the sentence was pronounced, he cried, "The Devil will take the Laird of Grant out of his shoes, and Donald Donn shall not be hanged!" He was executed, and the legend tells that as his severed head rolled from the block, his tongue uttered the appeal, "Mary, lift my head!" (MacKay 189–190).

Hearing this story, Claire shudders and squeezes Frank's hand. As she thinks, "As story after story of treachery, murder, and violence were recounted, it seemed as though the loch had earned its sinister reputation" (*Outlander,* ch. 2). For Claire, this becomes a prelude to the brutal history of cattle-stealing, clan feuds and executions in the Highlands, to say nothing of tragic love and ghost stories. Soon enough she finds herself living all of these, transformed from a modern tourist to a page in history.

Rat Satires

Roger insists that he can drive away rats by composing a spontaneous poem, satirizing the rats and telling them where they can find better prospects, concluding:

> Go and fill your bellies,
> Dinna stay and gnaw my wellies—
> Go, ye rats, go!" [*Dragonfly in Amber,* ch. 4]

This is yet another Scottish tradition that Gabaldon incorporates into her books. This can be considered a form of spell—words so strong the animals are compelled to obey. One wonders if the magic in Roger's lineage actually makes the spell more effective. John Gregorson Campbell writes:

> When a place is infested to a troublesome extent with rats or mice, and all other means of getting rid of the pests have failed, the object can be accom-

plished by composing a song, advising them to go away, telling them where to go, and what road to take, the danger awaiting them where they are, and the plenty awaiting them in their new quarters. This song is called the Rat (or Mouse) Satire, and if well composed the vermin forthwith take their departure.

When the islet of Calv (an Calbh, the inner door), which lies across the mouth of Tobermory harbour, was let in small holdings, the rats at one time became so numerous that the tenants subscribed sixpence a-piece, and sent for Iain Pholchrain to Morven, to come and satirize the rats away. He came and made a long ode, in which he told the rats to go away peaceably, and take care not to lose themselves in the wood. He told them what houses to call at, and what houses (those of the bard's own friends) to avoid, and the plenty and welcome stores—butter and cheese, and meal—to be got at their destination. It is said that after this there was an observable decrease in the number of rats in the island! [225–226]

An Ardnamurchan man, pestered with mice, herded them onto a ship and composed a rat satire for them:

> The sea roaring boisterously.
> The ocean heaving and weltering,
> The tearing sound of sails splitting.
> The creaking of the keel breaking.
> The bilge water through the hull splashing
> Like an old horse neighing.

According to legend, it was successful (J.G. Campbell 225–226).

The Sprightly Tailor

In *Voyager,* Claire and Roger quote from an old Scottish fairytale not found in Grimms:

> "'See'st thou this great gray head, with jaws which have no meat?'" Roger quoted. "You know the story? The little tailor who spent the night in a haunted church, and met the hungry ghost?"
> "I do. I think if I'd heard that outside my window, I'd have spent the rest of the night hiding under the bedclothes" [ch. 22].

The story they're referencing is called "The Sprightly Tailor," collected by Joseph Jacobs (1854–1916). The little tailor must sew a suit in a haunted church, but he bravely keeps sewing and ignores the giant who appears and rises through the floor. "I see those, but I'll sew this!" answers the tailor to each revealed limb, until he finally escapes, finished trews in hand, just ahead of his adversary. In the book's version, this is a ghost, nodding to Claire's many hauntings. In fact, she meets them all with courage and practicality, emphasizing her commonality with the tailor.

MAGICAL ANIMALS

Deer/Stag

Jamie has a prized cloak brooch of two deer chasing each other—Frank particularly notices this upon seeing Jamie's ghost at the story's beginning. Deer in legend feed saints in the forest and aid hermits in their cave, suggesting the deer as an embodiment of the magical, protective forest. In Celtic Europe "The Horned One," Cernunnos is depicted with ram horns or antlers. He is a god of fertility and wild animals, sharing those characteristic with Jamie himself. As Jamie "lives wild" in the forest or trains horses, he seems a part of nature as well as the story's romantic lead.

In myth, the deer is a magical creature, able to move between the worlds. Humans in legend are often transformed into deer—St. Patrick transformed himself and his companions into deer in order to escape a trap laid by a pagan king and Fionn Mac Cumhaill wed a deer-woman. Deer thus suggest a primitive link to the wilderness, and in Scotland, they are said to be the fairies' cattle. In the Welsh tale of "Culhwch and Olwen" from *The Mabinogion,* the stag is one of the oldest animals in the world. It stands for solitary nobility, as well as honor, stern justice, and protection of its herd, as it defends mates and children. Jamie of course offers all these qualities as well.

The antlers, compared to tree-branches, represent nature and fertility. Their regrowth each year symbolizes rejuvenation and rebirth. Cernunnos is also linked with the Celtic Underworld god who leads the Wild Hunt through the sky. Jamie of course has nearly died almost nine times and seems to have one foot already in the grave. And as he points out to Claire, in the twentieth century he's long dead (whatever the final cause), and only the possibility of his wandering ghost still exists. Nonetheless, his ghost appears to be watching over his family in an unearthly resurrection.

Plovers

Just after their wedding, Jamie tells Claire the tale that plovers were once human (*Outlander,* ch. 17). "Plovers have the souls of young mothers dead in childbirth," he says. "The story goes that they cry and run about their nests because they canna believe the young are safe hatched; they're mourning always for the lost one—or looking for a child left behind."

The plover guards her nest in a way that evokes a human woman protecting her children. At the same time the bird's sad-sounding cry makes its call an omen of death. "A cuckoo calling from the roof predicted the death of an inhabitant, as did the call of a golden plover at night" (Sutherland 47). J.G. Campbell adds,

"A golden plover (*Feadag, Charadrius pluvialis*), heard at night, portends the near approach of death or other evil. The cry of the bird is a melancholy wailing note" (256). While the scene provides local color and an opportunity for Jamie to allude to his mother, dead in childbirth, there is more foreshadowing. Dark moments follow, interrupting Jamie and Claire's brief wedded joy.

Ravens

Several times in the novels, ravens appear over battlefields, emphasizing the carnage to come. *Voyager* begins with the chapter "The Corbies' Feast," stressing the devastation of Culloden. On seeing crows (symbolically and biologically similar to ravens), Roger recalls the ominous lyrics of "The Twa Corbies," a ballad of a pair of crows picking over a corpse. Revolted, he hurls a stone at them and drives them off. "But his belly was still knotted, and the words of the corbies' mocking song echoed in his ears." As he leaves, the disembodied voices repeat to him: "Ye'll sit on his white hause-bane/and I'll pick oot his bonny blue e'en. Wi' ae lock o' his golden hair/we'll theek oor nest when it grows bare" (ch. 87). Doom, of course, is coming.

Ravens were most often an omen of death for eating carnage but also for their black feathers. *Bean Sidhes* (Banshees) could take the shape of ravens as they cried above a roof, foretelling death in the household below. The Scottish goddess of winter, the Cailleach, also appeared as a raven and brought death with her touch. In the late nineteenth century, the seer Angus McDonald prophesized, "The beginning of the troubles was to see a white raven. The next sign was to see a white crow" (Sutherland 131).

Tha gliocas an ceann an fhitich is a Gaelic proverb meaning, "There is wisdom in a raven's head." Ravens as birds of knowledge appear throughout myth, especially in Odin's two ravens, Huginn (Thought) and Muninn (Memory) who flew about the world, delivering messages, gathering knowledge and reporting back to him. Giving a child his first drink from the skull of a raven was said to give the child powers of prophecy and wisdom in the Hebrides. Scottish Highlanders also associate ravens with the gift of Second Sight.

In "The Legend of Eilean Donan Castle," the son of a chief in Kintail drinks from a raven's skull and acquires the power of communicating with birds. He goes to France and does marvelous feats for the king and returns home, fulfilling a prophecy he gave as a child that his father would serve him at their table. Thus he links the gifts of second sight, animal communication, and perceptive wisdom. As an acknowledgement of his great power, the laird asks him to build a great castle to defend their allies from the Norse invaders—he who is raised by the ravens becomes a protector of Scotland as well (Wilson 49–55).

White Raven

In the New World, the local tribes call Claire White Raven for her wisdom and gifts. The wisewoman Nayawenne's granddaughter tells Claire that Nayawenne dreamed of her: "She met you here, at night. The moon was in the water. You became a white raven; you flew over the water and swallowed the moon." In the dream, this raven lays an egg with a shining stone within, and Nayawenne knows that this is "great magic, that the stone could heal sickness" (*The Drums of Autumn,* ch. 20).

Nayawenne then shows Claire a large sapphire and gives Claire a special amulet of her own. She tells Claire that she will gain her greatest power when her hair is white, and in a later book, when Claire heals Henry Grey, "He looked up at her, a great white bird." More skill may be coming to her with the raven's blessings.

The Cherokee believe that her pale skin means she's supernaturally gifted and also better equipped to deal with the ghost bear that's troubling them. As Claire thinks to herself: "Evidently the people of Tsatsa'wi's town had heard of White Raven as well as the Bear-Killer. Any white animal was regarded as being significant—and often sinister. I didn't know whether the implication here was that I might exert some power over the ghost-bear—or merely serve as bait" (*The Fiery Cross,* ch. 81).

White ravens in myth might mean hope or terrible doom—to the Native Americans of the Midwest, seeing one presaged the end of the world. In Celtic lore, ravens with white feathers were a good omen of blessing and spiritual cleansing, especially if they had white on the wings. While many animals can be born albino, there is a genetic possibility for a white raven—from an incredibly rare gene, even less likely to be found in both halves of a mated pair. Thus its uniqueness, like Claire's with her own genetic components, makes it a bird of great omen.

White Animals

Young Ian adds later that white animals in dreams bring messages and he sees a white bird bringing him an arcane message:

> He'd dreamed during the night, and the dream was still on him, though he couldn't recall the details. He'd been in thick woods, and something was there with him, hiding among the leaves. He wasn't sure what it was, or even if he'd seen it, but the sense of danger lingered uneasily between his shoulder blades. He'd heard a raven calling in his dream, and that was certainly a warning of some kind—but then the raven had flown past him, and it wasn't a raven at all but a white bird of some kind. Its wing had touched his cheek in flight, and he could still feel the brush of its feathers.

White animals were messengers. Both the Mohawk and the Highlanders said so [*Written in My Own Heart's Blood*, ch. 57].

In danger, Brianna meets an owl and reflects that white animals meant good luck in Celtic folklore. As she adds to herself, "Owls are keepers of the dead but not just the dead. They're messengers between worlds" (*Written in My Own Heart's Blood,* ch. 36). Ian may be seeing a white raven, or he may be seeing the same white owl, bringing a message from Brianna in another time.

In the fourth book, Jamie and Claire acquire a ferocious white sow, known for terrorizing men and animals and mating with wild boars in the forest. In Celtic myth, the mother goddess Cerridwen is a white sow that eats corpses in a symbol of death and rebirth. As such, she's a symbol of the white moon, waxing and waning through the month. Claire and Jamie's pig suggests the untamed female spirit and also a powerful Old World goddess guarding their domain.

Celtic heroes pursue supernatural beasts from the Otherworld, and nearly all are white. Because of their coloring, they were considered intermediaries between the real and fairy worlds. King Arthur hunts a white deer, which leads him to Sir Pellinore. In the Welsh epic *The Mabinogion,* Prince Pwyll encounters King Arawn's otherworld dogs, which are "glittering bright white" with bright red ears (Ford 37). Pryderi and Manawydan pursue a "gleaming white boar" (Ford 80) into a magical trap while hunting, and the goddess Rhiannon enters the human world riding from a fairy mound on a white horse (Ford 42–45).

In book five, the Cherokee decide a ghost bear is menacing them. Jamie reports: "The thing was much bigger than the usual bear, he says—and pure white. He says when it turned to look at him, the beast's eyes glowed red as flame. They kent at once it must be a ghost, and so they werena really surprised that their arrows didna touch it" (*The Fiery Cross,* ch. 81). The ghost bear is revealed as most likely a real bear—yet still king of the forest and supernaturally ferocious, with more than a touch of magic.

In the sixth chapter of Book of Revelation, one of the Four Horsemen of the Apocalypse, Death, rides upon a pale horse. Lord John is called upon to exorcise a succubus by riding a white horse over its grave in "Lord John and the Succubus"—the first chapter is titled "Death Rides a Pale Horse" as a nod to this lore. This links with the Bible and its concept of the afterlife but also the banishing of ghosts through the power of the otherworld and its animal representative.

In a more mystical moment, Lord John describes the ordinary magic of a white deer that "looks as though it's made of silver" to explain that he wouldn't want to tame it, even if he could, though "it is a sight of rare beauty"—his affairs follow a similar course: "It comes for two nights, three—rarely, four—and then it's gone, and I don't see it again for weeks, sometimes months. And then it comes again, and I am enchanted once more," he concludes (*An Echo in the Bone*, ch. 95). He regards his visitor as a blessing, and indeed, it brings magic to his nights.

PEOPLE AND THEIR TALENTS
Blessings and Charms

Jocasta Cameron offers Brianna a charm to protect her new baby from fairies. This is "a small pierced-work tin brooch, rather tarnished, made in the shape of a heart." Jocasta calls it a deasil charm, and adds, "Keep it pinned to the lad's smock—always to the back, mind—and naught born of the Auld Folk will trouble him" (*The Fiery Cross*, ch. 41). "Deasil" is a Gaelic term meaning southward or sunward. "To walk deasil" means to walk in a circle clockwise with the sun—from east, towards the south, to west, to north, back to east. This gives the quester all the power of the heavens, together with the rightness of the right handed path. A pagan variant of drawing down the power of the sun, it is associated with blessings and good health. Though Brianna hesitates, the old motherhood ritual has a profound effect, welcoming her into the deeper mysticism of Scottish culture. "The hair on Brianna's forearms prickled slightly at the matter-of-factness in the old woman's voice" and she feels a sense of the ancient magic. Holding a small torch, she walks "sunwise" three times around the cradle, while Jocasta recites in Gaelic from the *Carmina Gadelica* Volume III:

> *Wisdom of serpent be thine,*
> *Wisdom of raven be thine,*
> *Wisdom of valiant eagle.*
> *Voice of swan be thine,*
> *Voice of honey be thine,*
> *Voice of the Son of the stars.*
> *Sain of the fairy-woman be thine,*
> *Sain of the elf-dart be thine,*
> *Sain of the red dog be thine.*
> *Bounty of sea be thine,*
> *Bounty of land be thine,*
> *Bounty of the Father of Heaven.*
> *Be each day glad for thee,*
> *No day ill for thee,*
> *A life joyful, satisfied* [240].

After following Jocasta's orders, she finds "to her fascination that she did not find any of this even faintly ridiculous. Odd, but very satisfying to think that she was protecting Jem from harm—even harm from fairies, which she didn't personally believe in. Or she hadn't, before this" (*The Fiery Cross*, ch. 41).

Unsurprisingly, the brooch and charm are traditional Scottish.

> Small brooches of silver in the form of a heart, such as were in common use in Scotland at the end of the seventeenth century and throughout the eighteenth as personal ornaments, were also believed to be endowed with the property of protecting children from witchcraft and enchantment. An interesting account of the manner in which such brooches were used in the beginning of this century is given by the Rev. James Hall, who states that he saw one fastened to an infant's clothes in a clergyman's house in Speyside, and adds, "This was done by the nurse; the clergyman was certain it could be of no use, but allowed it to continue, as one and all the females in the house were of a different opinion. They always fix it to girls, somewhere to the clothes about the left hip, and on boys about the middle of the left thigh, to protect his powers of generation" [Black].

Their world of witchcraft and magic held numerous charms for protecting one's loved ones and possessions from harm. Frequently this took the form of religion—baptism, the name of God, personal prayers. Other times, the rituals seem far more pagan in origin. While Jocasta's fairy charm mentions the "Father in Heaven," references to fairies as well as serpent, raven, and sea appear far older. One scholar mentions "It is still possible, in the Highlands, to serve two masters, and nowhere are all forgotten far-off things so intimately connected with our modern mysteries of faith."

> There are baptisms and sacraments, unknown to the strict authorities of the faith, and the charms in *Carmina Gadelica* prove how recently the western islanders still offered tribute to the unknown gods. "Three days before being sown, the seed is sprinkled with clear cold water, in the name of Father, and of Son, and of Spirit, the person sprinkling the seed walking sunwise the while"; and in harvest, "the father of the family took up his sickle, and, facing the sun, cut a handful of corn. Putting the handful three tunes round his head, the man raised the 'Iollach Buanat or reaping salutation."'... What, for example, could be at once more genuinely Christian, and at the same time Pagan, than this charm, with which they guarded their cattle from harm:
>
> > "The prosperity of Mary Mother be yours;
> > Active and full may you return.
> > From rocks, from drifts, from streams,
> > From crooked passes, from destructive pits,
> > From the straight arrows of the slender ban-shee,
> > From the heart of envy, from the eye of evil" [Morison Vol. IV, 206].

This charm similarly blends the newer Christian traditions with older fears of the banshee, a spirit of a wailing woman. Many more Christian-Pagan rituals abound in the series, all from authentic Scottish culture. In a late book, Jenny gathers goats with a Gàidhlig livestock charm from the *Carmina Gadelica* Volume 1, p. 289:

"The Three who are above in the City of glory,
Be shepherding my flock and my kine,
Tending them duly in heat, in storm, and in cold,
With the blessing of power driving them down
From yonder height to the sheiling fold"
[*Written in My Own Heart's Blood*, ch. 142]

This appears to begin with an appeal to the Trinity, but the longer version may invoke a far older power.

Some charms of course were far less benign. Mrs. Bug describes a well-known love spell from Scotland, noting, "There's some charms that take grave dust, ken, and some the dust of bones, or the ashes of a body." She adds that "seaweed, bones, and a flat rock" are a love charm ominously called "the Venom o' the North Wind." She recites it for Brianna, with a list of ingredients from foxglove and butterbur to "Three bones of an old man, newly torn from the grave" (*A Breath of Snow and Ashes*, ch. 49).

Gabaldon explains the source for many of her protective charms: The scholar Alexander Carmichael collected an enormous amount of traditional Gaelic oral lore: charms, chants, poems, prayers, and much more. Gabaldon adds, "I used small bits of several of the invocations and prayers from this huge collection, as seemed appropriate to the occasion" (*Outlandish Companion* 526).

In one of the late books, the school principal asks Roger to teach a Gaelic class for the children and he speedily agrees. He uses the *Carmina Gadelica* in a delightful homage:

He'd brought one volume of the *Gadelica* with him, and while he passed the ancient hymnal round the room, along with a booklet of waulking songs he'd put together, he read them one of the charms of the new moon, the Cud Chewing Charm, the Indigestion Spell, the Poem of the Beetle, and some bits from "The Speech of Birds" [*An Echo in the Bone*, ch. 46].

Here are the prayers and charms, taken from the authentic ancient lore to be said by Jamie and his friends in times of trial.

THE BATTLE TO COME

JESUS, Thou Son of Mary, I call on Thy name,
And on the name of John the apostle beloved,
And on the names of all the saints in the red domain,
To shield me in the battle to come,
To shield me in the battle to come.

When the mouth shall be closed,
When the eye shall be shut,
When the breath shall cease to rattle,
When the heart shall cease to throb,
When the heart shall cease to throb.

When the Judge shall take the throne,
And when the cause is fully pleaded,
O Jesu, Son of Mary, shield Thou my soul,
O Michael fair, acknowledge my departure.
O Jesu, Son of Mary, shield Thou my soul!
O Michael fair, receive my departure! [Vol. 1, 113]

SOUL PEACE

SINCE Thou Christ it was who didst buy the soul—
At the time of yielding the life,
At the time of pouring the sweat,
At the time of offering the clay,
At the time of shedding the blood,
At the time of balancing the beam,
At the time of severing the breath,
At the time of delivering the judgment,
Be its peace upon Thine own ingathering;
Jesus Christ Son of gentle Mary,
Be its peace upon Thine own ingathering,
O Jesus! upon Thine own ingathering.
And may Michael white kindly,
High king of the holy angels,
Take possession of the beloved soul,
And shield it home to the Three of surpassing love,
Oh! to the Three of surpassing love [Vol. 1, 121].

Gabaldon adds: "This is the prayer that Jamie recommends to Young Ian, for use when one has been compelled to kill in battle or in self-defense. Or, if time is too short to allow for this, he recommends the shorter version, "Soul Leading" (*Outlandish Companion* 528).

THE SOUL LEADING

By this soul on Thine arm, O Christ, Thou King of the City of Heaven. Amen.
Since Thou, O Christ, it was who brought'st this soul,
Be its peace on Thine own keeping. Amen.
And may the strong Michael, high king of the angels,
Be preparing the path before this soul, O God. Amen.
Oh! the strong Michael in peace with thee, soul,
And preparing for thee the w ay to the kingdom of the Son of God.
Amen [Vol. 1, 117].

Unfortunately, Jamie must pray for the dead quite often in his journeys. After a truly unsettling moment, he offers a very short traditional Celtic invocation, called "The Death Blessing" from *Carmina Gadelica*: "God, omit not this woman from Thy covenant, and the many evils that she in the body committed" (Vol. 1, 119).

On another occasion, he gives a longer funeral prayer: "Jamie took a deep breath and a step to the head of the grave. He spoke the Gaelic prayer called the Death Dirge, but in English, for the sake of Fanny and Lord John." This too is from *Carmina Gadelica* (Vol. 3, 383).

> Thou goest home this night to thy home of winter,
> To thy home of autumn, of spring, and of summer;
> Thou goest home this night to thy perpetual home,
> To thine eternal bed, to thine eternal slumber.
> Sleep thou, sleep, and away with thy sorrow,
> Sleep thou, sleep, and away with thy sorrow,
> Sleep thou, sleep, and away with thy sorrow;
> Sleep, thou beloved, in the Rock of the fold
> [*Written in My Own Heart's Blood,* ch. 134].

Of course, there are charms for good times and celebrations as well. In book four, Jamie and his friends dedicate a new house. Jamie forms a cross with his knife and asks God's blessing on his people and his farm. He then buries iron and places the hearthstone on it to ensure blessing and prosperity. The men circle the house with a torch, chanting words from a more Pagan time, this time in Gaelic, not English:

> The safeguard of Fionn MacCumhall be yours,
> The safeguard of Cormac the Shapely be yours,
> The safeguard of Conn and Cumhall be yours,
> From wolf and from birdflock
> From wolf and from birdflock.
> The Shield of the King of Fiann be yours
> The shield of the king of the sun be yours
> The shield of the king of the stars be yours
> In jeopardy and distress
> In jeopardy and distress
> The sheltering of the King of Kings be yours
> The sheltering of Jesus Christ be yours
> The sheltering of the spirit of Healing be yours
> From evil deed and quarrel
> From evil dog and reddog [*The Drums of Autumn,* ch. 19].

This comes from "House Protecting" (Vol. 1, page 103) and "The Driving" (Vol. 1, 43) in *Carmina Gadelica*. Both ancient folk heroes and the Christian trinity are summoned to bless and protect the house from all ills.

The Brahan Seer

A farm labourer called Coinneach Odhar, otherwise known as Kenneth Mackenzie from Lewis, started making predictions of the future around the same time as Nostradamus. He made many of his prophecies on the Brahan estates where the powerful Seaforth MacKenzies lived. The Brahan Seer's "Second Sight" was reputed to come from a small blue and black stone with a hole in the center, which a spirit had given to his mother. He predicted the Battle of Culloden and the demise of the Highland way of life; in one prediction he was walking on Drummossie moor when he said, "Thy bleak wilderness will be stained by the best blood of the Highlands. Glad I am that I will not live to see that day where heads will be lopped off in the heather and no lives spared." In another prediction he said that "the clans will become so effeminate as to flee from their native country before an army of sheep," referencing the Highland Clearances.

His powers finally ended his life: while his employer the Earl of Seaforth was in Paris, his wife Isabella called for Coinneach Odhar and asked him to tell her how her husband was. The seer reluctantly admitted that her husband was on his knees in front of a French lady fairer than herself. Lady Isabella had him executed.

As Frank Randall describes the incident in a letter, "The Seer came to a sticky end, as prophets often do (do please remember that, darling, will you?), burnt to death in a spiked barrel of tar at the instigation of Lady Seaforth—to whom he had unwisely prophesied that her husband was having affairs with various ladies while away in Paris. (That one was likely true, in my opinion.)" (*Written in My Own Heart's Blood*, ch. 42)

As he was being dragged off to meet his fate he made his last and most chilling prediction as a curse on the family of MacKenzie; "The line of Seaforth will come to an end in sorrow. I see the last head of his house both deaf and dumb. He will be the father of four fair sons, all of whom he will follow to the tomb. He will live careworn, and die mourning, knowing that the honours of his line are to be extinguished forever, that no future chief of the Mackenzies shall bear rule at Brahan or in Kintail." In 1783, Francis Humberston Mackenzie inherited the title. He was indeed deaf and mute due to a childhood attack of scarlet fever. He had four children all of whom died prematurely fulfilling the final prophesy.

The Brahan Seer's fame rests on a best-selling book by Alexander Mackenzie published in 1877—it's unclear whether the man ever truly lived. His prophecies, however, fit well into Scottish history: "Strange as it may seem to you this day, time will come, and it is not far off, when full-rigged ships will be seen sailing eastward and westward by the back of Tomnahurich, near Inverness." 150 years later, the Caledonian Canal was built, linking the Lochs along the Great Glen.

Frank Randall adds that the seer predicted "that when there were five bridges over the River Ness, the world would fall into chaos. In August 1939, the fifth bridge over the Ness was opened, and in September, Hitler invaded Poland. Quite enough chaos for anyone" (*Written in My Own Heart's Blood,* ch. 42)

Frank writes a letter to Brianna telling her some details that he guessed about Jamie and Claire. As he adds:

> I think you won't have heard of the Brahan Seer. Colorful as he was—if, in fact, he existed—he's not really known much beyond those circles with a taste for the more outlandish aspects of Scottish history....
>
> ...
>
> Amongst his lesser-known prophecies, though, was one called the Fraser Prophecy. There isn't a great deal known about this, and what there is is rambling and vague, as prophecies usually are, the Old Testament notwithstanding. The only relevant bit, I think, is this: "The last of Lovat's line will rule Scotland."
>
> ...
>
> The essence of what I'm saying is this: if you can indeed go back in time (and possibly return), you are a person of very great interest to a number of people, for assorted reasons. Should anyone in the more shadowed realm of government be halfway convinced that you are what you may be, you would be watched. Possibly approached. (In earlier centuries, the British government pressed men into service. They still do, if less obviously.)
>
> That's a very remote contingency, but it is a real one; I must mention it.
>
> There are private parties who would also have a deep interest in you for this reason—and evidently there is someone who has spotted you and is watching. The chart showing your line of descent, with dates, indicates that much. It also suggests that this person's or persons' interest may be a concern with the Fraser Prophecy. What could be more intriguing to that sort of person than the prospect of someone who is "the last of Lovat's line" and is also a time traveler? These sorts of people—I know them well—invariably believe in mystic powers of all sorts—nothing would draw them more powerfully than the conviction that you hold such power.
>
> Such people are usually harmless. But they can be very dangerous indeed [*Written in My Own Heart's Blood,* ch. 42].

Frank suggests that if Brianna is desperate enough, she might take refuge in the past, where no one can follow her.

Claire learns from the Reverend Campbell about the details of the Fraser prophecy. (*Voyager,* ch. 61). Geillis latches onto it as a source of power, but is silent on what she means to do about it. In *Voyager,* Jamie hears a rumor of the French gold meant for Prince Charlie and is told Geillis has saved the gold for "A MacKenzie, it is for Himself. MacKenzie. It is theirs, she says it, for the sake of him who is dead" (ch. 10)—could it be Brianna's MacKenzie son the gold is meant for?

In the twentieth century, there are still Jacobite descendants though they have not pursued their claim for centuries. Nonetheless, historically, Bonnie Prince Charlie's younger brother sent many Jacobite heirlooms to George III, acknowledging him as a Jacobite heir through his family's ancient claims. In today's political climate, it would make more sense for Brianna's son to use the gold to advance Scottish national pride or become Prime Minister rather than endeavor to put the hapless Jacobites on Britain's throne. Will this be the series end?

Fionn mac Cumhaill

Upon returning home at last, Jamie quotes from the poem "The Hounds of Fingal" describing his dogs, "Thus Fingal chose his hounds: Eye like sloe, ear like leaf, Chest like horse, hough like sickle And the tail joint far from the head" (*Outlander,* ch. 26). While this poem was published in 1761, it's alleged to be from the older oral tradition, so this need not be an anachronism. Fionn is indeed devoted to his hounds, Bran and Sceolan, who were once human themselves.

When Jamie visits Ireland, the legend follows him. There's speculation that a bog man is "Fionn Mac Cumhail, though why he should be lying in a bog and not having it away with the female denizens of Tír na Nog (fairyland), I don't know" (*The Scottish Prisoner,* ch. 19).

Fionn Mac Cumhaill (sometimes called Finn McCool in English or Fingal in the Scottish Gaelic tradition) is the epic hero of Irish legend, much like King Arthur or Odysseus from other traditions. His stories, called the Fenian Cycle, also appear in Scotland and on the Isle of Man. "Fionn," meaning fair-haired, has a heroic birth and gains magical powers from tasting the Salmon of Wisdom, a legend also ascribed to Taliesin from Welsh and Arthurian myth. He led a legendary war band, the Fianna, in many battles. It is the common idea among the peasantry that he and his band were of gigantic size. According to legend, he never died, but like King Arthur, sleeps in a cave until he and his band will be needed once more. The epic, of great battles and heroism entwined with love and magic, has several parallels with Jamie and Claire's story.

Fionn mac Cumhaill's wife, Sadhbh, had been turned into a deer by a druid. Fionn saved her from his hunting hounds, and when they reached his lands, she transformed into a human woman and dwelt together happily as husband and wife. When she fell pregnant, however, *Fear Doirich* (Dark Man) the druid returned and turned her back into a deer. Fionn spent seven years searching for her, only to find their human babe, Oisín, though his wife was lost to him forever. Like the selkie tale, this epic parallels Jamie and Claire, as he can keep his magic wife for a time, then must lose her to human villainy and the ill-luck of fate.

Oisín followed a beautiful fairy woman, Niamh of the Golden Hair, into the Otherworld, where they became lovers. Later, when he decided to return, Niamh warned him that if he touched the land, he would not be able to return. When he stepped down from his magical horse, he was instantly aged. As he soon discovered, all his companions had been dead for hundreds of years. This mythic pattern of travel to another world and return forms the basis for the standing stones legends in the series.

The other tale of Fionn's love, "The Pursuit of Diarmuid and Gráinne," has Fionn's greatest warrior, Diarmuid Ua Duibhne, falling in love with the wife of his aging chief. He bore that name ("Díarmait of the Love Spot") because a mark on his forehead made him irresistible to women. This mark would prove his undoing. The lovers ran away and Fionn pursued them through the land. Fionn finally made an uneasy peace with them, only to let Diarmuid die rather than saving him with water from his own hands when Diarmuid was wounded in a boar hunt. Claire's love triangle between the stately but less-passionate Frank and the powerful warrior Jamie (who is irresistible to several women in the series) has parallels, as Frank futilely hunts for them, especially on the show. In the books, he reveals in letters that he found Jamie in the past but refused to tell Claire and let her return to him, letting Jamie live alone out of a similar spite and possessiveness.

In December 1761, James Macpherson announced the discovery of an epic written by Oisín, Fionn's poet-son. He published *Fingal, an Ancient Epic Poem in Six Books, together with Several Other Poems composed by Ossian, the Son of Fingal, translated from the Gaelic Language.* The poem was much-celebrated, influencing writers as Goethe and the young Walter Scott. It had a massive cultural impact during the 18th and 19th centuries—Napoleon carried a copy into battle; the city of Selma, Alabama, was named after Fingal's home. However, one difficulty existed with the manuscript:

> James Macpherson claimed that Ossian was based on an ancient Gaelic manuscript. There was just one problem. The existence of this manuscript was never established. In fact, unlike Ireland and Wales, there are no dark-age manuscripts of epic poems, tales, and chronicles and so on from Scotland. It isn't that such ancient Scottish poetry and lore didn't exist, it was just purely oral in nature. Not much of it was committed to writing until it was on the verge of extinction. There are Scottish manuscripts and books in existence today which date as far back as the 12th century (some with scraps of poetry in them), but they are principally on subjects such as religion, genealogy, and land grants ["Index," Macpherson "Poems of Ossian"].

Using older oral sources, he may have invented the text himself. Nonetheless, the Fenian Cycle, from a multitude of ancient works, continues to influence legend, folklore, and modern fantasy.

Fortune Telling

Mrs. Graham is a fortune-teller, who's read tea leaves and palms like her grandmother before her and presumably back to ancient days. She pulls Claire into the kitchen to read tea leaves, in a scene mostly word-for-word identical to the book.

CLAIRE: Well? Am I going to meet a tall, dark stranger—and take a trip across the sea?

MRS. GRAHAM: Could be. Or could not. Everything in it's contradictory. There's a curved leaf, which indicates a journey, but it's crossed by a broken one,—which means staying put. And there are strangers there, to be sure. Several of them. And one of them's your husband, if I read the leaves aright. Show me your hand, Dear. Odd. Most hands have a likeness to them. There are patterns, you know? But this is a pattern I've not seen before.

CLAIRE: Oh.

MRS. GRAHAM: The large thumb, now, means that you're strong-minded and you've a will not easily crossed. And this is your mount of Venus. In a man, it means he likes the Lasses. But it is a bit different for a woman. To be polite about it, your husband isna likely to stray far from your bed. [Laughs] The life-line's interrupted, all bits and pieces. The marriage line's divided. Means two marriages. But most divided lines are broken. Yours is forked [Episode 101].

Tea leaf reading and the tea came from England, rare and expensive enough at the time to earn great mystique. J.G. Campbell notes:

After drinking the tea, the person for whom the cup is to be read, turning the cup deiseal, or with the right-hand turn, is to make a small drop, left in it, wash its sides all round, and then pour it out. The fortune is then read from the arrangement of the sediments or tea-leaves left in the cup. A large quantity of black tea grounds (smurack dii) denotes substance and worldly gear. The person consulting the oracle is a stray leaf standing to the one side of it. If the face of the leaf is towards the grounds, that person is to come to a great fortune; if very positively its back, then farewell even to the hope "that keeps alive despair." A small speck by itself is a letter, and other specks are envious people struggling to get to the top, followers, etc. Good diviners can even tell to their youthful and confiding friends when the letter is likely to arrive, what trade their admirer follows, the colour of his hair, etc. [266–267].

"A highly developed subject in India, which was perhaps its birthplace, palmistry was known in China, Tibet, Persia, Mesopotamia, and Egypt, and flowered, more or less in its present form, in Greece" (Rakoczi, "Palmistry" 1967). Hands, man's method of interacting with the world, have long fascinated ancient scholars, who began to believe one's ancestry, acts, and even astral self were carved into the lines of a hand, indicating the shape of past and future. In Western Europe, the three most important lines in the palm are the heart line, life line, and head line. The palm is divided into mounts for all the planets—the Mount of Jupiter stands for ambition, while the Mount of the Moon is creativity (Bruce-Mitford 110). The Mount of Venus represents "love, instincts, vitality, sensuality, fecundity, and bounty" (Rakoczi, "Palmistry" 1969). Mrs. Graham of course focuses on the romances Claire will find.

This scene is quite clear, even for new fans, who only know the show's most basic premise. Moore explains that it also adds the "creep factor" (Podcast 101). Mrs. Graham appears to have a link with the spiritual world as leader of the circle dancers—her fortunetelling is far more than a game. On the show, she adds to her own credibility by not only accurately predicting Claire's future, but telling Frank in episode eight that Claire may have traveled through the standing stones.

Beyond all this of course, many readers unconsciously believe in fortunetelling, at least a bit. There's a convention in fiction that fortunetelling indeed comes true, even in wholly nonmagical series (and *Outlander,* in fact, is far from that). Even Scarlett O'Hara mentions a fortuneteller once said she would marry a black-haired man, a prediction that functions as foreshadowing for the readers. Thus Mrs. Graham's scene establishes the romantic plot and Claire's love triangle dilemma even while hinting at deeper sources of power.

Late in the first book, Murtagh suggests Claire start fortunetelling when they're seeking Jamie, adding, "The more we can offer, the more folk will come to see us—and go back to tell others. And word will spread about us, 'til the lad hears of us. And that's when we'll find him. Game to try, are ye?" (ch. 32). Claire thus creates a reputation for herself as a seer, months before becoming White Lady. Using some of the techniques Mrs. Graham has mentioned, Claire the woman from the future ironically tells fortunes, though mostly innocuous things people want to hear. Divination of several forms was traditional. J.G. Campbell adds:

> The same causes which in other countries led to oracles, astrology, necromancy, card-reading, and other forms of divination, in the Scottish Highlands led to the reading of shoulderblades [of a slaughtered animal] and tea-cups, palmistry, and the artless spinning of tee-totums (dhdumari). In a simple state of society mummeries and ceremonies, dark caves, darkened rooms, and other aids to mystification are not required to bring custom to the soothsayer. The desire of mankind, particularly the young, to have pleasant anticipations ... of the future, supply all deficiencies in his artifices. One or two shrewd guesses establish a reputation, and ordinarily there is no skepticism or inquiry as to the sources of information [262–263].

Various divination rites traditionally worked best at Halloween or Hogmanay—countryfolk would climb up cairns then as they descended, the first creature they saw on the way home would suggest characteristics of their future spouse. At a Hogmanay party, Laoghaire spins round and round to see who she'll marry and finds herself staring at Jamie. The first person seen on Hogmanay indicated one's luck in the new year (Sutherland 47). There were many more casual games played at parties. Traditionally, one might toss an apple peel to see the name of a future husband scribbled in the dropped peel's curls. Mrs. Bug does this with the young girls "with much giggling and glancing over shoulders toward the young men (*The Fiery Cross,* ch. 35).

It's also said that the first head of kale a young person pulls up on Hallowe'en will resemble their future spouse (Daniels and Stevens 1486). Dipping one's shirt sleeve in the water of a south-running stream where three lairds' land meets and letting it dry will also summon a vision of them, in a tradition called the "sark sleeve" (Daniels and Stevens 1485).

In Jamie's life, fortunetellers are far more ominous. Claire tells Jamie Mrs. Graham's comment that lifelines reflect people's acts instead of predicting them. He notes that meeting Jack Randall and Claire, close together, were the defining moments of his life and may be close on his palm (*Voyager*, ch. 27). Surrounded by travelers Claire, Brianna, and Roger in the later books, he becomes resigned to hearing of the future world he will never see and trying to reconcile the knowledge with his own existence.

> The things Claire told him of her own time seemed often fantastic, with the enjoyable half-real sense of faery tales, and sometimes macabre, but always interesting, for what he learned of his wife from the telling. Brianna tended to share with him small, homely details of machinery, which were interesting, or wild stories of men walking on the moon, which were immensely entertaining, but no threat to his peace of mind.
>
> Roger Mac, though, had a cold-blooded way of talking that reminded him to an uncomfortable degree of the works of the historians he'd read, and had therefore a sense of concrete doom about it [*A Breath of Snow and Ashes,* ch. 10].

Considering this and mentally comparing Roger to "a particularly evil-minded fortune-teller," Jamie suddenly recalls an actual fortuneteller he met as a young university student in Paris. Filthy and ancient, she snatched his wrist tightly and gave him her prediction. She called him "A little red cat" and suggested that like a cat, he would have nine lives: "You have a nine in your hand. And death ... you'll die nine times before you rest in your grave" (*A Breath of Snow and Ashes*, ch. 10).

As fortunetelling conventions go in fiction, this must be taken as truth. Jamie abruptly asks Claire how many times he's nearly died, and she lists the axe to the head he took just before they met, the climaxes of the first and second books as well as his gunshot wound in book three, and a snakebite later on. This is five. Oddly, they do not bring up his hundreds of lashes at the hands of Jack Randall—he was ill for some time after, but apparently he doesn't feel it came close enough to killing him. Of course, after the conversation, the Battle of Saratoga and a near-miss at sea (both times at which Claire believes he's dead) likely brings this up to seven. Jamie is a violent person, called upon to be a soldier and lead men into battle many times. Readers begin to think he has a charmed life, as he manages to find his way back to Claire through impossible odds.

"You're a very hard person to kill, I think," Claire says to end their conversation. "That's a great comfort to me" (*A Breath of Snow and Ashes,* ch. 13). Nonetheless, it seems his number may finally come up.

Herbalism

The author's note in *Cross Stitch* reads:

I would also like to note that while the botanical preparations noted in the story were historically used for the medicinal purposes indicated, this fact shouldn't be taken as an indication that such preparations are necessarily either effective for such purposes, or harmless. Many herbal preparations are toxic if used improperly or in excess dosage, and should be administered only by an experienced practitioner.

While Claire uses all kinds of herbs in her medical treatments, Gabaldon notes, "I'm not by any means a professional botanist or herbalist. In fact, the sum total of my academic credentials is the six class-hours of botany required to get a B.S. degree in zoology at Northern Arizona University" (*Outlandish Companion* 284). Historically, medical practitioners of the time didn't know much more than she:

There was a great deal of irregular practice in the early part of the 18th century. The country was invaded by mountebanks, who came especially from Germany and the Low Countries, set up stages in the towns and treated people wholesale. Partly owing to the scarcity of doctors and partly perhaps from want of faith in some of those who were provided with University degrees, a great number of books on simple forms of medical treatment were also in vogue.

In Scotland several books were in use, designed for those who knew a little medicine, such as the clergymen, lairds or great ladies who took an interest in their retainers. Of these books, one of the best known was *The Poor Man's Physician, or the Receits of the Famous John Moncrief of Tippermalloch.* This, as its title-page records, is "a choice collection of simple and easy remedies for most distempers, very useful for all persons, especially those of a poorer condition." The first edition was published in 1712, and the third edition in 1731.
....
Some of these appear to be quite natural and salutary, and some can only be described as extremely disgusting. The following is a fair average sample of [one] book:
38. For the Colick.
The Hoofs of living Creatures are singularly good, being drunk. Rhasis. Or dry Oxdung drunk in Broth, or the Juice pressed from the Ox-dung drunk, is better. Gesnerus. 2. The Heart of a Lark bound to the Thigh, is excellent against the Colick, and some have eaten it raw with very good Success. A Spaniard. 3. This is certain, that a Wolf's Dung, Guts, or Skin eaten, will cure the Colick, or if yo11 do but carry them about you; for they strengthen the Choler [Comrie 113–114].

Towards the end of the 18th century, regular medicine such as quinine became more easily available, so ancient recipes like this one became ridiculous relics of the past. Nonetheless, Claire uses a great deal of herbalism, searching for plants with verified active ingredients. In the books, Claire makes marigold lotion and a burn salve of sarsaparilla and bittersweet. She has a lavender salve for diaper rash and poison ivy. Her willow bark tea contains salicylic acid, aspirin. Laudanum, an opium derivative, was popular at the time for pain, though the series uses alcohol nearly constantly for the same purpose. By the later books, she notes she always carries a gathering basket in spring and summer. She trades for ginseng and uses garlic and onions for poultices as well as for cooking. In *The Drums of Autumn,* Claire prepares a tea of valerian, catmint, root of a passionflower, and lavender to keep William calm while he journeys with Jamie (ch. 27).

When she finds a stable home at last, she begins experimenting with penicillin. Gabaldon notes that Claire doesn't slap moldy bread on everyone's wounds because she knows too much about medicine: many kinds of mold do not generate penicillin and may have many other contaminants (*Outlandish Companion* 288).

Futuristic medical knowledge of sterilization can always be used, while some conditions such as diabetes or Colum's congenital illness leave Claire helpless. Nonetheless, the alternative medicine popular among some people today provides a viable alternative. While she's not certain of all the cures, many compounds were still used in her time and today for their active ingredients.

On the show, Moore describes using real, correct herbs for Claire's picking expeditions and in her surgery to add a "sense of authenticity" and stay true to the spirit of the book ("Inside the World," 103). In the poison scene of that episode, Claire identifies lily of the valley as the poisonous plant possibly confused with wood garlic. When Geillis visits Claire in her surgery in the fourth episode, she notices that Claire has been working with valerian, and cautions her to boil it first before she knocks someone out with it. Rent collecting, Claire treats Ned Gowan's asthma with thornapple and jimson weed.

With Claire in the books, Geillis picks aspen bark. "The globules of dried sap on the papery bark looked like frozen drops of blood" (*Outlander,* ch. 24). Claire thinks she can smell cinquefoil and nightshade when she and Geillis share a summoning spell (ch. 24). Geillis tells Claire bloodwort or roseroot will make warts grow on someone's nose and that wood betony can turns toads into pigeons (ch. 9). Claire is suspicious of these, though she uses bloodwort for purging. The ill-wish bundle left under Claire's pillow contains thorny primrose.

Paris offers well-stocked apothecaries as well as a garden at L' Hôptial des Agnes. There, Claire uses St. John's wort and other herbs (*Dragonfly in Amber,* ch. 12). Monsieur Forez brings Claire raspberry leaves and saxifrage from Mother

Hildegarde. It is "a favorite remedy of les maitresses sage-femme (matters of midwives)" (ch. 23). Master Raymond sells bitter cascara, a diuretic, to people who want to buy poison. As he explains:

> The rival will fall sick tomorrow, suffer visibly in order to satisfy the Vicomtesse's desire for revenge and convince her that her purchase was a good one, and then she will recover, with no permanent harm done, and the Vicomtesse will attribute the recovery to the intervention of the priest or a counterspell done by a sorcerer employed by the victim [*Dragonfly in Amber,* ch. 8].

Claire is occasionally consulted on birth control. When asked, she recommends a sponge soaked in vinegar or breast feeding—both traditional methods in the eighteenth century. The Native Americans in North Carolina teach her about dauco seeds, their method of choice. *Daucus carota* is also called Queen Anne's Lace or wild carrot, used by some today.

In America, the Cherokee and Iroquois have many other remedies. They mix dried trillium with bear grease to heal cuts and make strong-scented mosquito ointment from bear grease and mint. In *The Fiery Cross,* it's revealed that the amulet Nayawenne gives Claire contains the herb arsesmart, known as waterpepper and known for creating blisters. Bree teases, "Arsesmart? Is that a comment on what she thought of you?" Claire uses gallberries to treat malaria when she can't find imported cinchona bark—both contain quinine. Jocasta, bothered by glaucoma, lights up a hemp cigarette as her doctor prescribed.

There are nonmedical herbal remedies as well. In *Dragonfly,* Claire washes her hair with yarrow to keep it clean and free of lice (ch. 26). On discussing toilet paper in the twentieth century, Claire mentions that people used mullein leaves, which "are very nice; quite as good as two-ply bathroom tissue" (ch. 2). Extensive research makes the past come alive with plants across the world, many beloved by herbalists today.

Second Sight

Jamie explains several times that Claire has second sight, though he knows the truth—he has no better way to explain why his sister must plant potatoes for the coming famine, or why he knows the Jacobites will never restore Bonnie Prince Charlie to the throne. Jamie insists in *The Scottish Prisoner* that he won't participate in another uprising because his wife was a seer and told him they would fail. "La Dame Blanche, they called her in Paris, and for good reason. She saw the end of the Cause—and its death. Believe me Thomas. This venture, too, is doomed, and I ken that fine. I wouldna have it take ye down wi' it. For the sake of our shared past, I beg ye—stand clear" (ch. 29).

When Jenny asks Claire for advice, Claire notes: "Being a prophet was a very uncomfortable occupation." Nonetheless, she resolves to do it, even in the eerie atmosphere: "On the crest of a Scottish hill, the night wind of an autumn storm whipping my hair and skirts like the sheets of a banshee, I turned my face to the shadowed skies and prepared to prophesy" (*Outlander,* ch. 33). Of course, Claire does not have second sight, only medical training and book knowledge of the future. Other characters, however, may be more gifted.

Old Lord Simon keeps a seer, who holds back his fate of a traitor's hanging in London. As Jamie describes her, "Her name's Maisri, and she's had the Sight since she was born" (*Dragonfly in Amber,* ch. 40). When Claire speaks to her, she bursts out: "Why! Why can I see what will happen, when there's no mortal thing I can be doin' to change it or stop it? What's the good of a gift like that? It's no a gift, come to that—it's a damn curse, though I havena done anything to be cursed like this!" (ch. 41).

These words of course mirror Claire's predicament on the edge of Culloden, as she knows exactly what will happen. Claire concludes, "Doom, or save. That I cannot do. For I have no power beyond that of knowledge, no ability to bend others to my will, no way to stop them doing what *they* will. There is only me."

In the short story "The Space Between," the girl Joan is revealed to have the gift—specifically, she can tell when someone is about to die. To her, they appear to have a "grey shroud," as if they're wrapped in mist. (Ironically, foretelling death is also one of Claire's powers, between the history books she's read and the medical knowledge she possesses.) Joan also hears voices. "They now and then tell me something's going to happen. More often, they tell me I should say thus-and-so to someone" ("The Space Between" 220). Her voices feel like Joan of Arc's to her, but she has no idea why she hears them or what their plan may be for her in the long term. By the point of "The Space Between," her knowledge afflicts her so far that she joins a convent. While she has an adventure in her one story, the larger mystery of her life goes unresolved. This fits neatly into the tradition—it's considered a talent like any other, rather than a puzzle needing unraveling.

Traditional aspects of Highland second sight include "spontaneous unsought vision; the precognition of impending disaster; the physical changes that affect the seer; the prophecy that looks to the far future" (Sutherland 17). The tradition of second sight likely originated with Neolithic tomb builders receiving messages from on high. Druids cultivated and valued the talent, believing it came from the fairie folk. As their religion faded, the famed Saint Columba treated his own power as a gift from God meant to be used—this is likely the tradition that labeled second sight as a benign gift through the centuries after. It was linked with Biblical prophecy rather than magic. Even those who considered it an affliction did not confuse it with witchcraft, as it was considered unsought and involuntary.

More subtly, Jamie has true dreams on occasion. Visions of his loved ones in the future appear to him—surprising as he specifically cannot travel the stones and there is no hint he has any other supernatural abilities. But he tells Claire of a vision he had one night:

> "I've seen ye there."
> The prickling ran straight down the back of my neck and down both arms.
> "Seen me where ?"
> "There." He waved a hand in a vague gesture. "I dreamt of ye there. I dinna ken where it was; I only know it was there—in your proper time."

He even sees electric light and recognizes it. When Claire asks how he could dream of someplace he's never seen, he replies, "I dream of the past; why would I not dream of the future?" As she concludes, "There was no good answer to a thoroughly Celtic remark of that nature" (*A Breath of Snow and Ashes,* ch. 68).

He also has moments that stick perfectly in his head—visions of the present rather than future or past. His second sight appears to be a family trait from his Scottish background, in contrast with Claire's different hereditary gift of traveling. Jamie also tells Claire that he's seen Brianna's birthmark in dreams, "a wee brown mark, shaped like a diamond.... Just behind her left ear" (*The Drums of Autumn*, ch. 21). After she leaves, he dreams about her, Jem, and Mandy, along with inventions he can barely describe. Jem and Mandy in turn feel his presence, though they know he died centuries before. In one heart-tearing moment, Jem is taught to use the telephone, so he picks it up and asks for Jamie, another moment Jamie sees in his dream. When asked about Jamie, Brianna, Mandy, and Jem sharing dreams of each other, Gabaldon admits there's a link with the second sight and "probably some of that" is responsible (*Outlander Podcast*).

Brianna also has a share in this gift. She was born with a caul—as Claire thinks, "A 'silly hoo,' the Scots called it; a lucky hood. A fortunate portent, a caul offered—they said—protection from drowning in later life. And some children born with a caul were blessed with second sight" (*The Drums of Autumn,* ch. 23). As early as *Voyager*, in one startling moment, Brianna's voice emerges from the medium Margaret Campbell and tells Jamie he must stay with Claire to protect her. As Brianna describes the incident: "There was one dream in particular.... I couldn't see his face very well, because it was dark, but I could see that he had red hair.... I turned to him, and I called to him to go with [Claire]— to save her from whatever it was. And he saw me!... He did, he saw me, and he heard me. And then I woke up" (*The Drums of Autumn,* ch. 40).

Jenny, another blood relation, is seen having a single vision on Jamie's wedding day, telling her that he and Claire are linked. Thus the Frasers seem to have the old Highland gift. Jenny also meets Maisri later and they discuss second sight, suggesting the gift comes from the Fraser side (*The Drums of Autumn,* ch. 33). If so, then Roger MacKenzie will not have inherited it. By contrast, Jem and Mandy's sense of each other is likely related to the time travel gene, which comes from Claire but not Jamie (*Outlander Podcast*). Dowsing, auras, and other extrasensory powers appear to correspond with the stones, as Claire displays growing powers in this area.

Margaret Campbell, another Highlander, appears to be a vessel for others if not gifted herself. She is shown to be traumatized into a chronic trance state, and while in it, able to channel the dead like a traditional medium. The extent of her gifts is not entirely clear.

Witches

"In Scotland, a suspected witch was treated no less indecently than cruelly, for she was stripped naked and "cross-bound," that is, her right thumb to the left toe and her left thumb to the right toe, and then thrown in the water; if guilty, it was believed to be impossible for her to sink" (Daniels and Stevens 1451). The townsfolk near Leoch plan exactly this for Claire. As Gabaldon adds:

> I wanted to have a witch trial, but looking into it, I could see that the last witch trial in Scotland took place in 1722. So I was telling my husband that I'd really like a witch trial, but it doesn't fit. He looked at me and said, "You start right off with a book in which you expect people to believe that Stonehenge is a time machine, and you're worried that your witches are 20 years too late?" [Laughs] So I did stretch that point. I figured that possibly this witch trial was an ad hoc affair that didn't make it into the record. That's the only place where I can remember I deliberately moved something that I knew was not quite there [DeLuca].

The Encyclopedia of Witchcraft and Demonology calls Scotland "second only to Germany in the barbarity of its witch trials" (Robbins 454). Historically, Mary, Queen of Scots (who was raised in France) introduced witchcraft and witch trials to the country. Her son King James VI had a far fiercer horror of witches. While traveling to Denmark in order to claim his bride, he was plagued by storms that he assumed was their plot to kill him. On returning to Scotland, the credulous twenty-four-year-old king oversaw the trials that were occurring in North Berwick, personally extracting confessions through torture until the accused women admitted they had gone to sea in sieves and tried to wreck the king's ship (Robbins 277). Impressed by how common witchcraft was growing, he set up royal commissions to hunt down witches in his realm. James decreed that since he was God's anointed, he was the first target of witchcraft, making the crime treason as well as heresy. In 1597, he wrote a book about witches and their threat to society entitled *Daemonologie*.

In 1604, following James' accession to the English throne, he added the death penalty for anyone who invoked evil spirits or communed with familiars (under his predecessor, Elizabeth I, witches could only be executed for causing great injury). Under both their laws, witchcraft was prosecuted by the judicial system, not the church. Nonetheless, torture and unproven accusations were common, leading to hanging for many women. In the 17th and 18th centuries Scotland put to death over 4,000 alleged witches, making the country likely their greatest persecutor. By the end of the 17th century, burning had gone out of fashion, so most of them were hanged, with the last hanging taking place in 1728.

These Witchcraft Acts were finally repealed in 1735—by the new law, anyone found practicing was penalized for being a vagrant or con artist, emphasizing rationality and the Enlightenment triumphing over superstition. Admittedly, Claire is tried in 1743. Gabaldon notes that this need not rewrite history as it's such a quick incident. Claire comments that she "had thought it a practice common to the seventeenth century, not this one. On the other hand, I thought wryly, Cranesmuir was not exactly a hotbed of civilization" (ch. 25). Indeed, fears of devilish arts lingered, especially in rural areas. In 1773 the divines of the Associated Presbytery passed a resolution declaring their belief in witchcraft, emphasizing the church's place in encouraging the mass hysteria (Robbins 457).

Episode three sees Claire trying to save a boy from poisoning, as the people around her fear demonic possession. Moore notes that most of this episode's plot is new, in an attempt to show her life at Castle Leoch and the conflicts within it. It also introduces Father Bain and his grudge against Claire, which returns when he condemns her later. Moore describes her as "Bumping up against society and social thinking and superstition and the social mores of the time" ("Inside the World," 103).

Mrs. Fitz asks Claire in surprise whether she actually knows how to keep wounds from festering, adding, "Are ye a charmer, then? A Beaton?" (Episode 102). The Scottish Beaton clan were famous healers. Colum notes at the end of the episode that Castle Leoch used to have a Beaton healer until he died some years back. Claire identifies herself as a doctor but admits she's more often called "wisewoman, or conjure woman. Or ban-lichtne" (Gaelic for female healer) (*A Breath of Snow and Ashes,* ch. 22). Dougal says, "Well, you're a healer. Surely ye believe in the powers of magic," linking the concepts (Episode 106).

Being taken for witchcraft is a constant threat in Claire's life, as she knows too much about medicine and the future, both areas the province of witchcraft. Of course, in medieval times any outspoken woman might be accused and murdered—the witchfinders inherited the women's property after all. In 1576, Bessie Dunlop of Ayr was burned alive for witchcraft, not for harming anyone but for healing people as a wise woman (Illes 818). The witch trials were a time of misogyny in which thousands of women were murdered for being leaders and wisewomen—something many men of the time reviled. "I've yet to see the auld woman believes in witches, nor the young one, neither. It's men think there must be ill-wishes and magic in women, when it's only the natural way of the creatures," Murtagh notes (*Outlander,* ch. 31). Father Bain bears a grudge in book and show, and he wields it as a weapon, quoting "Deliver thee from the strange woman, even from the stranger that flattereth with her words. For her house inclineth unto death, and her paths unto the dead" (Proverbs 2:16–18).

Historically, wisewomen were trailblazers of their community, guardians and guides as well as wielders of the ancient lore. The church's attack on them was an attack on all strong women in their world:

> The Inquisition persecuted witches (literally wise women), who had always been bastions of advice and cures for the village. Many of their remedies had a psychic component, leaving them open to accusations of magic. These women were natural leaders of the encroaching economy, first feudal and then industrial, and thus Church and State combined to target them as obstacles. These witches were accused of casting spells, having intercourse with the devil, cursing men and animals, and (rather tellingly) causing impotence or painless childbirth. Women were meant to suffer, and men to be virile and rule the household; any attack on that status quo was deemed deviltry [Frankel 289].

Imprisoned beside her, Geillis reminds Claire of how the witch trials work—mob rule and hysteria combined with the vindictive nature of the accusers see women tortured and killed on circumstantial evidence. As Ned Gowan explains it, "the worst of these trials take place in a climate of hysteria, when the soundness of evidence may be disregarded for the sake of satisfyin' blood-hunger" (ch. 25). There was no burden of proof. "The costs of the trial and execution had to be borne by the condemned person, paid out of his own property before it was confiscated by the king" (Robbins 455).

"Ye still dinna understand, do ye?" Geillis tells Claire. "They mean to kill us. And it doesna matter much what the charge is, or what the evidence shows. We'll burn, all the same" (ch. 25). At their trial, the evidence presented is flimsy and inflammatory, based on superstition rather than fact: Claire and Geillis found a dying baby and thus must have influenced it. A waterhorse appeared before Claire. The priest's wound festered as Claire predicted. However, Scotland was the only country to allow lawyers for the accused, a historical note Claire uses to her advantage.

Moore describes Geillis as Claire's "one female friend" in the early part of the series ("Inside the World," 103). She is also, by her own admission, an occult practitioner. "They say I'm a witch," she said, widening her brilliant eyes in feigned astonishment. She grinned. "But my husband's the procurator fiscal for the district, so they don't say it too loud" (ch. 9). On the show she greets Claire by noticing the mushrooms she's picking are poisonous and adds, "Who is it you're planning to do away with? Your husband, perhaps? Tell me if it works, and I'll try it on mine" (Episode 102). Of course, she's later revealed to be a poisoner when necessary for her schemes. Lotte Verbeek (who plays Geillis) notes:

> It is interesting how much of it is actually witchcraft. Geillis uses her knowledge of herbs in a different way than Claire does. I found myself to be quite the herbalist; I found myself knowing a lot about it and if you live in L.A. and everything is in organic, that definitely puts you in contact with nature. There are modern witches—I think it's wicca—but witchcraft has a negative [connotation] and back in the day you could get burned for being caught in witchcraft and for being too much of a lightweight, for not weighing enough. In Holland there are scales in marketplaces where you could be put on the scale and if you were too light or too odd or different, that was a way to prove one was a witch [Ng, "Lotte Verbeek"].

Geillis notes that she and Claire are both witches, a hereditary gift. She uses the infamous *Witch's Hammer* as a reference book and adds, "Some people can leave their bodies and travel miles away.... Other people see them out wandering, and recognize them, and ye can bloody *prove* they were really tucked up safe in bed at the time ... some people have stigmata ye can see and touch—I've seen one. But not everybody. Only certain people" (*Voyager*, ch. 60). On the show, she insists, "There are powers beyond our ken beyond what we can see and hear and touch. Demon, fairy, devil doesn't matter what name we put on them." When Claire looks skeptical, Geillis adds, "Have you never found yourself in a situation that has no earthly explanation?" (Episode 103). Remembering her trip through the stones, Claire is stunned into silence.

As revealed in her diary, Geillis has chosen this name for herself because of its heritage. She writes, "This is the grimoire of the witch, Geillis. It is a witch's name, and I take it for my own; what I was born does not matter, only what I will make of myself, only what I will become" (*The Drums of Autumn,* ch. 40). Gabaldon writes in her FAQ that "There's a 'real' female witch (late 16th century) named Geilis Duncane in *Daemonologie,* a treatise on witches by King James of Scotland." In fact, the historical Geilis Duncane exhibited healer's skills in 1590. A servant for the deputy of Tranent (near Edinburgh), she went out at night to practice her job, and her employer quickly accused her. Under torture, she confessed and implicated many others, who were then tried alongside her in James's famous North Berwick Witch Trials (Illes 819). Gabaldon adds:

> Geillis Duncan was a conscious choice.... I liked the name—and had also seen a passing reference in one of Dorothy Dunnett's novels (which I much admire) to Geillis as "a witch's name." Little did I realize that the woman who bore it in *Outlander* had also chosen it deliberately, and for the same reason! She so informed me, sometime later, when she chose to reveal her real name—or what I must presently assume to be her real name—Gillian Edgars [*Outlandish Companion* 137].

Thanks to Geillis, Claire barely escapes with her life. However, by book's end, she's chosen to own the label and the power it brings her: "Witch I am. Witch, and I curse you. I curse you with knowledge, Jack Randall—I give you the hour of your death," she says (*Outlander,* ch. 35). When Colum asks, she flippantly tells him, "Better call me a witch.... It's as close as you're likely to get" (*Dragonfly in Amber,* ch. 37). In the fourth book, she pours snow into her large cauldron, "feeling, as I always did, rather like a witch." She quotes "Double, double, toil and trouble" to finish off the allusion (*The Drums of Autumn,* ch. 21).

Young Ian and his brothers debate at one point whether Claire is a "bansidhe," a "conjure-woman" a "witch" or an "Auld One" (*An Echo in the Bone,* ch. 80). Jamie says the Scottish word for White Lady is "*ban-druidh*; it also means witch" (*Voyager,* ch. 10). By the later books, all of Jenny's children and grandchildren take it as fact that Claire is some kind of wisewoman or fairy woman, though they don't specifically call her a witch.

Gabaldon comments that the books take place just as magic was giving way to science, leaving Claire poised between these two worlds: "The dichotomy between magic and science occurs explicitly for the first time in the eighteenth century, as part of the evolution of the Age of Enlightenment" (*Outlandish Companion* 192). Thus superstition and rationality mix in cures and charms. As she concludes, "Claire, with her peculiar perspectives, personifies the practice of medicine, mingling the rational and the metaphysical, the traditional and the modern, in pursuit of the ancient goals of the healing arts: the preservation and restoration of health" (*Outlandish Companion* 194).

At the same time, Claire learns the truth of magic in her world: not just the standing stones, but also the power of Geillis and Raymond, who can harm and heal through powers beyond her understanding. The wisewoman Nayawenne of the Tuscaroras teaches her amulets and charms as well as healing herbs, and Claire begins to bridge these disparate worlds.

RITUALS AND RITUAL TOOLS

Blood Sacrifice

At the beginning of book one, Frank notes the townsfolk of Inverness are sacrificing black cocks and smearing the blood on their doorsteps to dedicate their homes. Sacrificing a black rooster appears in several Scottish traditions: George Henderson records a correspondent from Lewis's letter in *Survivals in Belief Among the Celts:*

> The cure for epileptic fits is more barbarous, and to my knowledge was used not three months ago in Barvas (4 1/2 miles from here). A black cock (the barn-door

variety), without a light-coloured feather, is buried alive on the spot where the patient experienced his or her first fit; that is all and the cure is effected by [inducing] the evil spirit causing epilepsy to leave the patient and enter into the body of the cock [267].

Frank, upon finding blood on the stoop, notes in the first episode, "We seem to be surrounded by homes marked with blood." While Claire makes a Moses joke and Frank describes pagan superstition in the Highlands, in fact, their story will become soaked in blood, especially from Frank's ancestor Black Jack. It also foreshadows the sacrifice Claire will make, passing through the stones. Blood indicates sacrifice, a pagan blessing upon the houses rather than a Christian one. While Claire does not literally travel back to a pagan era, she uses ancient magic and arrives at a time of beliefs in fairies and kelpies. Moore starts off the television adaptation with the blood as it "spoke a lot about paganism and the area" and begins the story in an appropriately spooky fashion.

The blood comes from a black cockerel in order to honor St. Orrin, as the book reveals. Also called Saint Odhran, he helped found the monastery of Iona off the west coast of Scotland. Today, the oldest church on Iona is dedicated to him, and the surrounding cemetery is called *Reilig Odhráin* in his honor. Odhran's feast day is October 27, close to Samhain.

In an ominous legend, Saint Columba's chapel was destroyed each night as he and the monks tried to build it. He had a vision that it could never be finished until a living man was buried below. Thus Odhran willingly offered himself and was buried alive. The chapel was completed and Columba piled more earth on his friend to make sure he couldn't reemerge into the world of sin (G. Henderson 281).

These grisly legends were common and in fact based in practice. In the fourth book, Roger tries to solve the mystery of Mountgerald House, another tale of foundation sacrifice to ensure the strength and protection of the building. Henderson adds that in the Arthurian stories, "A child without a father has to be found and slain, and the fortress is to be built in such a one's blood if the building is to stand" (278). This is Merlin, who only preserves his own life through magic. "Grimm tells us that in 1843, during the building of the new bridge at Halle, it was a popular superstition that one required to bury a child in the foundation, and he cites similar beliefs among the Danes, Greeks, and Servians" (G. Henderson 279). This tradition appears in Gabaldon's "Lord John and the Succubus" as John travels through Prussia and learns of Saint Orgevald who stopped this terrible practice.

Later on, libations of milk or ale appeared in place of human sacrifice, but these always symbolized the most sacred fluid—the blood of life. In the island of Valay, "There is a flat thick stone call'd Brownie's Stone, upon which the ancient inhabitants offered a cow's milk every Sunday" (G. Henderson 254). The sea-god Shony received libations in Lewis at Hallowtide:

> They gathered to the Church of St. Mulvay, Lewis: each family furnished a peck of malt, and this was brew'd into ale: one of their number was picked out to wade into the sea up to the middle, and carrying a cup of ale in his hand, standing still in that posture, cry'd out with a loud voice, saying: *Shony, I give you this cup of ale, hoping that you'll be so kind as to send us plenty of sea-ware, for enriching our ground the ensuing year*, and so threw the cup of ale into the sea [G. Henderson 254–255].

These gifts seem benign, but like the cock's blood, they nod to a darker time past.

Cup of the Druid King

The *Cupán Druid riogh* is the ancient possession of the kings of Ireland, given to him by the chief Druid. As a Jacobite conspirator adds in *The Scottish Prisoner*, "It's still spoken of in the legends, and 'tis a powerful symbol of kingship" (ch. 3). He plots to deliver it to Prince Charlie and have him claim Ireland in the court of Dublin Castle, cup in his hands. As is revealed later, the cup was found with an ancient corpse dug up in a bog. Jamie has an opportunity to examine it.

> It was made of a polished wood, to his surprise, rather than gold. Stained and darkened by immersion in the peat, but still beautifully made. There was a carving in the bottom of the bowl, and gemstones—uncut, but polished—were set round the rim, each one sunk into a small carved depression and apparently fastened there with some sort of resin.
>
> The cup gave him the same feeling he'd had in the abbot's study: the sense that someone—or something—was standing close behind him.

Jamie warns the abbot that it gives him "the cold grue" and sends a clear message to put it back. Then he sees something carved inside and asks the abbot what it is.

> "A *carraig myr*, or so I think. A long stone." The abbot turned the bowl, holding it sideways so that the lantern light illumined the dish. The cold grue slid right down the backs of Jamie's legs, and he shuddered. The carving showed what was plainly a standing stone—cleft down the center [*The Scottish Prisoner*, ch. 19].

Though little more appears on the origin of the cup, Jamie wonders if the standing stone carving means whoever created it was displaced in time. As such, its original owner may have been a wielder of true magic, rather than superstition. He may have been a primitive, or a man of science and education from Claire's time in the future.

In a moment much like a crowning, the priest takes him up to the druids' ancient seat and offers him the cup. "This is the High Seat—the *órd chnoc*— where the kings of this place were confirmed before the old gods," the priest says. Jamie is impressed despite himself. As he thinks, "It was a very old place, and the stone seemed to hold a deep silence; even the wind over the bog had died, and he could hear his heart beating in his chest, slow and steady" (*The Scottish Prisoner,* ch. 19). As the priest describes Jamie as a leader of men and urges him to rejoin the Jacobite cause, he's offering a symbolic anointing if not an actual one. Despite the ceremony of the gesture, Jamie firmly refuses.

Dagger Oaths

Jamie does not wear a cross, swearing on his dagger hilt when a cross is needed. Men likewise swear on their daggers at the Gathering, as these are the weapons they will use in their laird's service. There is another reason as well: iron was the tool of man, and thus protection against the fairyfolk and evil spirits.

> An oath on cold iron was deemed the most binding oath of any; when people swore on their dirks it was only because it was at the time the cold iron readiest to hand. A man who secreted iron, and died without telling where, could not rest in his grave. At Meigh, in Lochaber, a ghost for a long time met people who were out late. An old man, having taken with him a Bible and made a circle round himself on the road with a dirk, encountered it, and, in reply to his inquiries, the ghost confessed to having stolen a ploughshare and told where the secreted iron was to be found. After this the ghost discontinued its visits to the earth [J.G. Campbell 246–247].

Funerals

> At a funeral, a fall sustained by one of the bearers of the body was considered ominous of the person's speedy death. It was also esteemed very unlucky to look at a person's funeral from the door of a house or from windows having a stone lintel. On the death of a Highlander, the corpse being stretched on a board covered with a linen wrapper, the friends laid on the breast of the deceased a wooden platter containing a small quantity of salt and earth, unmixed. The earth was meant as an emblem of the corruptible body, while the salt was an emblem of the immortal soul. All fire was extinguished where a corpse was kept, and it was accounted so ominous of evil for a dog or cat to pass over it that the poor creature was instantly deprived of life [Guthrie, ch. 18].

Several minor characters have funerals, at which Claire and the other characters must consider their mortality. The myriad of Highland customs appear, emphasizing the culture of ghosts and superstitions. "It was customary to place a plate of salt, the smoothing iron, or a clod of green grass on the breast of a corpse, while laid out previous to being coffined" (J.G. Campbell 241). Other items were also bestowed on the corpse: "The boards on which it had been lying were left for the night as they were, with a drink of water on them, in case the dead should return and be thirsty. Some put the drink of water or of milk outside the door, and, as in Mull and Tiree, put a sprig of pearlswort above the lintel to prevent the dead from entering the house" (J.G. Campbell 241). Claire notes there are libations of bread, salt and wine at a funeral she attends and that "it was the custom for everyone to touch the body, so that the dead person should not haunt them" (*A Breath of Snow and Ashes,* ch. 39). The piece of bread is laid out for "the sin-eater," as Jamie says. Later, he arrives, a mysterious man who seems half apparition.

Claire adds that "Meeting his gaze gave me a queer feeling in the pit of the stomach, as though I looked for a moment into a distorting mirror, and saw that cruelly misshapen face replace my own" as she feels "something nameless pass between us" (*A Breath of Snow and Ashes,* ch. 39). While the visiting figure is human, he is stranger to the community, otherworldly enough to provoke chills. He, like many other characters and events in the series, adds a touch of the fantastical to the everyday, emphasizing the mystical world of the inexplicable.

There are many other traditions around a death. It's revealed in the later books that a new bride sews her own shroud, and then her husband's, preparing for a world of early mortality. Brianna is quite disturbed on receiving a wedding gift of embroidery thread for this purpose. One type of Scottish wake was the Lyke-Wake. "The evening after the death of any person, the relations and friends of the deceased met at the house, attended by bagpipes and fiddles. The nearest of kin, be it wife, son, or daughter, opened a melancholy ball, dancing and crying violently at the same time" (Guthrie, ch. 18). Finally, Jamie tells Claire that "The last person buried in a graveyard must stand watch over it ... until another comes to take his place" (*A Breath of Snow and Ashes,* ch. 39). This was called *Faire Chlaidh,* the graveyard watch. Indeed, "when two funeral parties met at the churchyard, a fight frequently ensued to determine who should get their friend first buried" (J.G. Campbell 242).

> At Kiel (Cill Challum Chille), in Morvern, the body of the Spanish Princess said to have been on board one of the Armada blown up in Tobermory Bay was buried. Two young men of the district made a paction, that whoever died first the other would watch the churchyard for him. The survivor, when keeping the promised watch, had the sight of his dead friend as well as his own. He saw both the material world and spirits. Each night he saw ghosts leaving the churchyard and returning before morning. He observed that one of the ghosts was always behind the rest when returning. He spoke to it, and ascertained it to be the ghost of the Spanish Princess. Her body had been removed to Spain, but one of her little fingers had been left behind, and she had to come back to where it was [J.G. Campbell 242].

In another tradition, "The Coronach, or singing at funerals, is still kept up, to some extent, in some parts of the Highlands. The songs are generally in praise of the deceased, or a recital of the valiant deeds of his ancestors" (Guthrie, ch. 18). The Coronach appears in the fourth book—Jamie insists the only rule is that it be loud, so he and his friends nearly howl down the walls of the pub. A final ritual in *A Breath of Snow and Ashes* unnerves the American-born Brianna: "An unearthly wail cut through the air, and Brianna froze, clutching Roger's arm. It rose to a shriek, then broke in a series of short, jerky gulps, coming down a scale of sobs like a dead body rolling down a staircase." This is the *ban-treim*, as Jamie calmly notes. Roger defines this job as "a mourning woman.... They, um, keen. After the coffin." Though this moment starts ominously, the *ban-treim* is less horrifying than the sin-eater. Mrs. Gwilty is well-known in the community, and more amusingly, she is training her teenaged niece to the job. The latter's wailing is "a high, thready sound, not the robust keening they'd heard before. And uncertain—like an apprentice ghost" (*A Breath of Snow and Ashes*, ch. 39). Together they emphasize the community's role in funerals and the everyday work of keeping tradition alive.

Sword Dance

Scotland has an enormous variety of "Sword Dances" including the Jacobite Sword Dance, the Argyll Broadswords, the Broadswords of Lochiel, the Clansmen Sword Dance, the Lochaber Broadswords, the Elgin Long Sword Dance and the oldest, the Papa Stour. In all, one or more dancers would dance over crossed swords, careful not to displace them.

The sword dance itself, an ancient dance of war, is said to date back to King Malcolm Canmore, illegitimate son of King Duncan of Scotland, who had been killed by MacBeth the Earl of Moray (detailed in Shakespeare's famous play). In 1054, Malcolm led an army against MacBeth, defeating him at the battle of Dunsinnan. Malcolm thus won back his own lands, then defeated and killed MacBeth in 1057 at Lumphanan in Aberdeenshire, reclaiming his father's throne. He founded the dynasty of the House of Canmore, which lasted 200 years until the House of Stewart.

> After defeating one of MacBeth's generals at the Battle of Dunsinane in 1054, Malcolm placed his sword over that of his enemy and performed a dance over and atop them symbolizing both his victory and his martial dexterity, a quality admired in leaders at this period. Since, in addition to being a test of skill and agility, this dance of exultation in triumph became a dance of prophesy among the highland warriors. The legend says that warriors would perform the dance over them in order to predict the outcome of the next day's battle. If the dancer finished without touching the swords, he was assured of victory, but touching the swords could forecast defeat and death [Béguinot].

The older meaning of the dance, foretelling the battle to come, appears in a scene with Claire and Jamie. Claire says, "Danced on the eve of a battle, the skill of the dancer foretold success or failure. The young men had danced between crossed swords, the night before Prestonpans, before Falkirk. But not before Culloden. There had been no campfires the night before that final fight, no time for bards and battle songs. It didn't matter; no one had needed an omen, then" (*The Fiery Cross,* ch. 35).

As Claire explains, "A Highland sword dance was done for one of three reasons. For exhibition and entertainment, as [Jamie] was about to do it now. For competition, as it was done among the young men at a Gathering. And as it first was done, as an omen" (*The Fiery Cross,* ch. 35). The sword dance may also have been "simply an exercise used to develop and hone the nimble footwork required to stay alive in swordplay" (Johnson, "Highland Dancing"). Today, the combined competition/performance is seen in modern Scottish Gatherings and Highland Games, performed 95 percent by young women rather than by men. It requires tremendous dexterity not to displace the swords, and grace and strength are also factors. "According to tradition, the old kings and clan chiefs used the Highland Games as a means to select their best men at arms, and the discipline required to perform the Highland dances allowed men to demonstrate their strength, stamina and agility" (Johnson, "Highland Dancing").

Primarily to make judging easier, the dances performed were narrowed down through the decades, until many were lost. "As far as competitive Highland dancing is concerned, until 1986 only four standard dances remained—The Sword Dance (Gille Chaluim), The Seann Triubhas, The Highland Fling and The Reel of Tulloch" (Johnson, "Highland Dancing"). The Highland Fling is notable for being originally danced over a small round shield with a spike projecting from the center, known as a Targe. One legend calls it a warrior's dance of triumph following a battle (Johnson, "Highland Dancing").

The single-performer competition dance, the "Ghillie Callum" (servant of Malcolm) is still popular. Its lyrics describe King Malcolm's tax collector seeking coins, as the speaker insists he can "get a wife for tuppence" (Béguinot). While the words are light and romantic, the song ridicules the new coin of Malcolm's reign, the new bawbee, a debased Scottish halfpenny. The hated tax collector or Ghillie Callum walks the streets, calling for the money. A Ghillie meant a young man-servant, but also a soft tongueless shoe worn for traditional Scottish Highland dances.

In the fifth book, Jamie is pressured to perform the sword dance for his people at a celebration. He reluctantly agrees, but Claire notes that it's an omen of war, much like the Fiery Cross that is the book's namesake. As he dances, she reflects that Jamie has danced this many times, in competition and as an omen on the eve of battles. "The old soldiers had asked him to dance, had valued his skill as reassurance that they would live and triumph.... But that was in the Old World, and in his old life." Now that world is vanishing forever with its omens and traditions. "This was a new world, and the sword dance would never again be danced in earnest, seeking omen and favor from the ancient gods of war and blood" (*The Fiery Cross,* ch. 35).

Weddings

Two types of Scottish wedding exist. One, the handfasting, lasts for a year and a day. This is a Celtic ceremony dating from at least the Middle Ages, and was generally used as a temporary measure, until a wandering priest would stop by to perform the ceremony. Any child produced during the handfasting time was considered legitimate.

Jamie specifically doesn't want this ... possibly because it will give Claire a way out. More likely, he wants his wedding to be religiously sanctioned and proper with finery for bride and groom, rather than a hasty, clumsy affair. In the wedding episode, Jamie insists he'll wed "in a way that would make my mother proud." The type of wedding he insists on, in a church with a priest, is meant to be permanent, on earth and beyond. (He's shown in the series to truly believe he and Claire will reunite in heaven.)

Many traditions and rules surround the Scottish wedding. When the date of the marriage was fixed, it was and still is necessary to post the banns or the public announcement of the upcoming marriage. (This Dougal sidesteps by means of a bribe.) While the handfasting ceremony is sometimes incorporated into modern Scottish weddings and the medieval wedding featured a Gaelic ceremony outside the church before the formal Catholic vows inside, the eighteenth century used a traditional Catholic Mass. Historically, there's no sign of the blood-sharing or Outlander vows:

> Ye are Blood of my Blood, and Bone of my Bone.
> I give ye my Body, that we Two might be One.
> I give ye my Spirit, 'til our Life shall be Done [*Outlander,* ch. 15].

"When asked for the origins of this wonderful blood vow, during the Surrey Gathering, in October 1998, Diana Gabaldon told us she had created it," the Ladies of Lallybroch report.

Certainly the book one wedding takes place in a rush, with little time for more than a gown and a priest. But there are an enormous collection of Highland traditions excluded, mostly games and practical jokes beforehand for the bride and groom. Friends would bathe the bride's feet with luck promised to the first woman to find the ring placed in the basin, while the groom would have to wear a heavy knapsack of stones, unless he could be relieved of it with a kiss from his bride. The townsfolk would line the streets to cheer for the happy couple before they entered the church for the Latin mass. Rings were traditional, as were various customs that have now made it into the mainstream. "Something old, something new, something borrowed, something blue, and a silver sixpence in her shoe" is seen in England and Scotland, and America without the sixpence. Carrying the bride over the doorstep was crucial, since evil spirits could inhabit thresholds. Following the ceremony, a bagpiper would frequently lead the wedding party down the streets to the home of a relative, where all would feast and dance.

Claire and Jamie have a high-spirited supper with Dougal's men in the inn, and in the books, there's even dancing the night after. As Claire notes, "Women being in short supply, the innkeeper's wife and I tucked up our skirts and danced jigs and reels and strathspeys without ceasing" until the men dance individually and as a group. Then Jamie leads Claire in "something fast and frantic called The Cock o' the North" (ch. 16) (a slight anachronism, as the tune was so-named after the Fourth Duke of Gordon's raising the Gordon Highlanders in 1794).

In old days, the entire village would get involved in preparations, as they particularly do on the show, collecting gown, ring, priest, and plaid in a scavenger hunt. The power of community is seen in the later books' weddings at the Cameron Plantation in North Carolina. Brianna's and Jocasta's weddings both involve an extraordinary number of well-wishers visiting the plantation and offering gifts and advice, though few actual traditions are shown. In fact, the story focuses on the political machinations and family drama at the receptions, rather than the rituals. By contrast, a few private handfastings—Brianna's and Lizzie's—stress the romance of the intimate ceremony.

Other Cultures' Folklore

CARIBBEAN-AFRICAN/VODOU

Obeah-Man

In "Lord John and the Plague of Zombies," John receives warnings from the Obeah-Man after the governor is murdered. With a great skill with herbs and poisons, the Obeah man was said to be able to "render someone invincible, resuscitate the dead, cure all diseases, protect a man from the consequences of his crimes, and cause great harm to anyone he wished" (Giraldo). He could create a powder, reportedly, that would make warriors impervious to white men's weapons. This practice likely evolved from the Ashanti and Koromantin tribes of Africa on the Gold Coast, with slaves bringing it to the Caribbean in the mid-seventeenth century.

> The practice of harnessing supernatural forces and spirits for one's own personal use, known in some parts of Africa as "Obeye" (an entity that lives within witches), has taken on many names in the Caribbean islands, such as Shango (Trinidad), Santeria (Cuba), Vodun or Voodoo (Haiti), Ju-Ju (Bahamas), Obeah (Jamaica). Although African slaves usually practiced Obeah for "evil" or rather self-interested, instrumental purposes, this faith also aided them as a source of strength and clandestine resistance. The practice of Obeah is the belief that one can use certain spirits or supernatural agents to work harm to the living, or to call them off from such mischief. Generally, the British used the term Obeah to describe all slave acts and practices that were considered supernatural or evil in nature, such as rituals and fetishes [Giraldo].

Religious dances and drumming often provided a cover for rebellions to form. The frightened slave owners enacted laws banning nocturnal "gatherings" forbidding "any slave any poisonous drugs, pounded glass, parrot's beaks, dog's teeth, alligator's teeth, or other materials notoriously used in the practice of Obeah or witchcraft." Nonetheless, the practice continued to flourish, and poisonings were common among the slave owners. These men slowly accumulated power and respect that rivaled the largest plantation owners. This power they used for the benefit of their people.

"It is believed that practitioners, called obeah-men, can cure any illness and eliminate evil spirits" (Foubister, Kindle Locations 4962–4963). Obeah man and women were community leaders and teachers of African cultural heritage. They also led in slave rebellions and the other forms of resistance in Jamaica. A white Jamaican planter, Edward Long, best describes the ritual that the Obeah man initiated in order to administer the oaths:

> "Their priests, or obeiah-man, are their chief oracles in all weighty affairs, whether of peace, war, or the pursuit of revenge. When assembled for the purposes of conspiracy, the obeiah-man, after various ceremonies, draws a little blood from every one present; this is mixed in a bowl with gunpowder and grave dirt; the fetish or oath is administered by which they solemnly pledge themselves to inviolable secrecy, fidelity to their chiefs, and to wage perpetual war against their enemies; as a ratification of their sincerity, each person takes a cup of the mixture, and this finishes the solemn rite. Few or none of them have ever been known to violate this oath, or to desist from the full execution of it, even although several years may intervene" [qtd. in Giraldo].

Snakes

In "Lord John and the Plague of Zombies," John is told by several mystics that a snake is riding on his shoulders. Lord John has adapted a harmless yellow constrictor by this point, to deal with vermin, though the snake on his shoulders may take the form of an otherworldly visitor. Geillis adds that some of the *loas* are snakes and asks John if he's been dreaming of them. At the book's climax, John must pick up a deadly African krait. He survives the challenge, and the headman rewards him by taking the snake *loa* from his shoulders, adding, "You have carried him long enough, I think" (368).

Loa, or Vodou spirits, are not gods but servants of God. These divinities of West Africa were transplanted through slavery to the Caribbean and North and South America. Damballa, the father of the other *loa*, is an enormous green and black snake associated with the patriarchy as well as primal sexuality and creativity. Vodou practitioners believe that the gods' parents are serpents— Damballah and his mate Aido-Hwedo, the rainbow serpent who encircled the world: "The sacred language of Voodoo, called Langage, is said to have originated with Damballah's hissing. As the mother and father of the gods, Aido-Hwedo and Damballah taught people how to procreate and how to make blood sacrifices so that they could obtain the wisdom of the serpent" (Foubister, Kindle Locations 856–861). Serpent *loa* include the Simbi family of spirits from the

West Central Africa/Congo region. These include Simbi Anpaka, a *loa* of plants, leaves, and poisons; Simbi Dlo (Simbi of the Water), Simbi Makaya (Simbi of Sorcerers and Secret Societies), Simbi Andezo (Simbi of Two Waters), and Gran Simba.

Other snakes as companions and possible holy avatars appear in France: St. Germain proves a snake won't bite him in *Dragonfly,* emphasizing his role as a person of power. Later, in "The Space Between," he feeds live rats to the white snake his friend Madame Fabienne keeps as a familiar. Madame Fabienne's snake may be the same one Lord John carries on his shoulders, as she acquired it in the West Indies. She describes the snake as a *mystère,* or *loa,* "a spirit, one who is an intermediary between the Bondye and us. Bondye is *le bon Dieu,* of course" (175–176). Whether her snake or Lord John's haunting reappear in the series or not, both have been linked with a primitive magic. "Snakes were considered immortal because they were believed to renew themselves indefinitely by shedding old skins" (Walker 387). Thus snake gods and goddesses thrive worldwide, teaching the wisest of initiates the secrets to immortality.

Vodou

Haitian Vodou is a religion of the Caribbean. Its practitioners pray to the creator god *Bondye* (likely derived from the French term Bon Dieu, or Good Lord), and to the *loa* who serve him and busy themselves with earthly matters. The religion began in the eighteenth century, when the slave owners pressured slaves to convert to Christianity and tried to suppress their own religions. The male priest is called a *houngan,* with the duty of preserving the rituals and songs and maintaining the relationship between the *loa* and the community.

After the revolution of 1804, the Vatican broke with Haiti, thus freeing *houngans* and *mambos* (female priests) to lead the people religiously. The new faith combined Catholicism and traces of African religions, and when the church returned to Haiti in 1860, the religions largely merged. Each *loa* became associated with a Catholic saint (Dumballah the snake *loa* is Saint Patrick; Erzulie the earth mother is the Virgin Mary). Thus the religion continues in a modernized form through today.

Zombies

Geillis tells Lord John and Claire on separate occasions that a *houngan* has taught her to make zombies—one gives a person poison made from the liver of a fugu fish (blowfish) and partially buries them with a rotting corpse. When the person awakes, he thinks he is dead, and will obey orders until he wastes away and dies. There is no cure ("Lord John and the Plague of Zombies" 337). While this is a scientific experiment, done with drugs rather than magic, it contains the horror of having one's body co-opted and placed in a state of living death. A zombie bites Lord John, adding to the revulsion of the tale.

According to Vodou, the soul consists of two aspects: the *gros bon ange* (big good angel) and the *ti bon ange* (little good angel). The former controls biological functions, and the latter, personality and individual identity. The concept of these being separated lies behind the lore of the zombie. In Haitian Vodou, zombies were corpses raised by a *bokor* (sorcerer) to be his slaves, as they lacked free will. In modern times, zombies have been rationalized as fanciful tales, as individuals with schizophrenia, or as a metaphor for the evils of slavery in Haiti.

Wade Davis, a Harvard ethnobotanist, had a different theory with which Gabaldon is clearly familiar. As he published in *The Serpent and the Rainbow* (1985) and *Passage of Darkness: The Ethnobiology of the Haitian Zombie* (1988), he believed a living person could be transformed into a zombie by introducing special powders into the bloodstream: The first included tetrodotoxin (TTX) from a blowfish and the second, dissociative drugs such as datura. These would unite to place a person at the sorcerer's mercy. The scientific community was doubtful of Davis's story, especially since tetrodotoxin produces paralysis and death but not a trance state. Nonetheless, the theory earned attention at the time and has been smoothly integrated into Gabaldon's fantasy novellas, in which magic is frequently revealed as science and hoax.

CHINA

Acupuncture

Acupuncture likely began in China a few centuries before the Common Era. The first work describing it is *The Yellow Emperor's Classic of Internal Medicine*, from about 100 BCE, though its traditions likely come from earlier.

> The concepts of channels (meridians or conduits) in which the Qi (vital energy or life force) flowed are well established by this time, though the precise anatomical locations of acupuncture points developed later. Acupuncture continued to be developed and codified in texts over the subsequent centuries and gradually became one of the standard therapies used in China, alongside herbs, massage, diet and moxibustion (heat).... Bronze statues from the fifteenth century show the acupuncture points in use today, and were used for teaching and examination purposes. During the Ming Dynasty (1368–1644), *The Great Compendium of Acupuncture and Moxibustion* was published, which forms the basis of modern acupuncture. In it are clear descriptions of the full set of 365 points that represent openings to the channels through which needles could be inserted to modify the flow of Qi energy [White and Ernst].

Jesuit missionaries brought reports back to France of acupuncture as early as the sixteenth century, and it gained popularity. In the first half of the nineteenth century, interest rose through America and Britain. Western medicine became popular in China at the start of the twentieth century, and acupuncture declined, finally outlawed in 1929. After the Communist government took over in 1949, acupuncture was reinstated in a nationalistic move but also to provide basic levels of health to the massive population. Traditional medicine, including both acupuncture and herbalism, reemerged in China and spread across the world. Today the science and its effectiveness are hotly debated (White and Ernst).

Gabaldon introduced the Chinese sailor Yi Tien Cho, also called Mr. Willoughby, in book three specifically so he could supply Jamie with this technique, though the character grew significantly from this initial purpose. Yi Tien Cho leaves Claire his gold needles (which she must replace after various unfortunate adventures) and he teaches her the technique, which she uses on Jamie in future books.

Astrology

Yi Tien Cho realizes Jamie was born in the Year of the Ox, which Claire thinks is appropriate because of his obstinacy. "The intelligent and hard-working ox can be stubborn. But once aroused, the ox's feelings are deep" (Bruce-Mitford 113). People of this sign are moral and conservative with deepset values, regardless of their surroundings. They tend to be honest, industrious, and cautious, talented leaders with devotion and staying power. Jamie labors hard and keeps his principles in the most trying situations, with indeed an old-fashioned, resolute view of life.

Claire, though it's not mentioned in this scene, was born in 1918, the year of the horse. Horses love life and are beautiful, sexual, and temperamental, a reasonable summation of Claire. "Freedom-loving, good-humored, and generous, the horse is a popular and rather unpredictable character" (Bruce-Mitford 113). Horses are honest and open-minded but may throw tantrums when situations don't go their way. Spontaneous as they are, they tend to fall fast and hard into relationships and give themselves fully, to the point of chipping away at their inner being. This trait mellows with age, however, leading to more stable relationships later in life. Claire is indeed seen flinging herself headlong into love as she tries to resist Jamie but finally commits to him, then returns to him in increasingly perilous situations. She's also seen having outbursts on many occasions.

Ghosts

Yi Tien Cho tells Claire that in China there is a prophecy "that one day the ghosts will come. Everyone fear ghost.... I leave China to save my life. Waking up long time—I see ghosts. All round me, ghosts." As he returns to consciousness on the docks of Edinburgh, one of the ghosts is Jamie. He adds that by renaming him Willoughby, Jamie has eaten his soul (*Voyager*, ch. 61).

In Chinese thought, the world is populated by a vast number of spirits, both good and evil. There are ancestor ghosts, demons (*oni*), and hungry ghosts from the Buddhist tradition. Ghosts appear in many aspects of life, from music and theater to philosophy to religion. Ghost culture goes back to the pre–Qin Dynasty age, first orally then as classics such as *Notes on Searching Deities (Sou Shen Ji)*, *The Story of Chinese Gods (Feng Shen Zhuan)*, *Journey to the West*, etc. By the time of the Qing Dynasty, *Strange Stories from a Chinese Studio* and *Notes of Yuewei Cottage* had been added to the canon. In these stories, clever and resourceful humans normally defeat the spirits.

Guǐ is the general Chinese term for ghost. *Guilao*, literally "ghost man," is a term used to refer to white people. Many Cantonese speakers frequently use the term for foreigners in general and consider it non-derogatory. The term, appearing during the Opium Wars, can also have a connotation of "foreign devil." While it may be natural for Yi Tien Cho to refer to Jamie as a ghost, this phrase emphasizes his disassociation from his home, as well as foretelling Jamie's future.

Pelican

Mr. Willoughby captures a pelican to fish with and names it Ping An, the peaceful one.

> Ping An, the peaceful one, soared to the limit of his line, struggled to go higher, then, as though resigned, began to circle. Mr. Willoughby, eyes squinted nearly shut against the sun, spun slowly round and round on the deck below, playing the pelican like a kite. All the hands in the rigging and on deck nearby stopped what they were doing to watch in fascination.
>
> Sudden as a bolt from a crossbow, the pelican folded its wings and dived, cleaving the water with scarcely a splash. As it popped to the surface, looking mildly surprised, Mr. Willoughby began to tow it in. Aboard once more, the pelican was persuaded with some difficulty to give up its catch, but at last suffered its captor to reach cautiously into the leathery subgular pouch and extract a fine, fat sea bream [*Voyager*, ch. 44].

As shown here, the pelican stores fish in its enormous bill, then brings them home to feed its young ... or possibly someone else. For the pelican to empty its bill, it must press its bill against its breast in order to force out the contents. This makes it appear as if the pelican is stabbing itself in its breast, leading to its use as an icon of self-sacrifice.

In the bestiaries of mediaeval Europe, the pelican was thought to nourish its young with its own blood and thus became a symbol of Christ-like self-sacrifice. I Ching decks use a picture of a pelican to symbolize faithfulness and constancy. In all these ways, the pelican comes to symbolize Mr. Willoughby himself, as he rushes to defend Claire on several occasions. As with many magical animals in fantasy, Ping An arrives to warn Claire help is coming, moments before his master comes to the rescue. As such, it's a force of blessing, like many prophetic birds.

Phoenix

> "I was a Mandarin," Mr. Willoughby began, in Jamie's voice, "a Mandarin of letters, one gifted in composition. I wore a silk gown, embroidered in very many colors, and over this, the scholar's blue silk gown, with the badge of my office embroidered upon breast and back—the figure of a feng-huang—a bird of fire."—*Voyager,* ch. 45

The mystical bird Feng Huang first appeared to the Chinese emperor Hung Ti around 2600 BCE, and returned in times of peace and prosperity, to salute new emperors in their glory. It rules the southern quadrant of heaven, with the dragon, the unicorn and the tortoise warding the others. Its name combines the male and female principles: Feng is the male bird and Huang is the female. It is a bird of longevity and grace, and indeed, Yi Tien Cho is a survivor, clinging to the civilization of his background while surrounded, as he thinks, by barbarians.

As Jamie notes, in Europe, the bird is called a phoenix, symbol of resurrection and immortality. The phoenix builds a pyre for itself, dies on it, and is restored through the flames (generally three days later). Along with its symbolism of rebirth, it represents mind and spirit seeking the heights of enlightenment, as it is a creature of flight. When the phoenix relinquishes its old and completed self, it does so because it feels it is ready to be transformed into a higher being. As such, it symbolizes creative destruction leading to rebirth within the mind. It reflects Mr. Willoughby's remaking of himself in a new land and culture but also Jamie and Claire's many renamings and struggles with identity in the third book. They too seek a new land and new adventures that will broaden them and show them a true purpose.

Worry Balls

> "Healthy balls," Mr. Willoughby explained, rolling them together in his palm. They made a pleasant clicking noise. "Streaked jade, from Canton," he said. "Best kind of healthy balls."
>
> "Really?" I said, fascinated. "And they're medicinal—good for you, that's what you're saying?"
>
> He nodded vigorously, and then stopped abruptly with a faint moan. After a pause, he spread out his hand, and rolled the balls to and fro, keeping them in movement with a dexterous circling of his fingers.

> "All body one part; hand all parts," he said. He poked a finger toward his open palm, touching delicately here and there between the smooth green spheres. "Head there, stomach there, liver there," he said. "Balls make all good."—*Voyager,* ch. 26

Baoding balls, also known as Chinese medicine balls, and "healthy balls" as Yi Tien Cho calls them, date back to the Ming dynasty, and were popular in Baoding, China. Two balls are rotated in the hand as recovery therapy or to improve manual dexterity and strength. Emphasizing the connection between all the parts of the body (also seen in acupressure and acupuncture), they are still popular today.

Europe

Alchemists and Wizards

In the second book, a servant says the Comte St. Germain "has a very bad reputation."

> "He has sold his soul to the Devil, you know," she confided, lowering her voice and glancing around as though that gentleman might be lurking behind the chimney breast. "He celebrates the Black Mass, at which the blood and flesh of innocent children are shared amongst the wicked!" [*Dragonfly in Amber,* ch. 7]

Nonetheless, Marguerite adds that he's rich enough that all the women chase him anyway.

The historical St. Germain was a figure of magic and mystery, as well as amazing longevity, so it's unsurprising to see him involved in the occult powers within this series. Other fantasy writers have linked Saint-Germain's mysterious life with the fantastical—Chelsea Quinn Yarbro made him an immortal vampire living as a romantic hero in different time periods. Gabaldon notes: "The Comte St. Germain was a real character of the times, and one with a reputation for being involved in occult matters—but very little else seemed known for sure about him. I consequently took nothing but his name and his unsavory associations, and beyond that, invented wholesale" (*Outlandish Companion* 139).

After appearing in the second book, the count, also known as Paul Rakoczy, plots through the short story "The Space Between." In addition, Geillis owns *Le Grimoire d'le Comte St Germain*—a handbook of magic (*Outlander,* ch. 24). She has already met Saint-Germain while calling herself Melisande Robicheau and staying in Paris. In World War II, a Polish pilot named Paul Rakoczy appears in "A Leaf on the Wind of All Hallows," suggesting he indeed learned to travel to the future.

The historical St. Germain has a vague origin. Possibly he was a son of Francis Racoczi II, Prince of Transylvania and was raised by the powerful and mystical Medici family of Italy. His contemporary, Prince Karl of Hesse, wrote:

> He told me that he was eighty-eight years of age when he came here, and that he was the son of Prince Ragoczy of Transylvania by his first wife, a Tékéli. He was placed, when quite young, under the care of the last Duc de Medici (Gian Gastone), who made him sleep while still a child in his own room. When M. de St. Germain learned that his two brothers, sons of the Princess of Hesse-Wahnfried (Rheinfels), had become subject to the Emperor Charles VI., and had received the titles and names of St. Karl and St. Elizabeth, he said to himself: 'Very well, I will call myself Sanctus Germano, the Holy Brother.' I cannot in truth guarantee his birth, but that he was tremendously protected by the Duc de Medici I have learnt from another source [Cooper-Oakley 11–12].

St. Germain was known for his love of jewels, which he carried about in a casket and had painted all over him in portraits. "His only luxury consists of a large number of diamonds, with which he is fairly covered; he wears them on every finger, and they are set in his snuffboxes and his watches. One evening he appeared at court with shoe buckles, which Herr v. Gontaut, an expert on precious stones, estimated at 200,000 Francs" (Cooper-Oakley 29). Jewels of course have mystical powers and are eventually revealed to be useful in Gabaldon's time travel.

"A man who knows everything and who never dies," said Voltaire of him. Saint-Germain created a great mystique around himself, insisting that he'd lived for centuries and met historical figures like Jesus. He never ate in public, adding to his legend. Though he was around fifty in his time in court in the 1740s, an old relative of a French ambassador at Venice insisted he'd known Saint-Germain to be the same age in 1710, and Mme. d'Adhémar (in her *Souvenirs sur Marie Antoinette*) reported him looking unchanged when he counseled the queen around the French Revolution. In addition, his death was unverified—rumors of Saint-Germain sightings followed over many years. An Englishman, Albert Vandam describes a meeting with someone occultists think may have been Saint-Germain in 1821:

> He called himself Major Fraser, lived alone and never alluded to his family. Moreover he was lavish with money, though the source of his fortune remained a mystery to everyone. He possessed a marvelous knowledge of all the countries in Europe at all periods. His memory was absolutely incredible and, curiously enough, he often gave his hearers to understand that he had acquired his learning elsewhere than from books. Many is the time he has told me, with a strange smile, that he was certain he had known Nero, had spoken with Dante, and so on.

This is a delightful coincidence (presumably) as in Gabaldon's work, he is a time traveler and business rival of Jamie's, who might conceivably take the name of an old acquaintance for his future endeavors. Thus Gabaldon makes him a master of the occult who can hear the stones, and indeed, he already fit the pattern quite well.

In Paris, Claire meets the herbalist "Maitre Raymond," a "wizard" as he's called, who dispenses cures and poisons of all sorts. When Claire lies ill, he heals her strangely by manipulating her aura. He also gives her an amulet to protect her from poison. With an unsavory reputation for sorcery, he takes an interest in Kaballah (Jewish mysticism), astronomy, and other subjects. Claire recognizes the symbols painted on a cabinet and notes, "While there was a strong interest in occult matters among some of the French literati and the aristocracy, it was an interest kept highly clandestine, for fear of the Church's cleansing wrath" (*Dragonfly in Amber*, ch. 16). He dispenses herbs and advice to Claire throughout the book like a mystical mentor. In the 1960s, several men train with a mysterious "Raymond" who tells them to use stones to protect themselves and concentrate on their destinations. It's likely this is the same man, a Traveler.

The most famous apothecary shops and cabinets of curiosities, and even cathedrals like the *Catedral* of Seville showed off a stuffed crocodile or alligator hanging from the ceiling. While they were ferocious creatures, they also represented evil (the primordial leviathan) kept in check "deriving from its resemblance to the dragon and the serpent, as a symbol of knowledge" (Cirlot 67). Thus, displaying one could ward off the evil eye. Master Raymond has one himself hanging from the ceiling. He tells Claire it's real, as it "gives the customers confidence" (*Dragonfly in Amber,* ch. 8).

Maitre Raymond and the Comte de Saint-Germain both dabble in alchemy, the predecessor to modern chemistry. This was "a richly symbolic science that united practical discovery with a mystical view of nature" (Bruce-Mitford 108). As such, it emphasized formulas and ingredients but also the transmutation of man from the crude to the spiritually perfect. Alchemists united opposing elements such as fire and water, and attempted to reach the fifth element, quintessence, which symbolized the spirit. Both men are seeking the truths of the world and (in their own ways) seeking to better themselves. Thus they make fascinating mentors and rivals for Claire, who stills struggles with her place in the world.

In a later story, Master Raymond helps the Count de Saint Germain to travel forward in time. Both men can see auras, and share Claire's blue aura, indicating magic (possibly healing, possibly traveling) and a family link ("The Space Between," 216). In 1739, a few years before the events of *Outlander,* Roger while time traveling meets the healer Dr. Hector McEwan, who also heals through auras. He reveals he's a time traveler from 1841 (*Written in My Own Heart's Blood*, ch. 37). It's unclear whether he's met Raymond, or simply has learned auras and touch-healing on his own. Claire may achieve this level of power as she continues to aid others.

Claire is struck by Raymond's skulls, which he calls "company of a sort."

> He had everything, it seemed. Tiny skulls, of bat, mouse and shrew, the bones transparent, little teeth spiked in pinpoints of carnivorous ferocity. Horses, from the huge Percherons, with massive scimitar-shaped jaws looking eminently suitable for flattening platoons of Philistines, down to the skulls of donkeys, as stubbornly enduring in their miniature curves as those of the enormous draft horses. They had a certain appeal, so still and so beautiful, as though each object held still the essence of its owner, as if the lines of bone held the ghost of the flesh and fur that once they had borne [*Dragonfly in Amber,* ch. 16].

One strange talent Claire has is in reading bones—Raymond with his massive collection of skulls may share her ability. In *Voyager,* examining an ancient skull in the twentieth-century, Claire feels "the shifting sadness, filling the cavity of the skull like running water. And an odd faint sense—of surprise?" Claire notes, "Someone killed her.... She didn't want to die" (ch. 20). Later, to her horror, Claire realizes she knew the skull's owner and how she perished.

Astrology/Zodiac

The Outlandish Companion contains horoscopes for Jamie and Claire, done by fan and astrologer Kathy Pigou.

> Jamie
> Birth date: May 1, 1721
> Time of birth: approx. 6:30 p.m.
> Birthplace: (near) Inverness, Scotland

Thus Jamie is a Taurus, "practical and reliable, yet with a stubborn streak" (Bruce-Mitford 112). Pigou finds many aspects of Jamie's chart fit the character very strongly, from his stubbornness and practicality to his future marriage. His sun is in the seventh house, indicating, "Marriage is important, and he may have increased success after marriage. His wife will be strong and loyal, as will his friends. He has a self-confident manner and deals well with the public, and is popular and easy to get along with." His moon in the ninth house suggests "He is a natural teacher and philosopher who is imaginative and fond of travel, and may live far from his birthplace. His religious beliefs are orthodox, and he has emotional attachment to the values instilled in childhood."

> Claire
> Birth date: October 20, 1918
> Time of birth: 2:09 p.m.
> Birthplace: London

Claire is a Libra, a champion for fairness and balance. Indeed, she worries over the lives she's saved and taken as she struggles to preserve the future as well as the past. Pigou adds: "This person performs best when part of a partnership, while maintaining her individuality. She is most likely to be married, sometimes more than once." Her sun in the ninth house indicates "a person who is interested in other cultures and traditions. She is adventurous, likely to travel widely, and may marry a foreigner." The charts, significantly longer than this, reflect many fascinating aspects of Jamie and Claire's characters, showing how well they correspond with the signs of their birthdates.

Auld Wife

It was a small chunk of stone, pale pink in color, and veined with gray, badly weathered. It had been crudely carved into the shape of a pregnant woman, little more than a huge belly, with swollen breasts and buttocks above a pair of stubby legs that tapered to nothing. I had seen such figures before—in museums [*The Fiery Cross,* ch. 34].

Roger mentions that the ones he's seen are "dated at thousands of years," and reverently touches the one Claire has been given. Claire stops Brianna from touching it. Though Claire is a rational scientist, she, like Roger, appears to sense the ancient power of the totem before them. Claire describes wishing Brianna wouldn't touch it, while Roger stares at the idol and Brianna. "I could almost imagine that he was willing her to touch the thing, as strongly as I was willing her not to. (*The Fiery Cross,* ch. 35).

This scene explores Brianna's interest in getting pregnant, but also suggests the magic of the fertility charm may be more than superstition, in a world with standing stones that transport people by magic. It is an artifact from a far more ancient time placed among the poems and charms of the Scots. A gift from the matriarch Mrs. Bug, it emphasizes the women's charms and ancient women's power pervading their homestead.

Decorating Geillis's house are ancient statues of women, "hugely pregnant, or with enormous, rounded breasts and exaggerated hips, and all with a vivid and mildly disturbing sexuality about them" (*Voyager,* ch. 60). Geillis comments that all men are obsessed with the female form, but only the former slaves worship it.

Made by Neolithic farmers thousands of years before the creation of the pyramids or Stonehenge, ancient figures across the world depict females with exaggerated breasts and hips. They mostly appear in the Near East and Egypt from as far back as 5000 BC, but also in Romania and the Ukraine, Greece, Crete, India, and Rome. They are often nicknamed "Venus figurines" or mother-goddess statues, and are thought to be fertility idols and charms meant to bring about pregnancy or safe birth. The Sheela na Gig is a common stone carving found in Ireland, Great Britain, and Europe as far out as the Czech Republic, but this depicts a trickster-crone rather than fertility goddess.

Auras

All living things (people, plants, animals, etc.) generate a magnetic field that many say can be sensed and even seen. Auras, particularly those around humans, appear in the teachings of Buddhists, Hindus, and Native Americans, as well as new age Wiccans. Mostly they appear nowadays in alternative medicine, treating mind-body-spirit as a unit. The aura of a person is bigger and brighter when they're healthy in terms of physical vitality, mental clarity, emotional well-being, and spiritual energies. In the books, Master Raymond, the Count de Saint Germain, and the doctor Hector McEwan can see and manipulate auras. Raymond explains, "All healing is done essentially by reaching the ... what shall we call it? the soul? the essence? say, the center. By reaching the patient's center, from which they can heal themselves" (*Dragonfly in Amber*, ch. 20).

When asked how Master Raymond heals Claire, Gabaldon responded on her Facebook page, "Though many years later, I happened to discover the art/science of jin shin jyutsu," which apparently syncs up perfectly with the scene in the book. Jin Shin Jyutsu involves redirecting life energy within the body and unblocking its pathways, gently balancing the flow of life energy. This laying of hands in more art than formula creates harmony between the self and the universe.

Raymond describes time traveler's auras as blue, for those who can perceive them. He calls Claire Madonna for her blue aura, linking her with the grace and peace of the Virgin Mary in her blue cloak. Claire sees blue when she operates on Henry Grey, and when she tries to save an unborn baby—she seems to be developing an understanding in this area, as relates to healing. To Saint Germain, this magic feels "like water—like lightning!" ("The Space Between," 240). A blue aura means a cool, calm, and collected personality. Its person is caring and intuitive. Bright royal blue can indicate clairvoyance or a highly spiritual nature.

By contrast, Raymond calls Jamie the "Red Man." While he has red hair, this term sounds like one of alchemy or auras. A red aura relates to the physical body, with enormous friction that attracts or repels others with its high emotion. Deep red indicates its owner is realistic, active, and survival-oriented, while clear red is powerful, competitive, energetic, sexual, and passionate with a healthy ego. Gabaldon adds, describing Raymond:

> He is—or was—a shaman, born with the ability to heal through empathy. He sees auras plainly; those with his power all have the blue light he has—born warriors, on the other hand, are red (so yes, "the red man" is iconic). He has a rather strong aversion to Vikings, owing to events that happened in his own time; hence his nervousness when he sees Jamie. He's afraid of them, but he also realizes just what a strong life-force they have—that's why he makes Claire invoke it (using the sexual and emotional link between her and Jamie) to heal her ["FAQ"].

La Dame Blanche

In France, Claire becomes known as La Dame Blanche (French, "white lady"). As the French butler describes her in the second book: "She is called a wisewoman, a healer. And yet … she sees to the center of a man, and can turn his soul to ashes, if evil be found there" (*Dragonfly in Amber,* ch. 20).

It's soon revealed that Jamie told his drinking pals that being faithful to Claire wasn't just a whim—if he cheated on his wife, a White Lady, she'd "shrivel [his] private parts" (*Dragonfly in Amber,* ch. 20). The drunken men were suitably impressed and warned off, as Claire discovers later. In Scotland, Jamie compares Claire to Dame Aliset, a white witch at St. Mary's Well at Grampian, who cured a faery child with the well's healing water. Gabaldon comments: "Given Claire's naturally pale complexion, her healing arts (and the ruthlessness which is a natural part of them), and her supernatural connections (both real and perceived)," it seemed "only reasonable" to endow her with the title (*Outlandish Companion* 195).

In French, Dutch, and Germanic folklore, White Ladies were a type of vicious fairy. Thomas Keightley describes the Dames Blanches as a type of Fée known in Normandy "of a less benevolent character" who lurk in narrow places like ravines or bridges and make travelers show respect or block them from passing.

> One of these ladies named La Dame d' Aprigny, used to appear in a winding narrow ravine which occupied the place of the present Rue Saint Quentin at Bayeux, where, by her involved dances, she prevented any one from passing. She meantime held out her hand, inviting him to join her, and if he did so she dismissed him after a round or two; but if he drew back, she seized him and flung him into one of the ditches which were full of briars and thorns. Another Dame Blanche took her station on a narrow wooden bridge over the Dive, in the district of Falaise, named the Pont d' Angot. She sat on it and would not allow any one to pass unless he went on his knees to her; if he refused, the Fee gave him over to the *lutins,* the cats, owls, and other beings which, under her sway, haunt the place, by whom he was cruelly tormented.

Like many fairies and like Claire herself, La Dame Blanche makes a formidable friend or enemy and expects respect from the men who want her aid. Also like many fairies, White Ladies are most likely pre–Christian place guardians, spirits of lakes or mountains. An ancient statue of Bride (or possibly predating Bride) features early in *Voyager* as Jamie hears the tale of a White Lady, ventures there, and discovers a hidden treasure.

In Germany, the Weisse Frauen (White Women) likely derive from the Light Elves of Norse myth. They are guardians of treasure, often benevolent, but more powerful than man. Jacob Grimm believed that they might also derive from the pre–Christian goddess Mother Holda (ch. 32). Grimm notes the image of the Weisse Frauen basking in the sun and bathing "melts into the notion of a water-holde and nixie," semi-treacherous water spirits (ch. 32). Other writers associate the White Ladies with ghosts. Sometimes they capture travelers and make them dance themselves to death.

Near Lochem and Zwiep comes a legend about the "Wittewijvenkuil" (White Women pit) inhabited by three White Women who floated around in the area at night. The White Women came to enjoy the company of two children, Herbert and his sister Aaltje, who visited to play and pick flowers. At one point, the White Women saved Herbert's life, and he had his sister bake them a cake in thanks. In time, Herbert fell in love with a girl called Johanna. Her parents decided that Herbert and the other suitor should race on horseback to the White Women pit at night, Herbert to the western edge, and Albrecht to the southern edge. There they had to throw a spit into the pit while saying the rhyme, "Witte Wieven wit, hier breng ik oe het spit" ("White Women white, here I bring you the spit"), and the first one to return would be allowed to marry Johanna.

> Both boys accepted the challenge, though Herbert knew that he had no chance because Albrecht had a faster horse; they both rode off and Albrecht quickly led, but halfway through the forest Albrecht became afraid; he threw his spit into the bushes and went back.
>
> Herbert continued and he reached the White Women pit, he threw his spit into the pit and shouted; "Witte wieven wit, hier breng ik oe het spit!"; the rest of the White Women was disturbed and they came out of the pit screaming in anger, Herbert quickly turned his horse and rode off with the White Women in hot pursuit, one of them had caught the spit and held it in her hand, she was quickly coming closer and he could feel her hot breath in his neck, suddenly he saw light in the dark night; Johanna had lit a lamp to show him the way to her farm and she opened the doors to let him in; Herbert and his horse jumped through the opened doors and Johanna quickly closed it before the White Woman's nose.
>
> The White Woman saw her prey escaping and angry she threw the spit at Herbert, but it hit the door and pierced into it.
>
> Johanna's parents kept their word and when the spring came Herbert and Johanna married, after the marriage they returned to Johanna's farm and they found something on the ground; a plate similar to the one Herbert had used to offer the cake to the White Women and a spit, both were made of gold; despite the nightly disturbance the White Women favoured Herbert and Johanna and had shown this with a wedding gift [Reginheim].

In the city of Vorden, the White Women were called "Völeken," who inhabited hills and stones (another link with the Light Elves). They were believed to come into houses at night to turn furniture upside-down. A local tale from 1790 has a man suddenly yanked into a hill by the Völeken, never to return. Near the city of Hummelo are the Witte Kolk ("White Pool"), the Zwarte Kolk ("Black

Pool"), and the Wrangebult ("Thorn-hedge-hill")—a "wrange," or plaited hedge of thorns, was often created around a holy place. According to legend, twelve White Women would appear out of the Witte Kolk at midnight, and then travel to the nearby Wrangebult, where pagan sacrifices had once been offered (Reginheim).

However, in the Dutch, *witte* means both white and wise, casting their folkloric figures as a cross between the community's midwives and the French spirit women. Whichever the women were, folk believed they could foresee the future. After death, they were destined to travel the world, helping others in a cross between doctors, ghosts, and fairies. Gabaldon notes that the White Lady "presides over both birth and death—which, it struck me, was pretty much what a doctor does" (*Outlandish Companion* 195). As this guardian of life's borders, she identifies with the Crone aspect of the Goddess.

This emphasis on the White Lady as an elderly wisewoman stresses that she will grow into her full power late in life. The healer or midwife of a community was often mature and experienced. She was an unknowable figure, skilled in walking the pathways between life and death.

> She was "crone" in its original meaning, from Greek *cronos*, meaning time. Like Kali (from Sanskrit *kala*, also meaning time), she is mistress of the life cycle and of prophecy. The Dark Mother, the third of the trinity, is often seen as Time the Destroyer. She inhales all the worlds at the end and exhales them at time's beginning. She is beyond time and space and the whole of manifestation. She is called "dark" because she is mysterious—we, as mortal, time- and space-bound creatures cannot really conceive of Her [Frankel 290].

In tales, she would be the one to dispense advice on spells and charms as well. For Gabaldon, combining the skills of doctor and time traveler made perfect sense: "Given the circumstances of Claire's story—her disappearance through standing stones—there was plainly going to be an air of mystery and magic about it. What occupation could be more appropriate than that of healer—an occupation that has about it the same air of mystery and hint of magic?" (*Outlandish Companion* 194).

In a more sinister moment, King Louis of France calls on Claire to make a judgment as a Dame Blanche: a woman who sees through lies. Though Claire hesitates, she throws herself into the role: Her enemy and her friend are both accused of sorcery and she must decide who lives and dies. As she says: "I didn't know whether the pursuit of an honorable cause justified the use of dishonorable means. I didn't know what one life was worth—or a thousand. I didn't know the true cost of revenge. I did know that the cup I held in my hands was death" (*Dragonfly in Amber,* ch. 27). As White Lady, she makes the choice and learns to live with it after.

Succubus

In "Lord John and the Succubus," Lord John's friend Stephan von Namtzen explains, "The succubus takes possession of the body of a dead person, and rests within it by day." Thus it can hide within a churchyard and emerge to terrorize sleeping folk at night (59). The word is derived from the Latin *succubae*, "paramour," first seen in this form in 1387. This short story is not the only reference: the chapter title in *Written in My Own Heart's Blood*, "The Succubus of Cranesmuir," refers to Geillis Duncan, who shares much of the fabled personality. Francis Barrett, a believer in demonology, wrote *The Magus* to describe these creatures:

> And, seeing the Faunii and Nymphs of the woods were preferred before the others in beauty, they afterwards generated their offspring amongst themselves, and at length began wedlocks with men, feigning that, by these copulations, they should obtain an immortal soul for them and their offspring; but this happened through the persuasions and delusions of Satan to admit these monsters to carnal copulation, which the ignorant were easily persuaded to and therefore these Nymphs are called Succubii: although Satan afterwards committed worse, frequently transchanging himself, by assuming the persons of both Incubii and Succubii, in both sexes; but they conceived not a true young by the males, except the Nymphs alone [qtd. in Robbins 490].

Succubae were known for tempting saints such as St. Anthony of Egypt and his disciple St. Hilary. The former was tempted by a devil "throwing filthy thoughts in his way" while "imitating all the gestures of a woman" while the latter was "encircled by naked women" when he lay down to sleep (Robbins 491). St. Hippolytus was lured to impurity by a naked woman, but when he resisted and covered her modestly with his cloak, she transformed into a corpse (Robbins 491). Consorting with succubae appears as a common accusation in sixteenth and seventeenth century witch trials.

The German equivalent is the *mare* or *mara*, a beautiful woman who rides on people's chests while they sleep, crushing them and bringing on bad dreams (hence the word nightmare). Sometimes she tortures them with desire, and drags the life out of them. In the story, the Prussian Princess Louisa calls it *Der Nachtmahr*, the Nightmare (110). Jamie too links dreams with this evil spirit: Trapped in terrible nightmares of Jack Randall, and then waking, Jamie feels "the wounds bleed clean again as the succubus drew its claws from his heart" (*The Drums of Autumn*, ch. 48).

In Serbia, the *mora* could be repelled through exotic means, from turning the pillow and making a sign of cross on it to leaving a broom upside down behind the door, or putting a belt on top of the sheets. Lord John is told that riding a white stallion over the grave will lay the demon to rest. As it turns out, the succubus is a hoax. Nonetheless, as the story brushes against magic and superstition, John must involve himself in an extensive investigation amid bats and ethereal charms in the haunted outskirts of future Germany.

NATIVE AMERICAN

Scots and Native Americans

> The tribalism of the Native Americans in the eastern part of North America was quite similar in many respects to that of Gaeldom, and maintained its independence for about as long (the Ulster Scottish or Scotch-Irish immigrants who settled the territory west of the Appalachians had practiced the techniques of fortifying their farms against hostile tribes during their tenure as settlers in Northern Ireland around 1600). Indications of early contact between the North American Indians and the IndoEuropeans are further suggested by the physical anthropology of the former. Their pre–Columbian physical remains have even been described as being less Oriental and more relatively European the more easterly their provenance—Cairney 22

The later books take the main characters to North Carolina where they encounter Tuscarora, Cherokee, and Iroquois, along with other tribes. When Claire is called on to minister to a dying man of the Tuscarora, Ian urges her to mix her customs with his and paint her face like a wisewoman. Several shared traditions appear: Ian advises Claire not to say the dying man's name: it will call demons. As he adds, she should sing to speed him on his way. "Tantum ergo, maybe; it sounded a wee bit like that" (*The Drums of Autumn,* ch. 26). Thus Claire eases the man with a Catholic prayer, one that his culture can accept as much as hers. Ian's warning that using the man's name will summon him is paralleled in comments about ghosts several times in the series.

Both cultures also share a belief in the fairyfolk:

> "Little People? Will that be like the faeries?" Jamie sounded surprised.
> "Something of the kind." Bonnet shifted his weight and the seat creaked as he stretched. "The [Cherokee] Indians do say that the Nunnahee live inside the rocks of the mountains, and come out to help their people in time of war or other evil."
> "Is that so? It will be something like the tales they tell in the Highlands of Scotland, then—of the Auld Folk."
> "Indeed." Bonnet sounded amused. "Well, from what I have heard of the Scotch Highlanders, there is little to choose between them and the red men for barbarous conduct."
> "Nonsense," said Jamie, sounding not the least offended. "The red savages eat the hearts of their enemies, or so I have heard. I prefer a good dish of oatmeal parritch, myself" [*The Drums of Autumn,* ch. 2].

Cherokee medicine men would travel to the rock caves to meet the Little People and sing songs for good crops and hunting in the coming year. On the seventh night, they'd dance together. These long-haired spirits were known for benevolence and gentleness. If one heard their drums in the distance, it was best not to follow, for the people often did not wish to be disturbed in their revels.

While Jamie considers the "red savages" far different from himself, he soon learns differently. He first encounters a few hunters and communicates with them using signs—as hunters and warriors they understand each other clearly without words. Claire notes, that he has seen their rituals "so like his own—and known them at once for fellow hunters; civilized men" (*The Drums of Autumn,* ch. 15). Jamie observes that the tribes and Scots have many traditions in common, beginning with the prayers they both say upon killing animals. Their loyalty to the larger group is also a parallel. Gabaldon comments:

> The clan system itself is particularly compelling, with its tradition of loyalty and self-sacrifice (and its interesting parallels to the Native American tribal cultures; there's a reason why Scottish immigrants often lived with and intermarried with Indians)—people are always intrigued by the notion of people living for something greater than themselves [Brittain].

The Tuscarora sprinkle whiskey in the four directions after killing a bear, an act Jamie understands perfectly. He tells Claire: "It's a charm. Ye scatter holy water to the four airs of the earth, to preserve yourself from evil" (*The Drums of Autumn,* ch. 15). A similar discussion follows in the next book:

> "Aye, well, I shouldna say it's anyone, so to speak. Only that the shamans say there is a spirit who lives in each o' the four directions, and each spirit has a color to him—so when they go to singin' their prayers and the like, they'll maybe call the Red Man o' the East to help the person they're singing for, because Red is the color of triumph and success. North, that's blue—the Blue Man, to give the spirit of the North his right name—that's defeat and trouble. So ye'd call on him to come and give your enemy a bit of grief, aye? To the South, that's the White Man, and he's peace and happiness; they sing to him for the women with child, and the like."
> Jamie looked both startled and interested to hear this.
> "That's verra like the four airts, Peter, is it no?"
> "Well, it is, then," Peter agreed, nodding. "Odd, no? That the Cherokee should get hold of the same notions as we Hielanders have?"
> "Oh, not so much." Jamie gestured to the dark wood, beyond the small circle of our fire. "They live as we do, aye? Hunters, and dwellers in the mountains. Why should they not see what we have seen?" [*The Fiery Cross,* ch. 81].

The two cultures find other opportunities to share their legends. "The Cherokee were in fact a great deal like the Scottish Highlanders, particularly in terms of liking stories," Claire notes (*The Fiery Cross*, ch. 82). As with the Scottish folktales, stories often appear to add local color and show the vibrant traditions of each culture. Young Sungi tells Claire a story of a ball game, that describes how bats were first given wings (*The Fiery Cross,* ch. 82)—this story appears in different collections of Cherokee tales.

Another connection lies in the Scots' persecution by the English, as they were chased from their lands and dismissed as barbarians. There is a Kahnyen'kehaka legend of hunters finding two snakes, one gold and one silver. While they seemed beautiful and the hunters brought them home, disaster struck. They ate everything and grew truly enormous, so much so that they swelled bigger than mountains. The warriors dragged them some distance away, where they continued to grow. However, the wise ones of the tribe prophesized that one day a great bowman would be able to vanquish the powerful serpents: Canada and the United States. Claire must decide whether to warn their friends about the similar doom of the mass relocations and the Trail of Tears. She and Jamie decide the situation is like Culloden—history cannot change, but perhaps a few people, warned, might escape.

Young Ian and Brianna compare dream-lore, important to the Kahnyen'kehaka and the Scots as well. Ian tells her, "The Kahnyen'kehaka set great store by dreams. More even than Highlanders." When she tells him she dreamed of birds, he adds, "That's good, to dream of live birds, especially if they sing. Dead birds are a bad thing, in a dream." (*A Breath of Snow and Ashes,* ch. 70)

At the same time, the Native Americans and Scottish have several widely different traditions. Young Ian notes that a woman invites a man to live in her house for as long as she wishes, then may dismiss him, unlike the Scottish marriage traditions. Ian also notes, "The Kahnyen'kehaka think to have a likeness of someone gives ye power over them. That's why the medicine society wear false faces—so the demons causing the illness willna have their true likeness and willna ken who to hurt, aye?" (*A Breath of Snow and Ashes,* ch. 55). A visiting scholar offers to sketch the chief's wife and is driven from the village.

Wisewoman

Claire mostly doctors people with medicine, prescribing plants with quinine to treat malaria or opium for pain. However, on occasion she's called to offer something deeper and more mysterious. After Jamie has been tortured, Claire reenacts his nightmares to give him a chance to break through them and heal. She sits at deathbeds and comforts however she can. The wisewoman Nayawenne of the nearby Tuscarora tribe brings her a charm that she treasures and teaches her deep secrets of healing magic. Gabaldon explains she incorporated this into the story because "there is a magical aspect to the practice of medicine, and always has been, though this aspect was decried and ignored for some time" (*Outlandish Companion* 194). Placebos work, and so do inexplicable practices and folk medicine beyond Claire's official medical training.

Nayawenne teaches Claire a great deal about the New World and the mystical. Like many Native American nations, the Tuscarora have no word for religion. They consider all aspects of life as being religious in nature. On the East Coast, a popular creation story tells of the Woman Who Fell From the Sky, or Ataensic. Sky Woman lived far above the Earth. However, one day she grew curious and pulled up a large plant that grew there, creating a hole. She fell far to the vast ocean below. Floating there, she watched as Turtle, Muskrat, and other animals brought earth for her to lie on. Soon after, Sky Woman gave birth to twins, one evil and the other good. The evil one burst through her side and killed her. While the good one created the sun, moon, stars, mountains, and many animals and plants, the evil one created darkness, monsters, and storms. This story parallels Claire, as she too, gives in to curiosity and tumbles through to a new land. More importantly, it establishes woman as the source of all life and knowledge in the world. Nayawenne, a leader of her community, parallels Sky Woman in her own way. In the fourth book, several evil children are created, as genocide and despair lead several men to follow the path of war and savagery. It's the job of Claire and Nayawenne to heal their peoples, as much as possible.

Each identifies the other as a magical woman. Such mysteries were often reserved for the elders of the community—it was thought that women past menopause hoarded their personal magic rather than spending it on procreation. "Many cultures believed that by retaining menstrual blood within, the crone claimed power over her magical energy and became an awesome figure....The crones are mentors or soothsayers, prophesying the triumphs of kings and the downfall of kingdoms" (Frankel 275). Claire is in her fifties and sixties in the late books and has become a crone and wisewoman as well as matriarch. Gabaldon explains:

> It is quite possibly not coincidental that Ishmael (*Voyager*) asks Claire whether she "still bleeds," explaining that only old women can work real magic—nor is it coincidental that the Tuscaroran seer, Nayawenne, told Claire that she would achieve her full power "when your hair is white" (*Drums*). On the other hand, it was purely coincidental that Geillis Duncan's hair should have been a blonde so pale as to be "almost white, the color of heavy cream." Or at least I think it was [*Outlandish Companion* 196].

The Wendigo

This is a human being turned into an endlessly hungry cannibal monster in the belief systems of several Algonquian peoples. Brianna calls it "an Ojibway cannibal spirit that lives in the wood. It howls in storms and eats people" (*A*

Breath of Snow and Ashes, ch. 55). Some of the legends describe it as possession and others a transformation more like a werewolf's (Either way this is not a sasquatch). A dreadfully skinny giant, it stands fifteen feet tall, with glowing eyes, long, yellowed canine teeth and a hyper-extended tongue, sometimes with matted fur or a deer's head.

"The Wendigo" by Algernon Blackwood (1907), introduced the legend to Americans and helped create the modern version of this trope. In the original story, the guide Défago is seized by madness and runs from the camp. The hero Simpson notes that "the man's footsteps in the snow had gradually assumed an exact miniature likeness of the animal's plunging tracks," and secretly remembers "that they measured a *wholly* incredible distance."

Dr. Cathcart, the psychologist among them, insists that both guide and protagonist were delusional. "For the Wendigo is simply the Call of the Wild personified, which some natures hear to their own destruction."

> "The allegory *is* significant," he remarked, looking about him into the darkness, "for the Voice, they say, resembles all the minor sounds of the Bush—wind, falling water, cries of the animals, and so forth. And, once the victim hears *that*—he's off for good, of course! His most vulnerable points, moreover, are said to be the feet and the eyes; the feet, you see, for the lust of wandering, and the eyes for the lust of beauty. The poor beggar goes at such a dreadful speed that he bleeds beneath the eyes, and his feet burn."
>
> As Dr. Cathcart adds, according to legend, "The Wendigo," he added, "is said to burn his feet—owing to the friction, apparently caused by its tremendous velocity—till they drop off, and new ones form exactly like its own."
>
> ...
>
> "It don't always keep to the ground neither," came in Hank's slow, heavy drawl, "for it goes so high that he thinks the stars have set him all a-fire. An' it'll take great thumpin' jumps sometimes, an' run along the tops of the trees, carrying its partner with it, an' then droppin' him jest as a fish hawk'll drop a pickerel to kill it before eatin'."

In the *Outlander* books, the group meet a traveler named Wendigo. Claire describes his monstrous namesake, remembering the gruesome picture Brianna once drew of one:

> Done in a reverse technique, the basic drawing done in white crayon, showing through an overlay of charcoal. Trees, lashing to and fro in a swirl of snow and wind, leaf-stripped and needle-flying, the spaces between them part of the night. The picture had a sense of urgency about it, wildness and movement. It took several moments of looking at it before one glimpsed the face amid the branches. I had actually yelped and dropped the paper when I saw it—much to Bree's gratification [*A Breath of Snow and Ashes*, ch. 31].

It appears a manifestation of the wild woods, moving in the shadows. Later, hearing howling, Brianna pictures a wendigo in the forest, adding to its eeriness

(*A Breath of Snow and Ashes,* ch. 39). In fact, the man named Wendigo is a Native American from the 1960s who travels back in time to improve things for his people, since he burns for justice. In his violence and desperation he mirrors the creature.

NORSE MYTH

Norse and Gaelic Crossovers

Frank tells Claire that Fionn and the Feinn are "Gaelic folktales ... probably from Norse roots. There's a lot of the Norse influence round here, and all the way up the coast to the West" (*Outlander,* ch. 1). The Norse invaded between 500 and 1300. For centuries, much of Scotland was part of the Kingdom of Norway, with the Western Isles only returned to Scottish rule in 1266. "The Norsemen also left an enormous legacy of superstition. No expedition was undertaken without consulting the runes. Belief in witchcraft, spells, and the power of omens and dreams became –like the mingling of blood—inextricably mixed with Celtic belief and custom" (Sutherland 31). As Frank adds, "And they brought their own myths along. It's good country for myths. They seem to take root here" (*Outlander,* ch. 1).

The god Odin, especially, appears in some of the Scottish customs and lore. He was the father-god of wisdom and the heavens, known for the ravens Thought and Memory, which sat upon his shoulders. "These ravens, in the superstitious belief of the people, appear to have survived the days of paganism, and have figured in our trials for witchcraft during last century," Guthrie writes (ch. 1). Odin also helped to inspire the Celtic concept of magic, and traces lingered for some time:

> An oath by Odin was formerly deemed legal as well as sacred. In some parts of Orkney it was the custom for all young couples meditating matrimony to go by moonlight to the Standing Stones of Stenness, known as the Temple of Odin, whom the woman, kneeling on the ground, must invoke. The lovers afterwards plighted their troth by clasping hands through the perforated stone of Odin. In the course of last century the elders of the local church punished a faithless lover because he had broken the promise thus made [Guthrie, ch. 1].

Likewise, Claire thinks of Jamie as coming from "Mrs. Baird's legends of the race of giants who once walked Scotland" (*Outlander,* ch. 24). Many times, she compares him to a berserk Viking warrior, and he may share biological ties to the Vikings, with his red hair and blue eyes. Certainly, this would help to explain his red warrior's aura and Master Raymond's fear of him.

Conclusion

The world of *Outlander* is rich with mythology, from the fairyfolk with their waterhorses and wild hunts to the tiny everyday superstitions. The Highlanders would cross themselves when seeing a plover on her nest or pause by a sacred spring to offer a quick blessing. The Fair Folk had their domain and the humans had theirs ... but every so often, the two would intersect.

In the Highlands, Catholicism and Celtic practices were fully integrated—one might swear by Jesus, Mary, and Bride. Churches stood over far more ancient sacred springs, and the solstices corresponded with feasts of saints. The devil tempted witches to follow his path and sent out demons, malicious fairyfolk from ancient days.

Across the land, standing stones dotted the high hills, surrounded by burial cairns, long-barrows and hill-forts. Ley lines connected these, through the still-present straight roads of Neolithic man. Through it all swam the Loch Ness Monster, whether mythic waterhorse or prehistoric plesiosaur. Older traces of foreign invaders remained, of Roman forts and Viking raiders, with runes to cast and traces of far-off myths and deities.

Outlander takes place on the cusp of the Age of Enlightenment, as folk cast superstition aside for medicine, demons for science. Nonetheless, the ancient world of fairies and folk wisdom lives on, side by side with the modern one of law and medicine. Across the ocean, obeah-men create zombies and use snakes in their rituals, while ghost bears prowl the forests of North Carolina. Literature and books of science dominate the land, spread by the powerful printing press. Other symbols fill the series in the plants and animals that offer deeper meanings, along with colors and talismans. Above all is the presence of jewels, each with a different ancient significance, protecting travelers on their journey through the stones.

Appendix 1: Titles in the Outlander Series

Main Series

1. *Outlander* (titled *Cross Stitch* in the UK)
2. *Dragonfly in Amber*
3. *Voyager*
4. *The Drums of Autumn*
5. *The Fiery Cross*
6. *A Breath of Snow and Ashes*
7. *An Echo in the Bone*
8. *Written in My Own Heart's Blood*
9. Book Nine (untitled, TBA)

Prequel about Brian and Ellen Fraser in the first uprising (untitled, TBA)

Lord John Novels

These take place during *Voyager* between 1756 and 1761, while Jamie is at Helwater and feature Lord John Grey, who is briefly introduced in *Dragonfly in Amber* and becomes more significant in the later books.

- *Lord John and the Hellfire Club* (1998), a novella. Originally published in the 1998 British anthology *Past Poisons: An Ellis Peters Memorial Anthology of Historical Crime* (edited by Maxim Jakubowski). Also in *Lord John and the Hand of Devils* (2007).
- *Lord John and the Private Matter* (2003). Published as a novel.
- *Lord John and the Succubus* (2003). Originally published in the 2003 Del

Rey anthology *Legends II: New Short Novels by the Masters of Modern Fantasy* (edited by Robert Silverberg). Also in *Lord John and the Hand of Devils* (2007).

- *Lord John and the Brotherhood of the Blade* (2007). Published as a novel.
- *Lord John and the Haunted Soldier* (2007). Originally published in *Lord John and the Hand of Devils.*
- *The Custom of the Army* (2010). First published in the 2010 anthology *Warriors*, edited by George R.R. Martin and Gardner Dozois. Also available as a standalone eBook, and in Gabaldon's collection *A Trail of Fire* (United Kingdom, Australia, Germany and New Zealand only), U.S. and Canada TBA.
- *The Scottish Prisoner* (2011). Published as a novel. This novel, unlike the others, is half-told from Jamie's perspective.
- *Lord John and the Plague of Zombies* (2011). First published in the 2011 anthology *Down These Strange Streets*, edited by George R.R. Martin and Gardner Dozois. Also available as a standalone eBook, and in *A Trail of Fire.*

OTHER SHORT FICTION

- "A Leaf on the Wind of All Hallows." The story of Roger MacKenzie's parents, in *Songs of Love and Death,* eds. George R. R. Martin and Gardner Dozois, 2010. Also available in *A Trail of Fire.* Takes place during book eight.
- "The Space Between." The story of minor characters Michael Murray and Joan MacKimmie in 1778 Paris, in *The Mad Scientist's Guide to World Domination,* ed. John Joseph Adams, 2013. Also available in *A Trail of Fire.* Takes place just after book seven.
- "Virgins." The story of Jamie and Ian's time as young mercenaries in 1740 France, before the events of *Outlander,* in *Dangerous Women,* edited by George R. R. Martin and Gardner Dozois, 2013.

OTHER

- *The Exile* (graphic novel adaptation of the first half of book one) 2010.
- *The Outlandish Companion Vol. I* (guide to books 1–4, titled *Through the Stones* in the UK) 1999.
- *The Outlandish Companion Vol. II* (guide to books 5–8, TBA)

Appendix 2: The Starz Series Cast and Creators

CAST

Caitriona Balfe as Claire Beauchamp Randall Fraser
Sam Heughan as James (Jamie) Alexander Malcolm MacKenzie Fraser
Tobias Menzies in the dual roles of Frank Randall and Jonathan (Black Jack) Randall.
Stephen Walters as Angus Mhor
Grant O'Rourke as Rupert MacKenzie
Annette Badland as Mrs. FitzGibbons
Graham McTavish as Dougal MacKenzie
Gary Lewis as Colum MacKenzie
Duncan Lacroix as Murtagh Fraser
Lotte Verbeek as Geillis Duncan
Bill Paterson as Ned Gowan
Finn Den Hertog as Willie
John Heffernan as Brigadier General Lord Oliver Thomas
Roderick Gilkison as Young Hamish MacKenzie
James Fleet as the Reverend Wakefield
Laura Donnelly as Jenny Fraser Murray
Steven Cree as Ian Murray
Nell Hudson as Laoghaire
Kathryn Howden as Mrs. Baird
Tracey Wilkinson as Mrs. Graham
Liam Carney as Auld Alec
Aislin McGuckin as Colum's wife, Letitia

Prentis Hancock as Uncle Lamb
Simon Callow as the Duke of Sandringham

CREATORS

Producer/Showrunner—Ron Moore
Series Composer—Bear McCreary
Costume Designer—Terry Dresbach

Bibliography

Primary Sources

Bell, Carrie. "*Outlander* Wedding: All the Details on Mr. and Mrs. Fraser's Attire, Plus See the Sketch of Claire's Dress." *Yahoo TV* 20 Sept 2014. https://tv.yahoo.com/blogs/tv-news/outlander-wedding-all-the-details-on-claire-s-dress—ring-jamie-s-kilt–023451554.html.

Bertone, Stephanie. "Graham McTavish Discusses Episode Five ('Rent') with Access Hollywood." *Access Hollywood* 4 Sept 2014. http://outlandertvnews.com/2014/09/graham-mctavish-discusses-episode-five-rent-with-access-hollywood.

Brittain, Jean. "The Outlander Lady." *Scottish Memories* May 2009. http://www.dianagabaldon.com/resources/interviews-articles-and-panels/the-outlander-lady-interview.

DeLuca, Ashleigh N. "Fictional Outlander Series Has Real Links to Scotland's Newly Unearthed Neolithic Ruins." *Book Talk National Geographic* 8 Aug 2014. http://news.nationalgeographic.com/news/2014/08/140808-outlander-scotland-orkney-islands-stonehenge-neolithic.

Dresbach, Terry. *Terry Dresbach: An 18th Century Life.* 2014. Blog. http://terrydresbach.com.

Friedlander, Whitney. "'Outlander' Costume Designer on Wedding Dresses, Kilts and Corsets." *Variety* 20 Sept 2014. http://variety.com/2014/artisans/news/outlander-wedding-costume-designer–1201309495.

Gabaldon, Diana. *A Breath of Snow and Ashes.* New York: Random House, 2005.

_____. *Cross Stitch.* London: Arrow Books, 1994

_____. "Diana Gabaldon, Author." Facebook Comment 10 Dec. 2013. https://www.facebook.com/home.php?ref=h...ed_comment

_____. *Dragonfly in Amber.* New York: Random House, 1992.

_____. "The Doctor's Balls." *Chicks Unravel Time: Women Journey Through Every Season of Doctor Who.* Edited by Deborah Stanish and L.M. Myles. USA: Mad Norwegian Press, 2012. Kindle Edition.

_____. *The Drums of Autumn.* New York: Random House, 1996.

_____. *An Echo in the Bone.* New York: Random House, 2009.

_____. *The Exile: An Outlander Graphic Novel.* New York: Del Ray, 2010.

_____. "FAQ." *Diana Gabaldon's Official Webpage.* 2014. http://www.dianagabaldon.com/resources/faq

_____. *The Fiery Cross.* New York: Random House, 2001.

_____. "A Leaf on the Wind of All Hallows." *Songs of Love and Death*, eds. George R. R. Martin and Gardner Dozois, USA: Gallery Books, 2010. 429–468.

_____. *Lord John and the Brotherhood of the Blade.* New York: Random House, 2011.

_____. "Lord John and the Plague of Zombies" *Down These Strange Streets.* Ed. George R.R. Martin and Gardner Dozois. New York: Penguin, 2011.

_____. "Lord John and the Succubus." *Lord John and the Hand of Devils.* New York: Random House, 2007. 45–156.

_____. *Outlander.* New York: Bantam Dell, 1992.

_____. "Outlander Reread Thoughts." *Books and Writers Community. Compuserve.* November 2010. Board Post. http://forums.compuserve.com/discussions/Books_and_Writers_Community/Diana_Gabaldon/Outlander_reread_thoughts/ws-books/69201.1?nav=messages#a1

_____. *The Outlandish Companion.* New York: Delacorte Press, 1999.

_____. *The Scottish Prisoner.* New York: Random House, 2011.

_____. "The Shape of the Books." *Books and Writers Community. Compuserve.* November 2005. Board Post. http://forums.compuserve.com/discussions/Books_and_Writers_Community/Diana_Gabaldon/The_shape_of_the_books/ws-books/49936.2?redirCnt=1&nav=messages

_____. "The Space Between." *The Mad Scientist's Guide to World Domination: Original Short Fiction for the Modern Evil Genius.* John Joseph Adams, ed. New York: Tor, 2013. 161–243.

_____. *Voyager.* New York: Random House, 1993.

"An Interview with Diana Gabaldon." *Outlander Podcast.* Episode 49. http://outlanderpod.wordpress.com/2014/08/03/episode-49-an-interview-with-diana-gabaldon.

Ladies of Lallybroch. "Jamie and Claire's Blood Vow." *Ladies of Lallybroch.* http://www.lallybroch.com/LOL/bloodvow.html.

Loughlin, Elenna. "Outlander TV Adaptation Won't Shy Away From Spanking." *Geek's Guide to the Galaxy. Wired.com.* 28 June 2014. http://www.wired.com/2014/06/geeks-guide-diana-gabaldon.

McCreary, Bear. "Comic Con 2014 Highlights." *Bear McCreary Official Site* 29 July 2014. http://www.bearmccreary.com/#blog/blog/films/comic-con-2014-highlights.

_____. "Outlander: Sassenach." *Bear McCreary Official Site* 29 July 2014. http://www.bearmccreary.com/#blog/blog/outlander-sassenach.

_____. "Outlander: The Garrison Commander, The Wedding, Both Sides Now." *Bear McCreary Official Site* 28 Sept 2014. http://www.bearmccreary.com/#blog/blog/outlander-the-garrison-commander-the-wedding-both-sides-now.

Moore, Ron. "Inside the World of Outlander." Episodes 101–108. *Starz Extras. Starz.com.*

Ng, Philiana. "'Outlander': Caitriona Balfe on Claire and Jamie's Steamy Connection (Q&A)." *Hollywood Reporter* 16 Aug 2014. http://www.hollywoodreporter.com/live-feed/outlander-caitriona-balfe-claire-jamie-725840.

_____. "'Outlander': Lotte Verbeek on Geillis' Darkness and 'Ballsy' Nature." *Hollywood Reporter* 23 Aug 2014. http://www.hollywoodreporter.com/live-feed/outlander-lotte-verbeek-geillis-darkness-727197.

Prudom, Laura. "'Outlander': Ron Moore on Adapting the Bestseller for Starz, Dispelling 'Game of Thrones' Comparisons." *Variety* 6 August 2014. http://variety.com/2014/tv/news/outlander-ron-moore-starz-book-game-of-thrones-1201277009.

_____. "Starz's 'Outlander' Woos Women with Strong Female Protagonist." *Variety* 7 Aug 2014. http://variety.com/2014/tv/news/starz-outlander-woos-women-with-strong-female-protagonist-1201277091.

Secondary Sources

Bede. *Ecclesiastical History of the English People.* Trans. Leo Sherley-Price. Rev. R. E. Latham Hamondsworth: Penguin, 1990.

Béguinot, Stéphanie. "Ghillie Callum (Sword Dance)." *History of Traditional Airs for Bagpipe and Contra Dance.* 2014. http://corne-musique.free.fr/ukghilliecallum.php.

Black, Geo. F. *Scottish Charms and Amulets. Electric Scotland.* http://www.electricscotland.com/history/articles/charms.htm.

Blackwood, Algernon. "The Wendigo." 1910. *The Gutenberg Project.* http://www.gutenberg.org/files/10897/10897-h/10897-h.htm.

Brickell, John. *The Natural History of North Carolina.* USA: Raleigh, 1911. https://archive.org/details/naturalhistoryof00bric.

Bruce-Mitford, Miranda. *The Illustrated Book of Signs and Symbols.* USA: DK Publishing, 1996.

Cairney, C. Thomas. *Clans and Families of Ireland and Scotland: An Ethnography of the Gael AD 500–1750.* Jefferson, NC: McFarland, 1989.

Campbell, J. F. *Popular Tales of the West Highlands Volume I-IV.* London, Alexander Gardner, 1890. *The Sacred Texts Archive.* http://www.sacred-texts.com/neu/celt/pt2/pt200.htm.

Campbell, John Gregorson. *Superstitions of the Highlands & Islands of Scotland. Collected Entirely from Oral Sources* Glasgow: James MacLehose and Sons, Publishers to the University, 1900. http://archive.org/stream/ cu31924029909896/cu31924029909896_ djvu.txt.

Carmichael, Alexander. *Carmina Gadelica.* Edinburgh: T. and A. Constable, 1900. *The Sacred Texts Archive.* http://www.sacred-texts.com/neu/celt/cg1/index.htm.

Cavendish, Richard, editor. *Man, Myth, and Magic: The Illustrated Encyclopedia of Mythology, Religion, and the Unknown.* New York: Marshall Cavendish Corporation, 1995.

Child, F. J., comp.; Sargent, H. C., and G. L. Kittredge, eds. *The English and Scottish Popular Ballads.* Boston, Mass: Houghton Mifflin, 1904.

Cirlot, J.E. *A Dictionary of Symbols.* New York: Routledge, 1971.

Comrie, John D. "General Practice in the Seventeenth and Eighteenth Centuries." *History of Scottish Medicine to 1860.* London: Bailliere Tindall and Cox, 1927.

Cooper-Oakley, Isabel. *The Comte de St. Germain,* Milano: G. Sulli-Rao, 1912. *The Sacred Texts Archive.* http://sacred-texts.com/sro/csg/index.htm.

Daniels, Cora Linn Morrison, and Charles McClellan Stevens, eds. *Encyclopedia of Superstitions, Folklore, and the Occult Sciences of the World: A Comprehensive Library of Human Belief and Practice in the Mysteries of Life, Volume 3.* USA: J. H. Yewdale & Sons Company, 1903.

Evans-Wentz, W.Y. *The Fairy-Faith in Celtic Countries.* London and New York: H. Froude, 1911. *The Sacred Texts Archive.* http://www.sacred-texts.com/neu/celt/ffcc/ffcc122.htm.

Folk-Lore and Legends of Scotland. London: W. W. Gibbings, 1889.

Ford, Patrick K., trans. *The Mabinogi and Other Medieval Welsh Tales.* Berkeley: University of California Press, 1977.

Foubister, Linda. *Goddess in the Grass: Serpentine Mythology and the Great Goddess.* USA: Spirrea, 2011.

Frankel, Valerie Estelle. *From Girl to Goddess: The Heroine's Journey in Myth and Legend.* Jefferson, NC: McFarland, 2010.

Giraldo, Alexander. "Obeah: The Ultimate Resistance." *Slave Resistance: A Caribbean Study.* University of Miami. http://scholar.library.miami.edu/slaves/Religion/religion.html.

Grant, James. "The Tartans of the Clans of Scotland." *Electric Scotland.* http://www.electricscotland.com/webclans/dress_arms. htm.

Grimm, Jacob. *Deutsche Mythologie.* Germany: Dietrich, 1835. Transcribed by Aaron Myer Grimm's Teutonic Mythology Translation Project Northvegr. 2007. http://www.north vegr.org.

Guthrie, E. J. *Old Scottish Customs.* Glasgow: Thomas D. Morrison, 1885. https://archive.org/details/oldscottishcusto00guth.

Henderson, George. *Survivals in Belief Among the Celts.* London: Macmillan and Co., 1911. *The Sacred Texts Archive.* http://www.sacred-texts.com/neu/celt/sbc/index.htm.

Henderson, Helene, ed. *Holidays Symbols and Customs,* 4th ed. Detroit: Omnigraphics, 2009.

"The Highland Garb." The Gaelic Society of Inverness. *Electric Scotland.* http://www.electricscotland.com/history/articles/garb. htm.

Hill, Douglas. "Stones." Cavendish 2489.

Hole, Christina. "Springs and Wells." Cavendish 2472–2473.

Illes, Judika. *The Element Encyclopedia of Witchcraft.* London: Harper Collins, 2005.

Jacobs, Joseph. *Celtic Fairy Tales.* London: D. Nutt, 1892. http://www.sacred-texts.com/neu/celt/cft.

Johnson, Ben. "Highland Dancing." *Historic UK.* http://www.historic-uk.com/HistoryUK/HistoryofScotland/Highland-Dancing.

Jones, William. *History and Mystery of Precious Stones.* London: Richard Bentley and Son, 1880.

Keightley, Thomas. *The Fairy Mythology: Illustrative of the Romance and Superstition of Various Countries,* 1870. *The Sacred Texts Archive.* http://www.sacred-texts.com/neu/celt/tfm/tfm177.htm

Keltie, John S., ed. "The Living Conditions in the Highlands." *History of the Scottish Highlands, Highland Clans and Scottish Regiments.* Edinburgh: Grange Publishing Works, 1887.

Kirk, Robert. *The Secret Commonwealth of Elves, Fauns & Fairies.* London: David Nutt, 1893. *The Sacred Texts Archive.* http://www.sacred-texts.com/neu/celt/sce/index.htm.

Linklater, Eric. *The Prince in the Heather.* New York, Harcourt Brace, 1966.

MacCulloch, J.A. *The Religion of the Ancient Celts.* Edinburgh: T. & T. Clark, 1911.

MacKay, William. *Urquhart and Glenmoristox: Olden Times in a Highland Parish.* Inverness: The Noetherx Counties Newspaper and Publishing Company, Ltd., 1914.

Mackinlay, James M. *Folklore of Scottish Lochs and Springs*. Glasgow, William Hodge and Co., 1893.

Macpherson, James. *The Poems of Ossian*. Boston: Phillips, Sampson & Co., 1773. http://www.sacred-texts.com/neu/ossian/index.htm.

Morison, J. L. *The Scottish Highlander*. Toronto: Canadian Institute for Historical Microreproductions, 2000. https://archive.org/details/cihm_88424.

Mountain, Harry. *The Celtic Encyclopedia, Volume 4*. USA: Universal-Publishers, 1998.

Poison, A. "Highland Folk-Lore of Luck." *Electric Scotland*. http://www.electricscotland.com/history/articles/luck.htm

Rakoczi, Basil Ivan. "Palmistry" Cavendish 1969.

Reginheim. "Heathen History of the Achterhoek." 2002. http://web.archive.org/web/20050524111821/http://geocities.com/reginheim/dutchlegendsachterhoek.html.

Robbins, Rossell Hope. *The Encyclopedia of Witchcraft and Demonology*. New York: Crown Publishers, 1959.

Sutherland, Elizabeth. *Ravens and Black Rain: The Story of Highland Second Sight*. Corgi Books, Great Britain, 1985.

Thomas, William, and Kate Pavitt. *The Book of Talismans, Amulets and Zodiacal Gems*. London: William Rider & Son, Ltd., 1922. *The Sacred Texts Archive*. http://www.sac red-texts.com/sym/bot.

Vandam, Albert D. *An Englishman in Paris. Notes and Recollections*. New York: Hovendon, 189?.

Varner, Gary R. *Menhirs, Dolmen and Circles of Stone: The Folklore and Mythology of Sacred Stone*. USA: Algora Pub, 2004.

Walker, Barbara G. *The Woman's Dictionary of Symbols and Sacred Objects*. San Francisco: HarperSanFrancisco, 1988.

Watkins, Alfred. *The Old Straight Track: Its Mounds, Beacons, Moats, Sites and Mark Stones*. London: Abacus, 1925.

White, A., and E. Ernst. "A Brief History of Acupuncture" *Rheumatology* (2004) 43 (5): 662–663. http://rheumatology.oxfordjournals.org/content/43/5/662.long.

Williams, Peter N. "The Traditions of the Northern Celts." *Britannia Internet Magazine* 1998. http://britannia.com/celtic/celtictraditions.html.

Wilson, Barbara Ker. "The Legend of Eilean Donan Castle." *Scottish Folk-Tales and Legends (Oxford Myths and Legends)*. Oxford: Oxford University Press, 1990. 49–55.

Index

Abbey of Ste. Anne de Beaupre 2, 58, 60, 127, 134
accent 52, 78, 79
acorns 23
acupuncture 176
Adam and Eve 64
adamant 32
Adams, John 68
The Adventures of Rodrick Random 58, 59
Africa 87, 94, 173, 174, 175
Alban Elfed 95, 100
alchemy 2, 9, 182, 185
Alice in Wonderland 72
All Hallows' Eve 95, 101
All Saint's Day 102
American Revolution 3, 6, 11, 13, 14, 16, 24, 59, 67, 79
amethyst 31, 88, 90
amulets 7, 89, 91, 141, 157, 164, 182
Angus Mhor Grant 44, 140
animal spirits 109
Aphrodite 34, 40, 122
apothecary 182
Ardsmuir 62
arisaid 24
Arnold, Benedict 57
Asia 90
astrology 177, 183
astronomy 182
athame 82
Auld Alec 65
auld wife 184
aura 2, 64, 105, 160, 182, 185, 195
autumn 11, 19, 96, 100, 147, 158
Autumn Equinox 11, 12, 95
Aztecs 90

Baal 98
Babylon 63, 87, 94
bagpipes 1, 29, 76, 168
Balfe, Caitriona 36, 55

"The Ballad of Paul Revere" 67
ballads 1, 46, 57, 77, 78, 107
ban-treim 1, 169
baoding balls 179–180
baptism 131, 144
bards 106, 170
barrows 86, 196
Battle of Saratoga 56, 114, 154
Beaker Folk 81, 95
Bean Sidhe 107
Beaton 161
Beefsteak Club 17
belt 19, 24, 26, 29, 189
Beltane 2, 95–99, 102, 115
Bible 1, 54, 62, 63, 103, 109, 110, 142, 167
birds 23, 37, 38, 87, 140, 179, 192; *see also* crows; ravens; songbirds
birth control 157
bitter cascara 157
black 28, 29, 32, 33, 40, 41, 48, 51, 90, 92, 98, 103, 115, 110, 111, 115–117, 120, 122, 140, 148, 152, 153, 164, 165, 174
Black Mass 180
black rooster 164
blood 2, 9, 13–16, 21, 37, 42, 48, 64, 66, 69, 83, 90, 91, 93, 95, 109, 123, 124, 146, 148, 156, 159, 162, 164–166, 171, 174, 178, 180, 193, 195
Blood of my Blood 171
blue 2, 6, 18, 19, 28, 29, 43, 64, 90, 120, 140, 148, 172, 179, 182, 185, 191, 195
blue vase 47
bodhrán 1, 76
bodice 20, 21, 22, 24
bonfires 96, 98, 101
Bonnie Prince Charlie 1, 6, 27, 42, 66, 75, 76, 79, 83, 123, 124, 149, 157, 166
Boston 50, 133
bracelet, pearl 35, 64
bracelet, silver 36–37
bracelets, boar tusk 36
Brahan Seer 2, 7, 147–149

breacan-feile 26
bread 100, 106, 156, 168
breasts 22, 34, 107, 134, 184
A Breath of Snow and Ashes 14, 53, 54, 59, 63,
　64, 66–68, 71, 78, 79, 85, 94, 101, 111, 114,
　116, 123, 132, 134, 145, 154, 155, 159, 161,
　168, 169, 192, 194–195
Brian Fraser 3, 37, 53, 73, 122, 133
Brianna Fraser 3, 8, 12, 15, 16, 36, 37, 39, 40,
　42, 52–55, 57, 59, 62, 64, 66–71, 79, 80, 85,
　86, 90, 91, 96, 99, 102, 105, 111, 117, 120, 136,
　142, 143, 145, 149, 150, 154, 159, 168, 169,
　172, 184, 192–194
Bride (goddess) 89, 125, 132
Brigadoon 85
Brigid (goddess) 53, 95–97, 120, 125–126, 133
Bronze Age 92, 93, 112
brooch 10, 13, 15, 24, 26, 29, 31, 33, 91, 113,
　128, 139, 143
brothel 46
Brother Anselm 58, 63, 134
brown 18–20, 22, 28, 29, 41, 45, 48, 49, 136, 159
brownie 111
Browning, Robert 71
Buddha 12
Buddhism 178, 185
Burns, Robert 2, 72, 73, 89

Caesar's *Commentaries* 59
Cailleach (goddess) 126, 140
calligraphy 16
caltrop 15
Cameron Plantation 172
Candlemas 97
Canterbury Tales 72
Caribbean 94, 173, 174, 175
Carmina Gadelica 41, 82, 143–147
Castle Leoch 19, 39, 46, 49, 50, 63, 84, 105,
　135, 161
cat 38–39
Catholicism 2, 50, 63, 77, 97, 100, 102, 126,
　133, 135, 171, 175, 190, 196
cattle 35, 106, 109, 110, 133, 137, 139, 144
Catullus 60
caul 159
Celtic 1, 2, 9, 10, 39, 40, 46, 50, 53, 79, 82, 83,
　86, 89, 92–95, 97, 100, 101, 106, 108, 112,
　125–127, 129–133, 139–142, 146, 159, 164,
　171, 195, 196
Cernunnos (god) 126, 139
Cerridwen (goddess) 127, 142
chalice 9, 166
changeling 2, 85, 108, 109
chanties 78
charms 2, 35, 97, 106, 135, 144–147, 164, 184,
　188, 190
Cherokee 111, 115, 141, 142, 157, 190, 191, 192
China 91, 122, 152, 176, 177, 180
Chinese 2, 51, 59, 86, 177–180
Christian 34, 94, 102, 105, 106, 111, 125, 128,
　131, 133, 144, 147, 165, 186, 187

Christmas 40, 64, 96, 102, 127
chrysoberyl 91, 92
circle dancers 74, 76, 81, 105, 106, 153
circle symbolism 10
Claire Beauchamp: dressing up 20–21; gender
　36; name 52; White Lady 186–188; White
　Raven 141; as witch 161–164; zodiac 177,
　183–184
clan badge 13, 121
clava cairns 83, 84, 86, 92, 93, 112, 153, 196
cleft stone 93, 94
clothes *see* arisaid; breacan-feile; collars;
　corset; feileadh breacan; hats; hose; kilt; mob
　cap; peignoir; petticoats; plaid; shift; tartan;
　underwear; utility suit; wedding gown
Coleridge, Samuel 70
collars 20
Colum MacKenzie 3, 21, 33, 37, 69, 73, 129,
　135, 156, 161, 164
comic book 19, 21, 29, 37, 122
Common Sense 57
compass 16
Conan Doyle, Arthur 72
constancy 6, 35, 43, 91, 92, 178
corn 78, 97, 99, 106, 144
Coronach 1, 168
corset 21, 23
courage 13, 35, 37, 43, 55, 85, 90, 101, 138
Craigh na Dun *see* standing stones
Cranesmuir 30, 160, 161
credits 74, 76, 82
Cro-Magnon 94
Cross Stitch 5, 6, 19, 22, 28, 29, 155
crown 6–7
crows 140
crucifix 115, 135
crystal 9, 89, 90, 116
Culloden 11, 13, 25, 42, 69, 70, 73, 75, 77, 115,
　136, 140, 148, 170, 192
Cup of the Druid King 9, 166
The Custom of the Army 17

Da mi basia mille 60
Dagda (god) 101
dagger *see* dirk
Dame Aliset 186
Danu (goddess) 53, 126, 133
dauco seeds 157
deamhan 109
deasil charm 143
Death Dirge 147
deer 33, 74, 124, 128, 139, 142, 150, 194
De Foe, Daniel 59
Demeter 12, 126
demons 92, 106, 109, 111, 178, 190, 192, 196
de Sade, Marquis 67
devil 14, 39, 48, 64, 69, 105, 109, 129, 137, 162,
　163, 178, 180, 189, 196
diamond 32, 33, 37, 88, 89, 91, 92, 159
The Diary of Samuel Pepys 58
Dickens, Charles 70

dirk 26, 29, 57, 74, 109, 167
disabilities 56
DisKilting Act 25, 30
Doctor Who 50, 68, 69
doctor's kit 33
Don Quixote 59
Donne, John 72
Dougal MacKenzie 2, 3, 19, 20, 25, 29, 33, 34,
    38, 39, 44, 45, 46, 62, 77, 132, 161, 171, 172
dowsing 87, 160
dragonfly in amber 7–9
Dragonfly in Amber 6–8, 11, 21, 26, 29, 33, 42,
    44, 49, 51, 54, 58, 59, 62–64, 66, 70, 72–74,
    79, 88, 112, 113, 116, 133, 134, 137, 156–158,
    164, 180, 182, 183, 185, 186, 188
dreams 8, 34, 40, 42, 53, 57, 58, 64, 66, 70, 91,
    92, 102, 124, 141, 159, 189, 192, 195
Dresbach, Terry 18, 19, 22, 23, 24, 30, 44
drugs 173, 175, 176
Druids 9, 82, 94, 95, 99, 100, 101, 105, 130,
    158, 166
drums 11, 76, 191
The Drums of Autumn 9, 11–14, 25, 31, 32, 37,
    39, 42, 43, 55, 59–61, 64, 67, 70, 71, 78, 79,
    82, 83, 88, 91, 92, 99–101, 105, 106, 109, 111,
    114, 115, 117, 134, 141, 147, 156, 159, 163, 164,
    189–191
Duke of Sandringham 58
Dunbonnet 136
Duncan Innes 55
dyeing 28, 120

Easter 40, 96, 97, 121, 127
Easter eggs 58
An Echo in the Bone 9, 15, 22, 24, 49, 57, 61, 65,
    66, 71, 72, 83, 86–88, 102, 107, 112, 114, 120,
    130, 143, 145, 164
Edinburgh 22, 25, 61, 126, 163, 178
eggs 40, 97, 98
Egyptian 90, 127, 152, 184, 189
18th century 19, 23, 27–28, 30, 48, 58, 62, 66–
    70, 78, 151, 155–157, 161, 164, 171, 175
Elizabeth I 161
Ellen MacKenzie Fraser 3, 33, 35, 36, 53, 122
Ellen's roses 49, 114
Elliot, T.S., 72
emerald 32, 37, 88–90
England 6, 32, 51–53, 79, 87, 94, 126, 152, 172
Enlightenment 161, 164, 196
Eostre (goddess) 97, 127
episode one 1, 6, 42, 49, 77, 78, 81, 94, 95, 152,
    153, 165
episode two 161, 163
episode three 2, 84, 106, 129, 156, 161–163
episode four 39, 45, 68, 77
episode five 68, 72, 77
episode six 25, 161
episode seven 28, 44, 68, 78, 171
episode eight 7, 8, 35, 51, 54, 68, 77, 88, 102,
    117, 119, 153
Eppie Morrie 79

Esus (god) 130
Europe 2, 46, 49, 87, 91, 94, 126, 139, 152, 178–
    181, 184
evil eye 89
The Exile see comic book

fairies 1, 23, 46, 81, 84–86, 89, 92, 94, 101,
    105–115, 120, 122–124, 136, 139, 142–144,
    150, 163–165, 186, 188, 196
fairy queen 107, 111, 123, 127
fairy tale 23
faith 10, 50, 90, 102, 111, 144, 155, 173, 175
family tree 12, 52
Fanny Hill 59
fans 21, 168, 183
Father Bain 161–162
Father Michael FitzGibbons 129
fedora 18
feileadh beg 27
feileadh breacan 26
female space 46–47
feminine 5, 6, 11, 33–35, 38, 44, 94, 95, 122,
    135
Fergus 3, 55, 57, 134, 135
Fielding, Henry 59
The Fiery Cross 11–13, 24, 31, 37, 38, 40, 52, 58,
    59, 67, 73, 79, 102–104, 107, 141–143, 153,
    157, 170, 171, 184, 191, 192
fiery cross (symbol) 12, 13
Fionn Mac Cumhaill 1, 94, 112, 115, 139, 147,
    150, 151
Fire Feasts 1, 88, 93, 95
firstfoot 103–104
fish 27, 33, 40, 100, 117, 175, 178, 194
fish pin 33
Flora MacDonald 75
fly 38
forest (symbolism) 12
forget-me-not 42
'40s music 77
fortunetelling 151–154
foundation sacrifice 165
France 2, 13, 21, 34, 43, 44, 49–51, 55, 93, 94,
    122, 126, 131, 140, 160, 175, 176, 186, 188; *see
    also* French
Frank Randall 1, 3, 8, 18, 19, 21, 22, 35, 36, 38,
    40, 41, 51, 53, 54, 57, 58, 62, 63, 65, 70,
    71, 73–78, 81, 93–95, 102, 105, 113, 118, 133,
    136, 137, 139, 148–151, 153, 164, 165, 195
Franklin, Ben 67
Fraser *see* Brian Fraser; Brianna Fraser; Ellen
    Fraser; Germain Fraser; Jamie Fraser; Marsali
    Fraser; Master of Lovat; Simon Fraser
Fraser Prophecy 149
Fraser tartan 28, 29
Frasers of Lovat 7
Fraser's Ridge 59
freedom 17, 38, 44
French 43, 48, 52, 60, 72, 103, 115, 148, 149,
    175, 181, 182, 186, 188; *see also* France
French Revolution 63, 181

Frost, Robert 67
funeral 15, 64, 147, 167, 168

Gaelic 6, 45, 50–52, 66, 76, 82, 86, 94, 96, 98,
 105–107, 110–112, 115, 118–121, 129, 140, 143,
 145, 147, 150, 151, 161, 171, 195
garnet 83, 91
Gathering 13, 19, 21, 24, 45, 47, 77, 167, 170,
 171
Geillis 2, 3, 18, 24, 30, 32, 46, 66, 67, 82, 88,
 90, 91, 93, 101, 106, 108, 109, 149, 156, 162,
 163, 164, 174, 175, 180, 184, 189, 193
gemstones 83, 88, 90, 166
George II 123
George III 149
Germain Fraser 122, 180, 181, 182, 185
German 53, 86, 94, 186
Germany 160, 186, 190
ghost 1, 2, 11, 12, 13, 16, 18, 31, 42, 65, 95, 102,
 106, 110, 113–116, 137–139, 141, 142, 167–
 169, 177, 178, 183, 187, 188, 190, 196
ghost bear 142
giants 94, 105, 195
gifts 7, 33, 40, 41, 42, 47, 97, 104, 131, 140, 141,
 160, 166, 172
Glaistig 108
goats 99, 144
gold 2, 20, 22, 23, 31–36, 83, 88, 106, 149, 150,
 166, 187, 192
gold ring 36
Gone with the Wind 76, 153
gowns 2, 20, 21, 23
gralloch prayer 106
Grandfather Tales 57
grandparents 14, 114
graveyard 168
gray 18, 19, 20, 22, 24, 38, 81, 116, 138, 158, 184
Great Mother 12
Greek myth 7, 47, 62
Greeks 1, 7, 24, 32, 47, 50, 60–62, 90, 93, 94,
 105, 106, 128, 152, 165, 184, 188
green 18, 21, 28, 29, 38, 43, 74, 98, 109, 115,
 167, 174, 180
Gwyllyn the bard 84

Halloween 95, 153
Hamish MacKenzie 73
handfasting 37, 171, 172
hats 22, 25, 71
Hawthorne, Nathaniel 67
healing 6, 7, 14, 31, 48, 76, 89, 93, 105, 126, 131,
 132, 161, 164, 182, 185, 186, 192
heart 9, 15, 17, 20, 27, 35, 36, 43, 44, 49, 63, 67,
 71, 90, 97, 101, 124, 143–145, 152, 159, 167,
 189
hearthstone 147
heather 28, 30, 42, 43, 89, 148
heaven 63, 65, 71, 88, 98, 111, 114, 126, 132, 171,
 179
Hebrew 59
Hector McEwan 182, 185

Helen of Troy 50, 53
Helwater 39, 54, 59, 102, 114, 135
Henry Gray 185
herbs 2, 42, 47, 155, 156, 163, 164, 173, 176,
 177, 182
Highland Clearances 148
Hines, Frazer 70
Hippocrates 61
The History of Tom Jones 58
Hogmanay 7, 95, 102, 103, 153
holy wells 105
Holyrood Palace 28
Homer 59
honor 9, 13, 43, 97, 101, 123, 134, 139, 165
horses 15, 39, 40, 74, 86, 106, 110, 116, 117, 120,
 126, 133, 139, 183
hose 26, 29
Hoskyns, John Moses 72
Hounds of Fingal 1, 150
The House of the Spirits 52
household spirit 136
Housman, Alfred Edward 70, 71
Hugh Munro 7–8, 55, 59–60
The Hunger Games 20

Ian Murray 3, 9, 52, 55; see also Young Ian Mur-
 ray
identity 8, 16, 51, 76, 176, 179
The Iliad 62
ill-wish bundle 156
Imbolc 95, 96, 104
Incas 86, 90
inventions 107, 159
Inverness 50, 92, 112, 118, 119, 132, 148, 164,
 183
Invernesshire 83, 108, 110, 115, 121, 136
Ireland 40, 53, 86, 93, 94, 123, 126, 130, 133,
 134, 150, 151, 166, 184, 190
iron 27, 36, 44, 45, 110, 112, 116, 117, 134, 147,
 167
Iroquois 11, 115, 157, 190
Ishmael 67, 193
Isle of Lewis 92, 110
Isobel Dunsany 59
Ivanhoe 57, 74; see also Scott, Sir Walter

Jack Randall 3, 19, 20, 38, 47, 51, 53, 62, 78,
 154, 164, 189
James I 163
James VI 160
James Francis Edward Stuart 42
Jamie Fraser: as Christ 64; dressing up 22; Dun-
 bonnet 136; as horse trainer 39; name 50–51;
 second sight 159; zodiac 177, 183
Japan 34, 91
Jared Fraser 44, 62
Jem Fraser MacKenzie 15, 40, 53, 91, 99, 102,
 120, 143, 159, 160
Jenny Fraser Murray 3, 21, 31, 33, 46, 52, 57, 62,
 63, 103, 116, 135, 144, 157, 159, 164
Jeremiah (Bible) 53

Jeremiah MacKenzie (sr) 18
Jesus 9, 21, 50, 64, 89, 97, 99, 101, 102, 125, 127, 128, 132–134, 146, 147, 178, 181, 196
jet 135
Joan MacKimmie 18, 48, 85, 132, 134, 158
Job 64, 128
Jocasta MacKenzie Cameron 3, 13, 31, 37, 143, 144, 157, 172
Joe Abernathy 68, 90
John Grey see Lord John Grey
Johnson, Samuel 59
journey 10, 12, 14, 18, 36, 38, 39, 48, 49, 60, 76, 78, 82, 83, 89, 102, 152, 196
Judas 127
Jung, Carl 5, 39

Kahnyen'ke-haka 192
Keats, John 71
kelpies 105, 110, 116–119, 165
key to Lallybroch 36, 44
keys 17, 44
kilt 25–29, 68, 79; history of 25–26
King Arthur 72, 87, 94, 123, 142, 150, 165

Lallybroch 21, 29, 36, 43, 44, 46, 49, 51, 52, 55, 57, 63, 89, 96, 107, 112, 114, 135
lambs 97
Laoghaire MacKenzie 62, 68, 103, 153
lapis lazuli 88, 90
Latin 1, 38, 59, 60, 61, 99, 106, 132, 171, 189
leaf on the wind (symbolism) 18
"A Leaf on the Wind of All Hallows" 17, 180
ley lines 67, 86, 87, 196
Lia Fáil 93
library 58, 59, 77, 127
Lizzie Wemyss 59, 109, 172
loa 2, 174, 175
Loch Ness Monster 2, 105, 118, 196
Longfellow, Henry Wadsworth 10, 67
Lord John books 16–17
"Lord John and the Plague of Zombies" 16, 17, 67, 173–175
Lord John and the Private Matter 17, 74
"Lord John and the Succubus" 16, 135, 165, 189
Lord John Grey 16, 53, 58–59, 61, 66, 175, 189
love spell 145
lover's eye 24
Lowlands 30, 86, 106, 113, 116, 131
Lugh (god) 100, 126
Lughnassadh 95, 100, 126
The Lymond Chronicles 58

The Mabinogion 139, 142
Mac Dubh 51
Macbeth 50, 65, 164, 169
MacKenzie see Colum MacKenzie; Dougal MacKenzie; Ellen MacKenzie; Jem MacKenzie; Mandy MacKenzie; Old Alec MacKenzie; Roger MacKenzie; Rupert MacKenzie
MacKenzie tartan 28, 29

Madame Fabienne 175
Madonna 64, 185
Maimonides 59
Maisri (seer) 158–159
Malva Christie 59
Mandy Fraser MacKenzie 92, 99, 102, 159, 160
Marcus MacRannoch 35, 64
Margaret Campbell 159–160
"Marmion" 74
Marsali MacKimmie Fraser 3, 132, 134
martyrdom 37, 48
Mary see Virgin Mary
Mary Grant 136
Mary, Queen of Scots 160
Masefield, John 70
Masonic ring 92
Master of Lovat 70
matriarch 33, 184, 193
Mayans 86
McCreary, Bear 74, 77, 78, 82
McTavish, Graham 45
medicine 2, 93, 94, 99, 129, 155, 156, 161, 164, 177, 180, 185, 191–193, 196
The Meditations of Marcus Aurelius 59–60
memory 9, 18, 34, 35, 50, 106, 112, 181
menopause 193
Merlin 94, 165
Michael Murray 18, 63
Michaelmas 96, 100, 133
Middle Ages 31, 63, 91, 92, 161, 171, 178
Midsummer 95, 96, 99, 100
military 17, 26, 35, 51
milk 45, 64, 89, 96, 98, 108, 165, 166, 167
The Mists of Avalon 81
mobcap 24
modesty 24
Mohawk 111, 142
Molière 57
Monsieur Forez 156
moonstone 31
Moore, Ron 8, 20, 22, 42, 44, 45, 49, 77, 81, 119, 153, 156, 161, 162, 165
Morrigan (goddess) 101, 127
Mother Goddess 40, 94, 184
Mother Hildegarde 21, 63, 134
Mount Fuji 14
Mount of Venus 152
Mrs. Baird 105, 195
Mrs. Bug 145, 153, 184
Mrs. Crook 21
Mrs. Fitz 19, 20, 21, 46, 161
Mrs. Graham 34, 81, 82, 88, 106, 151, 152, 153, 154
Murray see Ian Murray; Jenny Murray; Michael Murray; Young Ian Murray
Murtagh FitzGibbons 3, 29, 36, 37, 78, 114, 122, 127, 130, 153, 162
myrtle 115

Napoleon 151
Native Americans 11, 31, 48, 59, 141, 157, 185,

190, 191, 192, 193, 195; *see also* Cherokee;
  Kahnyen'ke-haka; Mohawk; Nayawenne;
  Tuscarora
The Natural History of North Carolina 59
Nayawenne 2, 141, 157, 164, 192, 193
Ned Gowan 44, 72, 156, 162
Neolithic 81, 87, 92, 93, 94, 158, 184, 196
nicknames 51
19th century 106, 136, 140, 176
Norse myth 2, 7, 44, 81, 118, 130, 140, 186, 195
North Carolina 31, 50, 59, 157, 172, 190, 196
Norway 44, 195
Nouvelle Héloïse 58
Nuckelavee 120
Nunnahee 111, 115, 190
nuns 21, 36
nurse 1, 49, 69, 84, 85, 128, 144

oak 23, 97, 105, 128
oath 167, 174, 195
Obeah-Man 173–174
objects of vertu 53, 55
Ocracoke 94
octothorpe 16
Odin 2, 12, 105, 140, 195
The Odyssey 10, 60
Ogham (god) 126
L'Oignon 57
Old Alec MacKenzie 39
omen 38, 90, 139, 140, 141, 170, 171
opal 31, 32, 115
Order of the Thistle 44
Orkney Islands 92
Osiris 12, 100
Outlander (book) 1, 5–7, 19–21, 29, 30, 33–35,
  37, 41, 45, 48, 50, 53, 54, 58, 60, 62–67, 70,
  72, 73, 78, 83, 94, 96, 105, 108, 109, 113, 116–
  118, 121, 122, 127, 128, 131, 135, 137, 139, 150,
  153, 156, 158, 162, 164, 171, 172, 180, 195
Outlander (show) *see* episode one; episode
  two; episode three; episode four; episode
  five; episode six; episode seven; episode eight
Ovid 59
Oxford 35, 47, 52, 58, 76

Pagan 40, 53, 62, 81, 95, 97, 100–102, 105, 131–
  133, 139, 143, 144, 147, 165, 188, 195
painting 8, 71
palmistry 153–154
Pamela 58–59
Paris 2, 3, 18, 50, 59, 62, 94, 116, 148, 154–157,
  180, 182
pearl necklace 33, 35
pearls 33–35
peignoir 19
pelican 178
penicillin 156
penny whistle 1, 76
pentacle 88
perfection 33, 34, 40, 43
Persephone 12, 61, 100, 126

petticoats 20, 22
phoenix 179
Picts 81, 94, 95, 112
pig 142
piskies 120
pistols 26, 54
plaid 19, 24, 26–29, 172
Pliny 31, 91
plovers 139
Podcasts 8, 10, 14–16, 28, 42, 44, 77, 81, 95,
  119, 127, 153, 159, 160
poison 31, 55, 89, 91, 92, 156, 157, 173–175, 182
pregnancy 11, 64, 184
priest 44, 63, 79, 84, 129, 157, 162, 166, 167,
  171, 172, 175
printer 51, 57
printing press 61, 196
prophecy *see* Brahan Seer; fortunetelling;
  Fraser Prophecy; second sight
protection 2, 7, 36, 37, 45, 88–90, 92, 110, 114,
  120, 125, 134, 139, 159, 165, 167
purity 21, 33, 36, 48, 97
purple 28, 43

Quarter Day 21, 36

rabbits 40
rat satire 106, 137, 138
ravens 105, 126, 127, 140–144, 195
Raymond 2, 18, 30, 63, 64, 88, 89, 157, 164,
  182, 183, 185, 195
red 16, 21, 22, 28, 29, 42, 43, 48, 50, 91, 104,
  110, 115, 120, 121, 128, 136, 142, 143, 145,
  154, 159, 185, 190, 191, 195
Red Jamie 48, 51
Red Man 185, 191
relics 133, 135, 156
Reverend Wakefield 3, 55, 58, 68
rings *see* gold ring; ruby ring; signet ring; silver ring
rings, Jocasta's 37
ritual 2, 11, 40, 81, 83, 88, 93, 98–99, 105, 120,
  127, 143–144, 169, 172–175, 191, 196
Robbie McNabb 127
Robinson Crusoe 10, 58, 59
Roger MacKenzie 2, 3, 8–12, 15, 16, 18, 25, 36,
  42, 51–53, 55, 57–59, 62, 64, 67, 73, 78, 79,
  82, 83, 86–88, 91, 94, 96, 99, 100, 102, 106,
  107, 109, 112, 114, 115, 117, 120, 133, 134, 136–
  138, 140, 145, 154, 160, 165, 169, 182, 184
Romans 87, 90
romantic 2, 10, 23, 25, 31, 48, 50, 66, 75, 77, 83,
  85, 139, 153, 170, 180
rosary 54, 134, 135
roses 42–43; *see also* Ellen's roses; white roses
rowan 30, 97, 119, 120, 121
ruby 2, 37, 54, 88, 90, 91
ruby necklace 37
ruby ring 21, 37, 54
runes 2, 89, 195, 196
Rupert MacKenzie 44, 117

Sabbats 101
sacrifice 2, 15, 50, 56, 96, 100, 105, 124, 130, 165, 178, 191
St. Andrew 133
Saint Clare of Assisi 52
St. Columba 50, 89, 97, 118, 133, 158, 165
St. Dismas 134
St. Dominic 134
St. Finbar 133, 134
St. Germain 18, 88, 175, 180, 181
St. Michael 87, 100, 132, 133, 146
St. Michael's Ley 87
St. Ninian 131, 132
St. Orgevald 135, 165
St. Orrin 165
St. Patrick 105, 139, 175
St. Paul 62
saints 50, 126, 130–134, 139, 145, 189, 196
saints' springs 130–131
salt 63, 78, 103, 104, 116, 167, 168
Samhain 18, 84, 95, 96, 100–102, 115, 165
sapphire 32, 91, 92, 141
Sassenach 51–52
scars 55, 56, 123
Scott, Sir Walter 2, 30, 31, 57, 72, 74, 151
The Scottish Prisoner 9, 17, 31, 42, 54, 58, 59, 62, 78, 79, 102, 123, 125, 130, 150, 157, 166, 167
second sight 9, 53, 94, 140, 157–159
secrets 13, 15, 17, 44, 175, 192
selkies 105, 114, 118, 121, 122, 150
serpent 64, 96, 126, 143, 144, 174, 175, 182
17th century 58, 123, 144, 161, 173, 189
sgian-dubh (sock knife) 26
Shakespeare 1, 50, 65, 169
shapeshifters 110
Shelley, Percy Blythe 71
Sheriffmuir 73
Sherlock Holmes 16, 68, 71
shift 19–20, 104
shinty game 45, 77
shipwreck 10, 74
Sidhe 111, 112, 124; *see also* fairies
signet ring 16
silver 2, 23, 26, 29–37, 41, 43, 44, 48, 55, 83, 88, 89, 97, 106, 135, 142, 144, 172, 192
silver ring 36, 44, 45
Simon Fraser (Old Fox) 158
Simon Fraser (younger) 43, 83
sin-eater 168, 169
Skara Brae 93
skulls 88, 183
Skye 1, 25, 26, 75, 76, 107
"The Skye Boat Song" 74, 75, 77
Smollett, Tobias 59
snake *see* serpent
snow (symbolism) 15
snowflake 15
Solstices 93; *see also* autumn; spring; summer; winter
songbirds 37

Sorcha 52
soul 8, 10, 25, 31, 47, 55, 60, 63, 75, 76, 82, 99, 102, 128, 135, 146, 167, 176, 178, 180, 185, 186, 189
"The Space Between" 17, 18, 48, 83, 85, 88, 132, 158, 175, 180, 182, 185
space program 10
Spanish 51, 59, 78, 168
spirituality 32, 37, 38, 47
sporran 26, 29, 54
"The Sprightly Tailor" 138
spring 2, 19, 72, 97, 100, 104, 118, 127, 130–132, 135, 147, 156, 187, 196
Spring Equinox 95, 97, 127
squares 10
standing stones 1, 2, 5, 35, 42, 46, 68, 81, 83–88, 90, 92–95, 106, 121, 125, 151, 153, 164, 184, 188, 195, 196
"The Star-Spangled Banner" 67
Stephen Bonnet 190
Stevenson, Robert Louis 72, 74, 75
stone circle 86, 87, 88, 92, 93, 94, 131
Stonehenge 87, 92, 93, 94, 160, 184
stones singing 83, 88, 107
storyteller 65, 105, 106, 192
strawberry 2, 43, 52
succubus 189
suitcase 54
summer 42, 95–101, 147, 156
Summer Solstice 42, 95, 96, 99
sun feasts 76, 88, 95
superstition 17, 31, 96, 102, 109, 129, 131, 135, 136, 161, 162, 164–167, 184, 190, 195, 196
surgeon 16, 62
Sussex 53
sword 13, 26, 28, 29, 49, 57, 63, 85, 119, 133, 169, 170, 171
Sword Dance 169–170

talismans 7, 135, 196
Tam Lin 123
tannagach 115
Taranis (god) 130
targe 26, 170
tartan 25–30, 52, 73
tea leaves 81, 151–152
television *see* episode one; episode two; episode three; episode four; episode five; episode six; episode seven; episode eight
Tennyson, Alfred Lord 70
Teutates (god) 130
thistle 6, 36, 42, 44
Thomas the Rhymer 86, 111, 112
time (symbolism) 14
time travel 16, 18, 19, 32, 47, 68, 69, 83, 85, 87, 118, 160, 181
time travel gene 160
Tom Jones 59
A Trail of Fire 17
Trail of Tears 192
trinity 105, 125, 147, 188

Tristam Shandy 59
trows 106
turquoise 32, 88, 90
Tuscarora 92, 164, 190–193
20th century 20, 122, 139, 149, 157, 177, 183
two hundred years 85, 124

Uncle Lamb 22, 23
underwear 19–20
underworld 12, 48, 61, 95, 119, 126, 130
ursiq 109
utility suit 18

Verbeek, Lotte 163
Versailles 21, 58, 62
Victorians 30
Vikings 2, 10, 44, 103, 185, 195, 196
Virgil 59
Virgin Mary 90, 125, 127, 132, 135, 144, 175, 185
"Virgins" 51, 59
Vodou 2, 173, 174, 175, 176
Voyager 9, 10, 22, 32, 51, 54, 57, 58, 61, 62, 65, 67, 70, 74, 88, 89, 93, 103, 125, 133, 134–136, 138, 140, 149, 154, 159, 163, 164, 178–180, 183, 184, 186, 193

wake 49, 168
War of the Roses 42
water dripping 135
water spirits 110
waterhorse 2, 116, 117, 119, 162, 196
waulking songs 45, 46, 145
waulking wool 45, 46, 57
wedding 2, 19–23, 28–30, 33–41, 43, 45, 48, 49, 52, 54, 55, 60–63, 68, 78, 99, 102, 139, 168, 171, 172, 187
wedding gown 20, 22
wedding traditions 171–172
Wendigo 193–195
Wentworth 62, 127
werewolf 109, 111, 194
West Indies 2, 33, 51, 59, 69, 175
The Westmoreland Dynasty Saga 58
wet nurse 19
white 2, 19–23, 28, 29, 39–43, 48, 89, 97, 99, 110, 120, 125–128, 140–142, 146, 173, 175, 178, 186–189, 193, 194

white animals 141–142
white cockade 43
White Lady 2, 48, 89, 125, 153, 157, 164, 186–188
White Raven 48, 140–141
white roses 42–43, 123
Whitman, Walt 67
wife of Balnain 84
Wild Hunt 1, 123, 124, 130, 139
wilderness 7, 12, 37, 41, 42, 64, 133, 139, 148
William Ransom 9, 15, 39, 53, 114, 135, 156
William the Conqueror 43
wine 20, 44, 88, 99, 101, 168
winter 14, 87, 93, 95, 96, 100–102, 104, 140, 147
Winter Solstice 95
wise woman 2, 107, 141, 161, 162, 164, 186, 188, 190, 192, 193
witch 2, 3, 39, 46, 63, 89, 92, 96, 107, 120, 125, 129, 135, 160–164, 173, 186, 189, 196
Witchcraft Acts 161
The Witch's Hammer 163
wizards 24, 182
The Wizard of Oz 68
wolves 41, 42, 122, 147
The Woman Who Fell from the Sky 193
women's mysteries 81
wooden snake 54
World Tree 12
World War II 1, 9, 69, 180
Written in My Own Heart's Blood 9, 15, 22, 43, 52, 57, 61, 64, 67–68, 70, 72, 73, 86, 90, 134, 142, 145, 147, 149, 182, 189

Yankee Doodle 68
Yeats, William Butler 71, 124
yellow 20, 21, 28, 41, 43, 89, 120, 174
yew 97
Yi Tien Cho 2, 177–180
Young Ian Murray 3, 10, 12, 15, 18, 31, 41, 52, 59, 60, 79, 88, 111, 114, 141, 142, 146, 164, 190, 192
Young Jamie Murray 50, 52
Yule 95, 96, 102, 103

Zeus 130
zombies 2, 174–176, 196